Measuring Up®

to the

California Content Standards

English Language Arts

This book is customized for California and the lessons
cover the California Content Standards. The Measuring Up®
program includes instructional worktexts and
Diagnostic Practice Tests, which are available separately.

Early Preparation

800-822-1080
www.PeoplesEducation.com

Peoples Education™
Your partner in student success™

Publisher: Diane Miller

Editorial Development: e2 Publishing Services

Editorial Director: Marie Spano

Editor: Jasper Jones

Vice President, Marketing: Victoria Ameer Kiely

Vice President, Production: Doreen Smith

Pre-Press & Production Manager: Jason Grasso

Project Manager: Dawn Unterreiner

Senior Book Coordinator: Ismael Feliciano

Book Coordinator: Carolyn Edelstein

Designer: Jodi Notowitz, Jay Gobolos

Copy Editors: Dee Josephson, Michael O'Neill

Proofreader: Pat Smith

Photo Researcher/Permissions Manager: Kristine Liebman

Cover Design: Yadiro Henriquez, Cynthia Mackowicz, Michele Sakow

Illustrators: Armando Báez, Salvatore Esposito

Advisory Panel, High School:

Dr. Gregory J. Vallone, Principal, James Monroe High School, North Hills, CA LAUSD

Jeff Mirosavich, English Teacher, Department Chair, Glendale High School, Glendale, CA

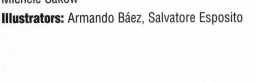

Your partner in student success™

Copyright © 2005
Peoples Education, Inc.
299 Market Street
Saddle Brook, New Jersey 07663

ISBN 978-1-4138-2188-8
ISBN 1-4138-2188-X

Printed in the United States of America.

11

Contents

Part I: Vocabulary, Reading Comprehension, and Literature

Chapter 1 Word Analysis

Lesson	California Content Standards Reading Vocabulary	

California Content Standards: RV 9.1.1, RV 9.1.2, RI 9.2.8
Build your intellectual stamina with these activities. Each question applies to the California Content Standards—standards addressed in Chapter 1 as well as ones dealt with in the chapters to come.

Chapter 2 Reading Comprehension

California Content Standards: RI 9.2.1, RI 9.2.3, RI 9.2.4, RI 9.2. 5, RI 9.2.7, RI 9.2.8
Build your intellectual stamina by practicing with passage and question types you will find
on tests. This section includes an information document with a map, graphic organizers, and
a broad range of questions that address the standards covered in Chapters 1 and 2.

Chapter 3 Literary Response and Analysis

It's time to practice more questions on the literary standards. The more experience you have reading and analyzing literature, the easier these questions will become.

Chapter 3   Literary Response and Analysis cont.

Part II: Writing

Chapter 4   Writing Strategies

Chapter 5   Writing Conventions

Chapter 6 Writing Applications

Selection: "The Day Grandfather Tickled a Tiger" by Ruskin Bond
California Content Standards: WS 9.1.1, WS 9.1.2, WS 9.1.4, WS 9.1.5, WS 9.1.9, WC 9.1.1, WC 9.1.2, WC 9.1.3, WA 9.2.2, WA 9.2.3
Here is an opportunity to practice all the elements of good composition and expository writing reviewed in this chapter. Build your stamina by completing both the writing tasks in this section.

Selection: "Zoo" by Edward D. Hoch
California Content Standards: WS 9.1.1, WS 9.1.2, WS 9.1.4, WS 9.1.5, WS 9.1.9, WC 9.1.1, WC 9.1.2, WC 9.1.3, WA 9.2.2, WA 9.2.3, WA 9.2.4
It's time to put it all together. Practice all the writing strategies and conventions covered in Part II in this **Building Stamina**™. This section contains practice with two writing prompts.

Selection: "To Catch the Wind: A Tale from the Marshall Islands" retold by Joyce Sidman
California Content Standards: RV 9.1.1, RV 9.1.2, RI 9.1.1, RI 9.1.2, RI 9.2.1, RI 9.2.3, RI 9.2.5, RI 9.2.8, RL 9.3.1, RL 9.3.3, RL 9.3.4, RL 9.3.5, RL 9.3.7, RL 9.3.8, RL 9.3.9, RL 9.3.10, RL 9.3.11, WS 9.1.1, WS 9.1.2, WS 9.1.4, WS 9.1.5, WS 9.1.9, WC 9.1.1, WC 9.1.2, WC 9.1.3, WA 9.2.2, WA 9.2.3, WA 9.3.4
Build intellectual stamina by practicing with this longer activity. This section includes practice answering questions on a reading passage, as well as practice revising and writing an essay.

Your teacher may choose to give Diagnostic Practice Tests that assess your understanding of skills and concepts that come from your California Content Standards. This will help you focus on areas where you need some extra help.

Teachers: Refer to WWW.CAStandardsHelp.com for teaching strategies and ELL teaching activities.

Correlation to the California Content Standards

This worktext is customized to the California Content Standards.

The correlation chart shows how Measuring Up® is vertically aligned to the California Content Standards because the lessons are customized for them. As the lesson for each student expectation is completed, place a (✓) to indicate Mastery or an (✗) to indicate Review Needed

Chapter 1: Word Analysis

	Lessons: 1	2	3	4	5	B
California Content Standard 1.0 Word Analysis, Fluency, and Systematic Vocabulary Development: Students apply their knowledge of word origins to determine the meaning of new words encountered in reading materials and use those words accurately.						
9.1.1 *Vocabulary and Concept Development:* Identify and use the literal and figurative meanings of words and understand word derivations.	★	★	★	★	✓	★
9.1.2 *Vocabulary and Concept Development:* Distinguish between the denotative and connotative meanings of words and interpret the connotative power of words.	○	○	○	○	★	★

Chapter 2: Reading Comprehension

	Lessons: 6	7	8	9	10	11	12	B
California Content Standard 2.0 Reading Comprehension (Focus on Informational Materials): Students read and understand grade-level-appropriate material. They analyze the organizational patterns, arguments, and positions advanced.								
8.2.1 Use features and Elements to Gain Meaning from Documents: Compare and contrast the features and elements of consumer materials to gain meaning from documents (e.g., warranties, contracts, product information, instruction manuals.).	★	✓	✓	✓	✓	✓	✓	★
9.2.1 *Structural Features of Informational Materials:* Analyze the structure and format of functional workplace documents, including the graphics and headers, and explain how authors use the features to achieve their purposes.	★	✓	✓	✓	✓	✓	✓	★
9.2.3 *Comprehension and Analysis of Grade-Level-Appropriate Text:* Generate relevant questions about readings on issues that can be researched.	○	○	★	✓	✓	✓	✓	★
9.2.4 *Comprehension and Analysis of Grade-Level-Appropriate Text:* Synthesize the content from several sources or works by a single author dealing with a single issue; paraphrase the ideas and connect them to other sources and related topics to demonstrate comprehension.	○	○	○	★	✓	✓	✓	★
9.2.5 *Comprehension and Analysis of Grade-Level-Appropriate Text:* Extend ideas presented in primary or secondary sources through original analysis, evaluation, and elaboration.	○	○	○	○	★	✓	✓	★
9.2.7 *Expository Critique:* Critique the logic of functional documents by examining the sequence of information and procedures in anticipation of possible reader misunderstandings.	○	○	○	○	○	★	✓	★
9.2.8 *Expository Critique:* Evaluate the credibility of an author's argument or defense of a claim by critiquing the relationship between generalizations and evidence, the comprehensiveness of evidence, and the way in which the author's intent affects the structure and tone of the text (e.g., in professional journals, editorials, political speeches, primary source material).	○	○	○	○	○	○	★	★

★ **STANDARD COVERED**   ✓ **STANDARD PREVIOUSLY COVERED**

○ **STANDARD TO BE COVERED**   B **Building Stamina™**

Correlation to the California Content Standards

This worktext is customized to the California Content Standards.

The correlation chart shows how Measuring Up® is vertically aligned to the California Content Standards because the lessons are customized for them. As the lesson for each student expectation is completed, place a (✔) to indicate Mastery or an (✗) to indicate Review Needed

Chapter 3: Literary Response and Analysis		13	14	15	16	17	18	19	20	21	22	23	B
Master Skill													
Review Skill													
Lessons		13	14	15	16	17	18	19	20	21	22	23	B
California Content Standard 3.0 Literary Response and Analysis: Students read and respond to historically or culturally significant works of literature that reflect and enhance their studies of history and social science.													
9.3.1	*Structural Features of Literature:* Articulate the relationship between the expressed purposes and the characteristics of different forms of dramatic literature (e.g., comedy, tragedy, drama, dramatic monologue).	★	✔	✔	✔	✔	✔	✔	✔	✔	✔	✔	★
9.3.3	*Narrative Analysis of Grade-Level-Appropriate Text:* Analyze interactions between main and subordinate characters in a literary text (e.g., internal and external conflicts, motivations, relationships, influences) and explain the way those interactions affect the plot.	○	★	✔	✔	✔	✔	✔	✔	✔	✔	✔	★
9.3.4	*Narrative Analysis of Grade-Level-Appropriate Text:* Determine characters' traits by what the characters say about themselves in narration, dialogue, dramatic monologue, and soliloquy.	○	★	✔	✔	✔	✔	✔	✔	✔	✔	✔	★
9.3.5	*Narrative Analysis of Grade-Level-Appropriate Text:* Compare works that express a universal theme and provide evidence to support the ideas expressed in each work.	○	○	★	✔	✔	✔	✔	✔	✔	✔	✔	★
9.3.6	*Narrative Analysis of Grade-Level-Appropriate Text:* Analyze and trace an author's development of time and sequence, including the use of complex literary devices (e.g., foreshadowing, flashbacks).	○	○	○	★	✔	✔	✔	✔	✔	✔	✔	★
9.3.7	*Narrative Analysis of Grade-Level-Appropriate Text:* Recognize and understand the significance of various literary devices, including figurative language, imagery, allegory, and symbolism, and explain their appeal.	○	○	○	○	★	★	★	✔	✔	✔	✔	★
9.3.8	*Narrative Analysis of Grade-Level-Appropriate Text:* Interpret and evaluate the impact of ambiguities, subtleties, contradictions, ironies, and incongruities in a text.	○	○	○	○	○	○	○	★	✔	✔	✔	★
9.3.9	*Narrative Analysis of Grade-Level-Appropriate Text:* Explain how voice, persona, and the choice of a narrator affect characterization and the tone, plot, and credibility of a text.	○	○	○	○	○	○	○	○	★	✔	✔	★
9.3.10	*Narrative Analysis of Grade-Level-Appropriate Text:* Identify and describe the function of dialogue, scene designs, soliloquies, asides, and character foils in dramatic literature.	○	○	○	○	○	○	○	○	○	★	✔	★
8.3.7	*Literary Criticism:* Analyze a work of literature, showing how it reflects the heritage, traditions, attitudes, and beliefs of its author (Biographical Approach)	○	○	○	○	○	○	○	○	○	○	★	★
9.3.11	*Literary Criticism:* Evaluate the aesthetic qualities of style, including the impact of diction and figurative language on tone, mood, and theme, using the terminology of literary criticism. (Aesthetic approach)	○	○	○	○	○	○	○	○	○	○	★	★
9.3.12	*Literary Criticism:* Analyze the way in which a work of literature is related to the themes and issues of its historical period. (Historical approach)	○	○	○	○	○	○	○	○	○	○	★	★

★ **STANDARD COVERED**   ✔ **STANDARD PREVIOUSLY COVERED**

○ **STANDARD TO BE COVERED**   B **Building Stamina**™

Correlation to the California Content Standards

This worktext is customized to the California Content Standards.

The correlation chart shows how Measuring Up® is vertically aligned to the California Content Standards because the lessons are customized for them. As the lesson for each student expectation is completed, place a (✓) to indicate Mastery or an (✗) to indicate Review Needed

Chapter 4: Writing Strategies	Master Skill				
	Review Skill				
	Lessons	24	25	26	27	B

California Content Standards 1.0 Writing Strategies Students write coherent and focused essays that convey a well-defined perspective and tightly reasoned argument. The writing demonstrates students' awareness of the audience and purpose. Students progress through the stages of the writing process as needed.

		24	25	26	27	B
9.1.1	*Organization and Focus:* Establish a controlling impression or coherent thesis that conveys a clear and distinctive perspective on the subject and maintain a consistent tone and focus throughout the piece of writing.	★	✓	✓	✓	★
9.1.2	*Organization and Focus:* Use precise language, action verbs, sensory details, appropriate modifiers, and the active rather than the passive voice.	✓	✓	✓	★	★
9.1.4	*Research and Technology:* Develop the main ideas within the body of the composition through supporting evidence (e.g., scenarios, commonly held beliefs, hypotheses, definitions).	○	★	✓	✓	★
9.1.5	*Research and Technology:* Synthesize information from multiple sources and identify complexities and discrepancies in the information and the different perspectives found in each medium (e.g., almanacs, microfiche, news sources, in-depth field studies, speeches, journals, technical documents).	○	○	★	✓	★
9.1.9	*Evaluation and Revision:* Revise writing to improve the logic and coherence of the organization and controlling perspective, the precision of word choice, and the tone by taking into consideration the audience, purpose, and formality of the context.	○	○	○	★	★

Chapter 5: Writing Conventions	Master Skill				
	Review Skill				
	Lessons	28	29	30	B

California Content Standards 1.0 Written and Oral Conventions: Students write and speak with a command of standard English conventions.

		28	29	30	B
9.1.1	*Grammar and Mechanics of Writing:* Identify and correctly use clauses (e.g., main and subordinate), phrases (e.g., gerund, infinitive, and participial), and mechanics of punctuation (e.g., semicolons, colons, ellipses, hyphens).	★	✓	✓	★
9.1.2	*Grammar and Mechanics of Writing:* Understand sentence construction (e.g., parallel structure, subordination, proper placement of modifiers) and proper English usage (e.g., consistency of verb tenses).	★	★	✓	★
9.1.3	*Grammar and Mechanics of Writing:* Demonstrate an understanding of proper English usage and control of grammar, paragraph and sentence structure, diction, and syntax.	★	✓	★	★

★ **STANDARD COVERED**   ✓ **STANDARD PREVIOUSLY COVERED**

○ **STANDARD TO BE COVERED**   B **Building Stamina™**

Correlation to the California Content Standards

This worktext is customized to the California Content Standards.

The correlation chart shows how Measuring Up® is vertically aligned to the California Content Standards because the lessons are customized for them. As the lesson for each student expectation is completed, place a (✓) to indicate Mastery or an (✗) to indicate Review Needed

Chapter 6: Writing Applications	Master Skill					
	Review Skill					
Lessons	31	32	33	34	35	B
California Content Standard 2.0 Writing Applications (Genres and Their Characteristics) Students combine the rhetorical strategies of narration, exposition, persuasion, and description to produce texts of at least 1,500 words each. Student writing demonstrates a command of standard American English and the research, organizational, and drafting strategies outlined in Writing Standard 1.0.						
9.2.1 Write biographical or autobiographical narratives or short stories: **a.** Relate a sequence of events and communicate the significance of the events to the audience. **b.** Locate scenes and incidents in specific places. **c.** Describe with concrete sensory details the sights, sounds, and smells of a scene and the specific actions, movements, gestures, and feelings of the characters; use interior monologue to depict the characters' feelings. **d.** Pace the presentation of actions to accommodate changes in time and mood. **e.** Make effective use of descriptions of appearance, images, shifting perspectives, and sensory details.	★	✓	✓	✓	✓	★
9.2.2 Write responses to literature: **a.** Demonstrate a comprehensive grasp of the significant ideas of literary works. **b.** Support important ideas and viewpoints through accurate and detailed references to the text or to other works. **c.** Demonstrate awareness of the author's use of stylistic devices and an appreciation of the effects created. **d.** Identify and assess the impact of perceived ambiguities, nuances, and complexities within the text.	○	★	✓	✓	✓	★
9.2.3 Write expository compositions, including analytical essays and research reports: **a.** Marshal evidence in support of a thesis and related claims, including information on all relevant perspectives. **b.** Convey information and ideas from primary and secondary sources accurately and coherently. **c.** Make distinctions between the relative value and significance of specific data, facts, and ideas. **d.** Include visual aids by employing appropriate technology to organize and record information on charts, maps, and graphs. **e.** Anticipate and address readers' potential misunderstandings, biases, and expectations. **f.** Use technical terms and notations accurately.	✓	✓	★	✓	✓	★
9.2.4 Write persuasive compositions: **a.** Structure ideas and arguments in a sustained and logical fashion. **b.** Use specific rhetorical devices to support assertions (e.g., appeal to logic through reasoning; appeal to emotion or ethical belief; relate a personal anecdote, case study, or analogy). **c.** Clarify and defend positions with precise and relevant evidence, including facts, expert opinions, quotations, and expressions of commonly accepted beliefs and logical reasoning. **d.** Address readers' concerns, counterclaims, biases, and expectations.	✓	✓	✓	★	✓	★
9.2.5 Write business letters: **a.** Provide clear and purposeful information and address the intended audience appropriately. **b.** Use appropriate vocabulary, tone, and style to take into account the nature of the relationship with, and the knowledge and interests of, the recipients. **c.** Highlight central ideas or images. **d.** Follow a conventional style with page formats, fonts, and spacing that contribute to the documents' readability and impact.	✓	✓	✓	✓	★	✓

★ **STANDARD COVERED**　　　✓ **STANDARD PREVIOUSLY COVERED**

○ **STANDARD TO BE COVERED**　　B **Building Stamina**™

Measuring Up®

to the
California Content Standards

Dear Student,

It's never too soon to prepare for your future. The same goes for learning skills in the area of English language arts. The lessons in the Measuring Up® book are geared to help you review and practice the California Content Standards and they describe the English language arts skills you need to acquire at your grade level.

Measuring Up® has six chapters. The first three chapters focus on reading skills and the last three chapters focus on writing skills. Each lesson consists of four main sections:

- **Focus on California Content Standards** introduces the skills covered in the lesson.

- **Guided Reading Instruction** shows you the skills you will need for successful learning.

- **Apply** helps you comprehend important concepts and skills by reading passages and answering open-ended or short-answer questions.

- **Assessment Practice** gives you experience in responding to questions in test format.

In addition to the lessons, other sections in the book are called **Building Stamina**™. They contain both multiple-choice and open-ended response questions that help build your intellectual brainpower.

Have a great and successful year!

PEOPLES®
PUBLISHING GROUP

to the
California Content Standards

To Parents and Families,

All students need reading and writing skills to succeed. California educators have created the California Content Standards for English Language Arts and have set the standards for reading and writing that all California students should meet at each grade level. The California Content Standards emphasize higher-level thinking skills. Students must learn to think on a higher level, to consider, analyze, interpret, and evaluate instead of just recalling simple facts.

Measuring Up® will help your children to learn the California Content Standards and prepare for all English language arts exams. It contains:

• lessons that focus on practicing the California Content Standards;

• **Guided Reading Instruction,** in which shaded numbers in text correspond to questions in the margin that guide reading by highlighting particular skills;

• writing responses to varied reading selections;

• revision exercises and writing prompts;

• **Assessment Practice**, which shows how individual Content Standards can be understood through multiple-choice questions;

• **Building Stamina**™, which gives practice in uncovering themes in passages and answering multiple-choice and open-ended questions that require higher-level thinking.

For success in school and the real world, your child needs good reading and writing skills. Get involved! Your involvement is crucial to your child's success. Here are some suggestions:

• Make sure your home shows that reading and writing are important. Keep bookshelves on display. Share stories from newspapers and magazines. Talk to your young adult librarian to find out what kids are reading. Bring books home from the library or bookstore and discuss them with your kids. Read book reviews and post interesting ones on the refrigerator. Listen to talk shows on books and talk about them with your kids.

• Treat reading as a pleasure, not a punishment. Give books as presents and show that you like to receive them, too. Respect each other's private reading time.

• Help to find appropriate Internet sites for literature, information, and reviews. Play recorded books together when riding in the car. Watch plays on television. Make a family outing of book signings and talks at your local library or bookstore.

• Encourage your kids to write and talk about what they have written.

Work with us this year to ensure your child's success. Reading and writing are essential skills for success and pleasure throughout your child's life.

This book was built for California students like you! Every lesson, every question, every selection is geared toward helping you master the California Content Standards and prepare for any rigorous exam you may be required to take in English language arts this year or the next.

About the California Content Standards

California educators have created the California Content Standards for English Language Arts. These standards describe exactly what is expected of all students at each grade level.

Reading Content Standards

California Content Standard 1.0 Word Analysis, Fluency, and Systematic Vocabulary Development: Students apply their knowledge of word origins to determine the meaning of new words encountered in reading materials and use those words accurately.

California Content Standard 2.0 Reading Comprehension (Focus on Informational Materials): Students read and understand grade-level appropriate material. They analyze the organizational patterns, arguments, and positions advanced.

California Content Standard 3.0 Literary Response and Analysis: Students read and respond to historically or culturally significant works of literature that reflect and enhance their studies of history and social science.

Writing Content Standards

California Content Standard 1.0 Writing Strategies: Students write coherent and focused essays that convey a well-defined perspective and tightly reasoned argument. The writing demonstrates students' awareness of the audience and purpose. Students progress through the stages of the writing process as needed.

California Content Standard 1.0 Written and Oral Language Conventions: Students write and speak with a command of standard English conventions.

California Content Standard 2.0 Writing Applications (Genres and Their Characteristics): Students combine the rhetorical strategies of narration, exposition, persuasion, and description to produce texts of at least 1,500 words each. Student writing demonstrates a command of standard American English and the research, organizational, and drafting strategies outlined in Writing Standard 1.0.

Measuring Up on Multiple-Choice Questions

You are probably familiar with the multiple-choice type of question. It has a question, or stem, followed by four choices. Your job is to pick the one correct choice. Here are some tips for answering multiple-choice questions:

- Many questions refer to a specific paragraph in a literature or informational selection. Go back and reread that paragraph to find the correct answer.

- Some multiple-choice questions may refer to a visual representation that accompanies an informational passage. Look at the text and graphics and how they work together. Think about the message they send. Then try to answer the specific question.

- Remember that many questions assess higher-order thinking skills. You will not find the exact answer right there in the passage. Instead you have to connect ideas and information to come up with the right answers.

- Rule out the wrong answers. Even if you don't know the answer to a multiple-choice question, you may still be able to guess and get the question right. Rule out answers that you know are definitely wrong. If you can narrow the possibilities to two choices, you can guess and have a good chance of picking the correct answer.

- Check your answers. Before you turn in a test, reread each question and the choices to double-check that you have chosen the correct one. In addition, make sure you haven't marked a wrong choice by mistake.

Getting a Head Start on Revising and Editing

The revising and editing portion of a test assesses your ability to spot and correct trouble spots in a written passage. Here are some tips for responding to revising and editing questions:

- Read the passage carefully. Note that all the sentences in the passage are numbered.

- Multiple-choice questions that follow the passage refer to a specific numbered sentence in the passage. Reread the sentence referred to in the question. Before you evaluate the choices, determine what error, if any, has been made in the sentence. Then read the choices and choose the correct answer.

Getting a Head Start on Writing in Response to a Prompt

A writing prompt on a test may consist of a writing topic and a suggestion on how you can write about it. The writing prompt on a test may relate to a literary passage or it may be a stand-alone task such as a persuasive essay on a given topic. Here are some tips for writing a response to a prompt:

- Read the prompt carefully. Think about what it asks you to do. If you misread a prompt or fail to interpret a prompt properly, your written response will be incorrect.

- Remember that the prompt may be linked to a reading passage. Think about the connection. If appropriate, use details from the passage in your response, but you are not required to do this.

- Read the reminder statements and take them seriously. They are meant to be a checklist. Read them before you write your response and after you write your response to make sure you have addressed them.

- Use the planning page to brainstorm ideas and organize them.

- Select an approach and an audience for your response. Remember that your audience can be anyone but yourself.

- Remember that you must show not only that you can write a correct answer but also that you can write a thoughtful and insightful one. In other words, show how well you have thought about the topic of the prompt. This is an opportunity for your higher-order thinking skills to shine.

- Let your own individual style show through. Develop a voice that sounds authentic and original and maintain this voice throughout your response.

- Revise and proofread your response. It will be evaluated based on how effectively it is written and how well it adheres to the conventions of standard written English. Check the organization. Consider whether or not it is focused. Scorers will use a four-point rubric to evaluate your writing.

Measuring Up® **with Building Stamina**™

A unique feature of this book is **Building Stamina**™, which is designed to give you practice and build your confidence and endurance for completing broad-based, higher-level thinking-type activities. These activities will include answering questions that cover multiple California Content Standards. Each chapter in Measuring Up® ends with a **Building Stamina**™ section. The challenging questions in this section will build your stamina to succeed on difficult activities.

 ## Higher-Level Thinking Skills

Many tests are designed to test your mastery of higher-order thinking skills. Questions move beyond asking you to recall simple information, and instead require you to analyze, interpret, and evaluate. For example, instead of being asked to recall where a story takes place, you might be asked to analyze the effect of the setting on the characters. Instead of being asked to identify what two things are being compared in a simile, you might be asked to interpret its meaning and its connection to the theme. Instead of being asked to identify the organizational pattern of a selection, you might be asked to evaluate how the organizational pattern helps the writer achieve his or her purpose. In this Measuring Up® book, all higher-order thinking skills questions in the **Building Stamina**™ sections are starred for easy identification.

- **Building Stamina**™ in Part I
  The **Building Stamina**™ sections in Part I are designed to give you practice on harder questions. They provide the type and length of selections you will be expected to read and the kinds of questions you will be expected to answer. They vary in length to help you build endurance. Following Chapters 1 through 3, the **Building Stamina**™ each consist of one selection with ten multiple-choice questions.

- **Building Stamina**™ in Part II
  The **Building Stamina**™ sections in Part II contain revising, editing, and writing practice.
- End-of-Book **Building Stamina**™
  At the end of the book is a **Building Stamina**™ that contains practice with both reading and writing questions. There are one proofreading passage, a reading selection with questions, and two writing prompts.

By the time you come to the end of this Measuring Up® book, you will have reviewed and practiced the California Content Standards and built up your stamina to answer tough questions. In other words, you will have all that you need to be a success. Now it's up to you!

Chapter 1 Word Analysis

In Chapter 1, you will study and practice how to:

- understand literal meaning
- interpret figurative meaning
- understand word derivatives
- use context clues
- understand connotation and denotation

Chapter 2 Reading Comprehension

In Chapter 2, you will learn how to:

- gain meaning from consumer documents
- analyze the structure of functional documents
- generate relevant questions
- synthesize and paraphrase
- analyze and evaluate
- critique functional documents
- evaluate an argument or defense

Chapter 3 Literary Response and Analysis

In Chapter 3, you will learn how to:

- understand the purpose and characteristics of dramatic literature
- analyze how characters interact in a literary text
- compare works that express a universal theme
- analyze and trace time and sequence
- observe and identify figurative language
- interpret symbolism and allegory
- understand how imagery and repetition are used
- interpret and evaluate ambiguity, subtlety, contradiction, irony, and incongruity
- understand voice, persona, and narrator
- observe the elements of drama
- use different approaches to analyze literature

Focus on California Content Standards

Reading Vocabulary 9.1.1 Identify and use the literal and figurative meanings of words and understand word derivations.

The **literal meaning** of a word is its dictionary definition. To be a successful reader you have to know what the individual words in a text mean.

The more you read and the more you listen carefully, the more new words you encounter and master. Developing a good vocabulary is an important indicator of success in both school and the business world.

How can you figure out the meaning of words? Sometimes, the **context**, or the words surrounding the unknown word, provides a clue. Other times, you can look at the word parts for clues to meaning. Also, knowing the origin of the word helps. Often, though, you have to look up the word in a dictionary to find its meaning.

When you use a dictionary, you will see more than one meaning. Then you have to choose the meaning that fits the context and adapt that meaning to the context. For example, nouns are defined in their singular form (*computer*). If you read the plural form of the word (*computers*), you have to make the definition plural too.

After you look up the word, put the definition in your own words. Reread the sentence containing the word to see if your definition makes sense. For example, if you found the word *garrulous* describing someone's speech, you would find on looking the word up that it means "talking too much, especially about unimportant things." Stated in your own words, the speaker might be called "talkative." Look up the word in a **thesaurus** to find synonyms and antonyms for the word. Then use the word as often as you can during the week in your speaking and writing.

Mnemonic devices are tricks you can use to remember the meaning of words. They include rhymes, silly sentences, and phrases built from the individual letters of the word you want to remember. Suppose you always confused the words *complement* and *compliment*. To remember that the word *compliment* spelled with *i* means "praise," you create a mnemonic: *I like to receive a compliment and I like to give compliments*.

Creating a **mental image** of a word can also help you remember its meaning. For example, to remember the word *frigid*, which means "extremely cold," you might think of the letters of this word as shaking with cold as they might in a cartoon caption. The sillier an image is, the easier it will be for you to remember.

Guided Reading Instruction

Directions Read the following passage. Use the questions in the margin to guide your reading. Then answer the questions that follow.

Amber
The Forty-Million-Year-Old Trap
by Marjorie Jackson

FORTY MILLION years ago, when the earth was much wetter and warmer, huge forests with many kinds of trees thrived in the far north. **1** Out of some of these trees, stretching as tall as ten-story buildings, oozed a sticky resin. Mosquitoes buzzed through the forests, grasshoppers and crickets leaped, and ants and spiders scurried by the trees in search of food. If they carelessly let a leg or wing touch the resin—zap!—they were stuck, preserved like mummies in an airtight trap.

Millions of years passed, and the climate of the earth altered dramatically. The northlands turned cold and icy. The giant trees fell, buried under the salt water that now covered the land. Far beneath the water, the globs of resin slowly changed, hardening into solid, glowing pieces of amber.

Still millions of years later, storms at sea broke the amber free and tossed it onto beaches for early cave dwellers to find. The cave dwellers wondered if the strange golden stone, warm to the touch, could be solid sunlight. Using flint and bone tools, they carved pieces of amber into the shapes of animals or the sun and wore them on cords around their necks for magical protection. When early Chinese people found amber the color of tigers' stripes, they believed it held the souls of dead tigers and they treasured it as a source of courage.

The ancient Greeks called amber *elektor*, which means "sun's glare." When they rubbed amber against cloth or animal skins to polish it and make it glow, they noticed that the amber would pull feathers or pieces of straw to it. **2** They had discovered static electricity.

[handwritten notes:] I before e except after c or in sanding like way as in neighbor and way

Guided Questions

1 Look up the word *resin* in the dictionary. Form a picture in your mind of trees oozing this semisolid goo. What color do you see?

2 *Static electricity* is an electric discharge that results from the buildup of an electric charge on an insulated body. What example in this paragraph can help you remember the meaning of static electricity?

For hundreds of years, people used amber in jewelry or to decorate warriors' weapons; some soldiers braided amber beads in their horses' manes to ensure success in battle. Amber was also ground fine and mixed with honey, oil of roses, and crabs' eyes or claws for use as medicine. Amber mixtures were believed to cure earaches, headaches, and any number of diseases. Even wearing buttons or beads carved from amber was thought to keep a person well. **3** As amber became more valuable, sea traders making money on the precious commodity protected their trade routes by inventing stories about giant serpents, evil sea witches, and other terrors of sailing in search of the golden substance.

3 Look up the word *commodity* in a dictionary. What is a synonym?

Product

In the early 1700s, King Frederick I of Prussia had an entire room built from 100,000 pieces of amber of many colors—yellow, orange, red, brown, and even blue and green—all fitted together like a giant jigsaw puzzle. When the sun shone through the windows, nobles said, they felt as if they were standing inside a jewel box. The room was used and admired for more than 200 years, but in the 1940s, during World War II, it was taken apart and loaded into boxes for storage in a safer place. The boxes were somehow lost, and where the amber room is today remains a mystery.

Some of the oldest pieces of amber are mined in Appalachia, in the eastern United States. **4** The Baltic seacoast also has large deposits. But the Dominican Republic, in the Caribbean, yields the most pieces with inclusions of insects, leaves, feathers, and other remains of life. In the Baltic, amber "catchers" still wade into icy seas during winter storms, carrying 30-foot poles with nets on the end. They scoop up seaweed torn loose by the storms and pull it to shore, where children wait to look through the weeds for pebbles of amber. Other catchers search from boats or ride horseback in rivers or lagoons at low tide.

4 In this sentence, what are *deposits*? Name two things you might find deposits of on the seacoast.

Some pieces of amber have air bubbles inside that keep the light from passing through, making it look cloudy, but many others are clear like glass. The pieces of amber with inclusions of early life or gas bubbles are the most valuable to scientists. They hold clues about the earth's ecology millions of years ago and enable scientists to compare early life forms with today's. More than a thousand kinds of insects have been found preserved in amber, from prehistoric flies that proved to be the ancestors of our houseflies to a 140-million-year-old weevil that lived at the time of the dinosaurs. Whole flights of insects were sometimes trapped in one glob of resin; one two-inch piece of amber has 2,000 ants in it! **5** Although most of the preserved insects are now extinct, their descendants may still survive, sometimes in new places. A termite found in Mexican amber now lives only in Australia.

5 Circle the word *extinct*. Find a word in this sentence that tells what happened to creatures that did not become *extinct* and underline it.

Scientists use X-rays to study skeletons of frogs and lizards, seeds inside fruit, and other inclusions without opening the amber. They also scan the surface of ancient mummified insects with electron microscopes, revealing such detail as preserved muscle fibers and the spinning glands of trapped spiders. **6** In addition, scientists can extract DNA directly from an amber inclusion. Amber is the only known fossil from which ancient DNA can be recovered.

6 Look up DNA in a dictionary. Why would scientists be interested in finding DNA from creatures that are now extinct?

Many natural history museums have pieces of amber on display. Look for them during your next visit. These golden traps, 40 or more millions of years old, are the closest thing we have to snapshots of our ancient past.

1. Find the word *thrived* in the first sentence. To look up *thrived* in a dictionary, take off the *d* to form the present tense. What does *thrive* mean? Adapt the meaning to fit the context.

   Thrive means to become very successful, or very strong and healthy.

2. How is the Greek word *elektor* in paragraph 4 related to amber and to electricity? You may use your dictionary to help you.

   the Greeks tried to make amber look like the sun, so they polished it and discovered static electricity

3. *Ecology* is the science of the relationships between organisms and the environment. Create a mnemonic that helps you remember this word.

   Ecology is you and me in RP.

4. Use a dictionary to find the meaning of the word *inclusions* in this sentence: "But the Dominican Republic, in the Caribbean, yields the most pieces with inclusions of insects, leaves, feathers, and other remains of life." Picture a fly encased in an orange-gold transparent egg to help you remember this word.

   An inclusion is a foreign body enclosed in a mineral or foreign rock.

Apply **Directions** Read the passage below. Then answer the questions that follow it.

from One Alaska Night
by Barrett Willoughby

A root tripped me and threw me flat in the trail that led through the blueberry thicket. For a moment I was too tired to stir. I lay there, face on my arms, feeling that I'd been foolhardy to start out alone on a ten-mile hike across an unfamiliar peninsula. Yet I comforted myself with the thought that it could not be much farther to the coast fox-ranch which was my destination. There Lonnie, a schoolmate of mine, was spending the summer with her father, who owned the place.

Suddenly, nose to the ground, I became aware of a rank, musky odor that brought my head up with a jerk. Something queerly crawling touched my cheek. I slapped my hand over it, and, with a chill of premonition, looked at what I'd caught—a long tuft of coarse brown hair dangling from a twig above.

One startled glance told me it had been raked from the side of an Alaskan brown bear—the largest carnivorous animal that walks the world today. With the tuft of hair clutched in my hand and sudden alarm sharpening my senses, I looked closely at the path leading forward under the leafy tunnel in which I lay.

All along it, evenly spaced in the damp, brown mold, were deep depressions, round and large as dinner plates.

The truth came with a shock—I had been following a bear trail! It was already getting dark, and I was unarmed.

I'm not a hunter. I'm not even a brave woman. And I'd never before been alone in a bear-infested forest with night coming on. I recalled that bears do most of their traveling after dark—and I was lying flat in the middle of one of their thoroughfares.

I leaped to my feet, turned off the trail, and began plowing through the brush, intent only on putting all possible distance between me and that place before dark.

Almost at once the bushes thinned out, and I was able to make good time through stretches of short ferns; but the light was fading fast. Oddly, it was only now, when I was safely away from the bear trail, that it dawned on me that I had no idea which way to go.

I was lost.

In that instant of realization all my strength seemed to ooze out of me. Then panic came upon me. I had a senseless, almost uncontrollable impulse to dash madly through the trees, regardless of direction, bears, or anything else. But I got hold of myself, decided on a course, and with forced calmness went forward, watching tensely for that breaking away of the timber which foretells an approach to the sea.

Every step took me deeper into the darkening wilderness. There was no wind. Not a thing moved except myself—not a leaf, not a twig.

The very silence began to frighten me. I found myself stepping furtively, trying not to make any noise, and straining to hear the slightest sound. I kept glancing back over my shoulder. Every few feet I'd stop suddenly, holding my breath while I studied a moss-grown log or the long arm of a thorny shrub, which I was sure had stirred a second before.

I was groping with my feet, my gaze fixed ahead, when out of the tail of my eye I saw a blurred stirring in the shadows under the hemlocks. I jerked my head around to look.

Nothing moved.

I wondered if the "woods-madness" that seizes lost persons was coming upon me so soon.

And then I paused to stare at a murky clump which I hoped was only bushes. The clump, big as a truck horse, started toward me. It kept coming, slowly, heavily, swinging a great, low head. Brush rattled under its shambling tread. I smelled the rank, musky odor of bear.

The next instant I had turned from the monster and was running madly through the semidarkness of the forest.

1. Look up the word *peninsula* in a dictionary. Based on the meaning, why does the narrator think it is not too far from the coast?

   A body of land surrounded by water on three sides.

   _____

2. Look up the word *raked* in the dictionary. Which meaning fits the way the word is used in paragraph 3? What is another meaning that does not fit this context?

   Raked means to comb through. The definition of raked that involves
   gathering would not fit the text

3. Find the meaning of the word *carnivorous*. What is the opposite of a carnivorous animal?

An herbivore, which is an animal that eats plants

4. What does the word *bear-infested* mean? What other things could *infest* a forest?

It means something is full of bears, insects, wolves, and deer.

5. What is a synonym for the word *panic*? What is an antonym? Create a mental image to help you remember the meaning of this word.

Freak out. A word that has a reverse meaning.

Assessment Practice

Directions   Answer the questions based on the passage you just read.

1.   **Read this sentence from the selection.**

> A root tripped me and threw me flat in the trail that led through the blueberry thicket.

What does the word *thicket* mean in the sentence above?

  A   a field with mixed vegetation

  B   a dense growth of underbrush

  C   the roots of a tree

  D   a trail or path

2.   **Read this sentence from the selection.**

> I slapped my hand over it, and, with a chill of premonition, looked at what I'd caught—a long tuft of coarse brown hair dangling from a twig above.

What is the meaning of the word *premonition* in the sentence?

  A   a freezing cold breeze

  B   the knowledge that something will happen

  C   a look back into the past

  D   a feeling that warns you about something

3. **Read this sentence from the selection.**

> All along it, evenly spaced in the damp, brown mold, were deep depressions, round and large as dinner plates.

What does the word *depressions* mean in the sentence?

A   sunken or hollowed areas

B   periods of economic decline

C   sadness and hopelessness

D   reductions in activity

4. **Read this sentence from the selection.**

> I had a senseless, almost uncontrollable impulse to dash madly through the trees, regardless of direction, bears, or anything else.

In the sentence above, what does the word *impulse* mean?

A   a feeling of great fear

B   the inability to move

C   a sudden urge or wish

D   the strength to run quickly

5. **Read this sentence from the selection.**

> I found myself stepping furtively, trying not to make any noise, and straining to hear the slightest sound.

What does the word *furtively* mean in the sentence above?

A   openly

B   quickly

C   carefully

D   stealthily

Focus on California Content Standards

Lesson 2 Interpret Figurative Meanings

Reading Vocabulary 9.1.1 Identify and use the literal and figurative meanings of words and understand word derivations.

The **literal meaning** of a word or phrase is its dictionary meaning. When words are used literally, they mean exactly what they say. The **figurative meaning** of words is more imaginative. When words are used figuratively, they mean something different from their simple dictionary definitions.

When you read, make sure you understand when words are used literally and when they are used figuratively. For example, read the sentence below:

He had a frog in his throat and so could not give his speech.

The literal meaning of this sentence is that there was an actual frog in his throat. Probably, the writer did not mean for you to take these words literally, but figuratively. The figurative meaning is that the speaker was hoarse.

Four types of figurative language are similes, metaphors, personification, and idioms.

A **simile** is a comparison between two basically dissimilar things that uses the words *as*, *like*, or *resembles*. For example:

His evil smile revealed large teeth that were *like polished tombstones*.
Upon hearing the bad news, she felt as broken *as a cracked egg*.

A **metaphor** is a comparison between two basically dissimilar things that does not use the words *as*, *like*, or *resembles*. For example:

Johnny's mind was a *powerful computer*, processing complex information with amazing speed.
The sun is a *soft-boiled egg* in a *frying-pan sky*.

Personification means giving human qualities to animals or things that are not human. For example:

The sky *threatened* us with a thunderstorm.
The wind *sang a lullaby*, lulling us to sleep.

Idioms are special expressions that are peculiar to themselves grammatically and cannot be understood if taken literally. Some idioms are based on figurative comparisons. For example:

It's raining *cats and dogs*.
The proof is *in the pudding*.

Guided Reading Instruction

Directions Read the following passage. Use the questions in the margin to guide your reading. Then answer the questions that follow.

from **Moon Tiger**
by Penelope Lively

> The narrator of this selection is a British war correspondent in Egypt in World War II. The man she loves is at the front. Erwin Rommel was the German general in command of German troops in North Africa. "Monty" was Bernard Law Montgomery, who led the British forces in North Africa to victory in 1942.

There were weeks and months when nothing happened. **1** All we knew was that out there the two armies were crouched motionless somewhere west of Tobruk, waiting to see what the other would do. There was little information because there was none to give. It was then that the myth of Rommel took shape: the cunning, unpredictable foe, larger than life, a Napoleon of the sand, eclipsing the weathered homely legends of our own generals. Even Monty never had Rommel's mystique.

2 There must have been realists in Cairo who expected the worst, yet never even later in the wilder moments of "the flap," when the Panzer Army was poised at Alamein and the ashes of burning documents rained down from the sky do I remember the smell of fear. Crisis, yes; alarm, no. Those with wives and children sent them to Palestine; a few families got on boats for South Africa or India.

3 There was plenty of the globe left into which to withdraw, and in any case it would only be a temporary measure, until things picked up again. I don't think anyone seriously envisaged Rommel's officers sitting around the pool at Gezira Sporting Club. Drinks were served at sundown, as they always had been; race meetings were on Saturdays; the amateur dramatics group did a production of *The Mikado*. Mother, writing from war-straitened Dorset, said she was so relieved I was somewhere safe, but thought the climate must be trying. Did she ever look at an atlas, I wonder? She had her own problems; patient endurance was the theme of her letters—shortages, the garden sadly neglected, her good saucepans nobly sacrificed to be rendered into war weapons. The flimsy aerograms with their neat script were eloquent with stoicism. Did she ever imagine German troops surging through Sturminster Newton?

4 But in those static months of early 1942 war seemed like a permanent condition—a chronic disease that while not life-threatening impeded progress of any kind. I went to Jerusalem to try to get an interview with de Gaulle, who was rumoured to have turned up there, failed to get near him and did a piece on the Stern Gang instead.

5 One or two of my colleagues, restless with the inactivity, took off altogether for more interesting centers and had to come belting back in a hurry when eventually the desert sprang into life again. It was a time that seemed even while it was in progress to go on forever. The winter inched into spring; the temperature rose; at some point—when or for how long I do not know—he was there again.

1 What is the narrator comparing the armies to when she describes them as crouching motionless? *A tiger.*

2 Underline the metaphor the narrator uses to show how the ashes fell to the ground.

3 Explain the meaning of the idiom "things picked up."

4 How can the situation of war be like a chronic disease? *It doesn't go away.*

5 What does the narrator mean when she says that the desert "sprang into life again." *The fighting picked back up again.*

1. What does the idiom "larger than life" mean? Name two things you can think of that are "larger than life."

   It overshadowed the British Guy; he eclipsed him.

2. The moon eclipses the sun when it passes in front of it. How can one general "eclipse" another?

   By being better than him.

Apply **Directions** Read the passage below. Then answer the questions that follow it.

from The Baroque Marble
by E. A. Proulx

Late autumn rain again. Sister Opal woke up in a Polaroid yellow light with her head hanging off the bed all sideways. Down in the street children's voices slid under the window muffled and changed by the damp morning. Sister Opal thought the children sounded as if they were speaking Russian or Basque—some queer, garbled language. She pretended she was in another country where she didn't know a word of the language and where she would have to make signs to get breakfast in a few minutes when she went downstairs. False panic began to rise in her, then subsided. From her position of suspension over the edge of the bed, the furniture looked darker, and the unfamiliar angle gave it a sinister look. The bureau loomed, a skyscraper in dull, dark varnish. Perhaps there were tiny people and offices inside. The chair arms seemed to have clenched hands at their ends, like brown old men sitting anxiously in the doctor's office waiting to hear the bad news.

Sister Opal twisted her head around toward the yellow window. On the sill was a square glass jar of marbles, reddish brown, yellow, and white glassies and a very large blue one. Most of them were mob marbles, as much alike as the faces of the crowd to a dictator on his balcony. Off to one side of the jar there was a white marble, deformed and not a true round—a lopsided freak of a marble—her favorite one. When this marble sat alone on the splendor of Sister Opal's blue-velvet best dress, it took on a silver, translucent glow. In the jar, it was dirty-white, opaque, and with more space around it than the other marbles, as if they avoided getting too close to it.

The jar of marbles was a kind of wealth. It was the most Sister Opal owned. Eight hundred and forty-three marbles. She took a miser's satisfaction in pouring them out onto the bed, watching them roll into the valleys, gathering up their heavy, glassy weight, cold but soon warming in her hand. Each marble was individually beautiful. A kind of classic Greek perfection shone in their roundness. Under Sister Opal's father's magnifying glass, the perfect marbles disclosed blemishes, pits, and scratches. Sister Opal liked them unmagnified; in their smallness she found their greatest value.

She touched the shade and it leaped up, startled, to the top of the wooden roller where it chattered a few seconds in fright, and then clung, tightly wound. Her warm breath made a milky fog on the window glass and her warm finger wrote, "All the sailors have died of scurvy, yours truly, Opal Foote."

Downstairs, Sister Opal's family sat at the table. Dark and sullen, they crunched toast, stabbed at their eggs, and made whirlpools in their coffee, with spoons. Except for Sister Opal, it was a bad-tempered family in the mornings, and the only conversations were mumbles to each other to pass the sugar or salt. By noontime the family would be chatty and warm, and by suppertime everyone was in high spirits. Sister Opal's four brothers (except for Roy, who worked on the night shift at GE) were very jovial at suppertime, when Sister Opal was weary. This morning Sister Opal's father asked about homework. Sister Opal thought of homework as yellow leaves dropping softly down, like the yellow blank pages she had dropped into the wastepaper basket last night. Guilty, Sister Opal went outside with jammy toast, hearing something from her father about being home right after school to make up Roy's dinner pail and to start supper because Mama had to work late. Sister Opal sang a private song as she walked along the wet sidewalk hopping the shallow puddles which were out to ruin her good shoes.

1. Why does the author describe the light as Polaroid yellow in the first paragraph?

   The light is dim and fading.

2. In paragraph 2, what simile does the writer use to describe the marbles? What impression does this simile create of the marbles?

   The marbles [looked like]...the faces of the crowd to a dictator.
   This means a blurred impression in a crowd.

3. How does the author make the marbles seem almost human in paragraph 2?

   She implies that the other marbles are rejecting the lopsided marble.

4. In paragraph 4, what words create an impression of the shade as something human?

   Leaped up, startled, chattered, and clung

Assessment Practice

Directions Answer the questions based on the selection you just read.

1. **Read this sentence from the selection.**

   The bureau loomed, a skyscraper in dull, dark varnish.

   What does the metaphor in the sentence above suggest about the bureau?

   A   It came to life and started moving.
   B   It appeared very large and threatening.
   C   It was filled with many different objects.
   D   It made Opal feel cheerful.

2. **Read this sentence from the selection.**

   The chair arms seemed to have clenched hands at their ends, like brown old men sitting anxiously in the doctor's office waiting to hear bad news.

   What feeling is created by the simile in the sentence above?

   A   uneasiness
   B   pleasure
   C   anger
   D   despair

3. **Read this sentence from the selection.**

   By noontime the family would be chatty and warm, and by suppertime everyone was in high spirits.

   In the sentence above, what does the idiom "in high spirits" mean?

   A   a little tipsy
   B   cheerful
   C   unusually sad
   D   hungry

4. **Read this sentence from the selection.**

   Sister Opal thought of homework as yellow leaves dropping softly down, like the yellow blank pages she had dropped into the wastepaper basket last night.

   What impression of homework is created by the simile in the sentence above?

   A   something of great value
   B   something fragile
   C   something useless
   D   something that is hard to do

5. **Read this sentence from the selection.**

   Sister Opal sang a private song as she walked along the wet sidewalk hopping the shallow puddles which were out to ruin her good shoes.

   Which impression is created by the figurative language in the sentence above?

   A   The world is conspiring to harm Opal.
   B   The world is a pleasant place in which to live.
   C   Sister Opal enjoys singing in the rain.
   D   The wet sidewalks are dark and gloomy.

Focus on California Content Standards

Lesson 3 **Understand Word Derivations**

Reading Vocabulary 9.1.1 Identify and use the literal and figurative meanings of words and understand word derivations.

A **prefix** is a letter or group of letters added to the front of a base word or root to change its meaning. Below is a list of some common prefixes and the meanings they add to a base word or root.

Prefix	Meaning
a-, an-	not, without
col-, com-, con-, cor-	together
de-	from, down
dis-	apart, away, reverse
em-, en-, im-, in-	in, into
il-, im-, in, ir-	not
per-	by, completely
pro-	forward, in favor of
re-	again
sub-	under
trans-	across, through
un-	not, reverse

A **suffix** is a letter or group of letters added to the end of a base word or root to changes its meaning or part of speech. Below is a list of some common suffixes and their meanings.

Suffix	Meaning	Part of Speech
-al, -ial, ual	relating to	adjective
-ant	one who	noun
-ar, -er, or	one who	noun
-cian	having a certain skill or art	adjective
-ful	full of	adjective
-ion, -sion, -tion	state of, result of	noun
-ic	nature of, like	adjective
-ist	one who, that which	noun
-less	without	adjective
-ly	like, manner of	adverb
-ity, -ty	condition of, qulaity of	noun
-y	quality, somewhat like	noun or adjective

Two special suffixes are *-er* and *-est*. The comparative suffix *-er* is used to compare two things. The superlative suffix *-est* is used to compare three or more things.
For example:

Regina is taller than Pedro.

Regina is the tallest person in the class.

A **root** is the base from which a word is built by adding word parts such as prefixes and suffixes. Many roots come from Latin and Greek. Below is a list of some common roots and their meanings.

Root	Meaning
aud	hear, listen
cogni	know
fin	end
hap	chance
mori, mort, mors	death
navi	ship
not	know, observe
pons, pos	place, put
poli, polis	city
pop	people
port	carry
scrib, script	write
sci, scins, scient	know
spec, spect	look, see
stell	star
stru, struct	build

Understanding word parts can help you figure out the meaning of a word you do not know. For example, suppose you don't know the meaning of the word *metropolis*. Look at the word parts. The prefix *metro-* means "mother" and the root *polis* means "city." Therefore, *metropolis* means "mother city" or "major or chief city of a region."

Guided Reading Instruction

Directions Read the following passage. Use the questions in the margin to guide your reading. Then answer the questions that follow.

Old Man Mad About Drawing: Katsushika Hokusai
by Kathleen Krull

The man history knows as Katsushika Hokusai was born in the Year of the Dragon in the bustling city now known as Tokyo.

1 **2** After working for eight stormy years in the studio of a popular artist who resented the boy's greater skill, Hokusai was finally thrown out. At first he earned his daily bowl of rice as a street peddler, selling red peppers and ducking if he saw his old teacher coming. Soon he was illustrating comic books, then turning out banners, made-to-order greeting cards for the rich, artwork for novels full of murders and ghosts, and drawings of scenes throughout his beloved Edo.

Changing one's name was a Japanese custom, but Hokusai carried it to an extreme—he changed his more than thirty times. No one knows why. **3** Perhaps he craved variety, or was self-centered (thinking that every change in his art style required a new identity), or merely liked being eccentric. **4** One name he kept longer than most was Hokusai, meaning "Star of the Northern Constellation," in honor of a Buddhist god he especially revered.

By Chance

He did like variety in dwellings. **5** Notorious for never cleaning his studio, he took the easy way out whenever the place became too disgustingly dirty: he moved. Hokusai moved a total of ninety-three times—putting a burden on his family and creating a new set of neighbors for himself at least once a year. He married twice and had seven children, most of whom died in their twenties.

A born showman, Hokusai attracted attention by staging public performances of his art. Spectators marveled when he drew birds in flight—on a grain of rice; crowds cheered when he sprawled on a huge sheet of paper to paint with a brush the size of a broom. Sometimes he painted while hanging upside down, or with the brush held in his mouth or between his toes.

6 Wealth didn't impress him. He was known to keep important clients waiting while he meticulously picked all the fleas off his kimono. He lived simply,

Guided Questions

1 Find the word *popular*. Underline the root. What does this word mean?

2 Underline the suffix that turns an adjective into an adverb. It tells when Hokusai was thrown out. Circle the root. What does the root mean?

3 Find the word *perhaps*. Circle the prefix. Underline the root. What is the meaning of each word part?

4 Find the word *constellation*. Underline the prefix. Circle the root. Put a box around the suffix. What is a constellation?

5 Find the word *notorious*. Circle the root. Underline the suffix. What part of speech does this suffix form? What does *notorious* mean?

6 Circle the four adverbs ending in -*ly* that you find in this paragraph. What adjectives are formed when you remove the suffix?

meticulous
simple   most
usual

usually in poor neighborhoods. Hokusai drank tea and ate little, mostly rice cakes; he enjoyed a bowl of noodle soup before he went to bed. In the style of the times, he slept on a straw mat brought out from the closet every night. Money held no interest for him. **7** When he had to pay bills, he would hand over one of the unopened envelopes of payments he had received for his art—sometimes the money in the envelope matched the amount of the bill, sometimes it didn't.

Hokusai once went bankrupt and, to escape arrest by creditors, changed his name yet again and went into hiding outside of town for a year. Though he nearly died of starvation, running out of paper and paints was his worst nightmare. **8** After dark he would walk fifteen miles into Edo for supplies, trying to return before anyone he owed money to recognized him.

The older Hokusai got, the harder he worked. Sitting on his heels, hour after hour, he completed over thirty thousand pieces of art—an average of one a day during the course of his life. He hoped for immortality but made it to age eighty-nine. **9** The inscription on his gravestone shows his final name, Gwakio Rojin, meaning "Old Man Mad about Drawing."

Guided Questions

7 Find the word *unopened*. Form the antonym by removing the prefix.

opened

8 Find the word *recognized*. Underline the prefix. Circle the root. Box the suffix. What does this word mean?

9 Find the word *inscription*. Underline the prefix. Circle the root. Box the suffix. How do the word parts help you determine the meaning of the word?

1. The word *spectators* is made of the root *spec*, meaning "look" or "see," and the noun-forming suffix *-or*, meaning "one who." Therefore, *spectators* are people who look. List as many words as you can that contain this root.

   spectate, spectacle, spectral, speculate, spectacular, inspect, spectacles,

2. What is the root of the word *immortality* and the meaning of this root? List as many words as you can that contain this root.

   mortuary, mortal, mortician, mortified,

3. What is the root in *disgustingly*? What is the meaning of the root? What does *gusto*, a word formed with the same root, mean?

   gusting to like or enjoy,

4. What two words that begin with the prefix *en-* are synonyms for *gusto*?

   enjoy, entertain,

Apply

Directions Read the passage below. Then answer the questions that follow it.

Around the World on Just One Cent, Rufus Porter: Forgotten Genius of the Nineteenth Century
by Jane Kaplan Naliboff

HOW IS IT POSSIBLE that an American artist, inventor, and publisher who produced an amazing body of work—including beautiful landscape murals, machines and tools we use every day, *and* one of the most highly acclaimed scientific journals of our time—remains virtually unknown?

Rufus Porter, born in 1792, was a genius. And he was restless. The son of a prosperous farmer in West Boxford, Massachusetts, he left his father's farm and began working with his brother as an apprentice shoemaker when he was fifteen. But Rufus soon tired of that and moved on to Portland, Maine, where he lived with his cousin and learned to paint—first as a house painter, and later he taught himself to paint portraits and landscapes.

In 1815 Porter decided to become an itinerant portrait painter and moved to New Haven, Connecticut. From there he traveled throughout New England and south to Virginia, where he got many ideas for the murals he would later paint on the walls of New England homes. By selling his portraits and landscapes to pay for passage, he traveled to the Northwest and even to the Hawaiian Islands.

To help him paint silhouettes, Rufus Porter devised a portable camera obscura into which he placed a mirror so that the image would appear right side up instead of upside down. Porter became a famous mural painter himself, using a combination of freehand painting, stenciling, and cork-stopper stamps to complete his murals.

Not content simply to create, Porter wanted to share his knowledge, so, in 1825, after his return to the mainland and New England, he wrote and published *A Select Collection of Approved, Genuine, Secret and Modern Receipts, For the Preparation and Execution of Various Valuable and Curious Arts*, a book that explained how to paint landscape murals on the walls of houses. This book was to be the first of many publications with which he is credited in his lifetime—the *Scientific American* magazine foremost among them.

Porter began publishing *Scientific American* magazine in 1845. The first issue was four pages long and contained poetry, religious news, technical news and instruction, and interesting tidbits from around the country. Ten months later, however, he sold the magazine to Alfred Ely Beach and Orson D. Munn for $800.00.

Porter's artistic ability and journalistic flair were equaled only by his prolific creativity as an inventor. It was Porter who invented the revolving cylinder barrel of the Colt 45 revolver. In 1844, he sold the idea to Samuel Colt for only $100.00. And it was Porter who, during the gold rush of 1849, proposed the idea of a "flying ship" that would take people from the East Coast to California in three days, and he wrote a book about it called *Aerial Navigation*. In 1852 he started his own navigational company but was never able to build a working model of his aircraft, because he couldn't find enough investors to make it a success.

Fifty-four years later, on 17 December 1903, two bicycle salesmen from Dayton, Ohio, flew their flying machine 852 feet into the air—a flight that lasted fifty-nine seconds. After that historic moment, it would have been fitting for Orville and Wilbur Wright to have acknowledged Rufus Porter's genius, for his "flying ship" design had greatly contributed to their success and to the history of aerial navigation in general.

Porter's creative genius as an inventor, artist, and journalist was greatly hampered by his inability to successfully market his inventions. His failure to rise from obscurity may be traced to Porter's lack of foresight. He often neglected to patent his inventions prior to selling them and was dismally inept at estimating project costs, leaving him without the necessary funds to bring his work from the drawing board to the production line.

When Rufus died in New Haven, Connecticut, in 1884, few people knew of his inventions and accomplishments. Few knew that he had designed waterwheels and windmills, had written poetry, had been a talented violinist, and played the fife as well.

Few knew that he was the inventor of a rotary plow, a double-hand rake, a sewing machine, a washing machine, a clothes dryer, a distance-measuring appliance, a horsepower mechanism, a churn, a life preserver, a cheese press, a fire alarm, a cord-making machine, a camera, prefabricated houses, and a steam carriage for common roads—a predecessor to the first automobile. Porter also left us a legacy of mural paintings that still exist in many New England houses.

During his lifetime, Porter was regarded as "too radical and progressive" in his hometown. But those who knew him well and admired his creative genius said he was "a man who could go around the world with only one cent in his pocket."

1. In paragraph 1, find three words describing Rufus Porter that end in a suffix that means "one who." Then, using suffixes that mean "one who," build five new words.

    A baker, a manufacturer, a producer, and a journalist.

2. Build the missing form of each word below by changing suffixes. You can use a dictionary for help.

Noun	Adjective
beauty	beautiful
rest	restless
content	contented
journal	journalistic
creativity	creativeness

3. The word *scientific* in paragraph 5 is built from the root *sci*, *scins*, *scient*, which means "know." What does the word *scientific* mean? How is this word related to *know*? Build at least two other words using this root.

_____ Scientific means _____ like knowing. _____

_____

_____

4. Find the word *instruction* in paragraph 6. If you provide instruction, you build a person's knowledge so that he or she can do something on his or her own. Change the prefix to build two other words from the root *struct*.

This is what happens when something is torn down. _____ destruction _____

This is what happens when pieces are put together to build something. _____ construction _____

5. Look at paragraph 7. Use word parts to figure out the meaning of each word below. Check your answer in a dictionary.

proposed _____ to come up with _____

navigation _____ to find something _____

_____

_____

Assessment Practice

Directions Answer the questions based on the selection you just read.

1. **Read this sentence from the selection.**

   > How is it possible that an American artist, inventor, and publisher who produced an amazing body of work—including beautiful landscape murals, machines and tools we use every day, and one of the most highly acclaimed scientific journals of our time—remains virtually unknown?

   An *inventor* is a person who makes an—

   A   invitation.

   B   inventory.

   C   invention.

   D   inversion.

2. **Read this sentence from the selection.**

   > To help him paint silhouettes, Rufus Porter devised a portable camera obscura into which he placed a mirror so that the image would appear right side up instead of upside down.

   What is the meaning of the word *portable*?

   A   able to be carried

   B   too large to carry

   C   auto-focus

   D   easily assembled

3. **Read this sentence from the selection.**

   > The first issue was four pages long and contained poetry, religious news, technical news and instruction, and interesting tidbits from around the country.

   If you receive instruction, you get—

   A   direction.

   B   incentive.

   C   freedom.

   D   acknowledgment.

4. **Read this sentence from the selection.**

   > He often neglected to patent his inventions prior to selling them and was dismally inept at estimating project costs, leaving him without the necessary funds to bring his work from the drawing board to the production line.

   Which of the following words is built from the same root as *production*?

   A   protect

   B   appropriate

   C   aqueduct

   D   docile

5. **Read this sentence from the selection.**

   > This book was to be the first of many publications with which he is credited in his lifetime—the *Scientific American* magazine foremost among them.

   A word based on the same root as *publications* is—

   A   vacation.

   B   creation.

   C   republic.

   D   puberty.

Reading Vocabulary 9.1.1 Identify and use the literal and figurative meanings of words and understand word derivations.

1 **Context clues** are words in a sentence or passage that help you find the meaning of an unknown word or phrase. In the examples below, the unfamiliar words are in italics, and the context clues are underlined.

2 **Synonym or Restatement**

Some stars look so <u>tiny</u> that they seem *infinitesimal* in the night sky.

The dresses the bridesmaids wore were an awful *ocher*, or <u>yellowish-brown</u> color.

3 **Antonym or Contradiction**

Rather than go *berserk*, Gabriella stayed <u>calm</u> when she saw that her little brother had eaten the last piece of pie.

4 **Definition or Description**

Who in our class would have known that *curling* is <u>a sport played on ice with brooms</u>?

Timmy couldn't fit his jacket in the *chifforobe*, which meant he needed an even larger <u>piece of furniture for storing his clothes</u>.

5 **Example**

The stew was pleasantly *piquant*. The <u>hot peppers</u> gave it just the right <u>taste</u>.

6 **Comparison and Contrast**

Hiroko is usually *succinct*. However, when she told me about the dream she had yesterday, she was surprisingly <u>long-winded and rambling</u>.

7 **Cause and Effect**

In order to *ameliorate* the housing shortage, the college <u>built two new dormitories</u> to improve living conditions.

Guided Reading Instruction

Directions Read the following passage. Use the questions in the margin to guide your reading. Then answer the questions that follow.

from **Feared, Revered King Cobras**
by Mattias Klum

As if lit from within, the mist-drenched rain forest of Borneo's Danum Valley awakens with me before sunrise. Somewhere below stirs the king cobra—the inspiration for my journey to the villages and forests of Southeast Asia. **1** **2** The longest venomous snake, it produces startling amounts of neurotoxin—enough to kill an elephant with a single bite. **3** But this serpent that can stand up like a man in a terrifying pose is shy and retreating, aggressive only if provoked. We know little about its populations, but fragmented forests and illegal wildlife trade may be putting it at risk. **4** Though snakes strike fear in many Westerners, in the East the cobra is often an object of worship and reverence—and, in some places, a part of peoples' livelihoods. **5** So I have come here to pay my respects to *Ophiophagus hannah*, with hopes that I might observe this king of snakes.

Guided Questions

1 Circle the word *venomous*. Underline the context clue that helps you figure out its meaning. What does *venomous* mean?

2 Circle the word *neurotoxin*. Underline the context clues that help you figure out its meaning. What is a neurotoxin?

3 Circle the word *aggressive*. Underline the antonyms, or words that mean the opposite, of *aggressive*. What does *aggressive* mean?

4 Circle the word *reverence*. What does *reverence* mean?

5 Which words in the sentence tell you what an *Ophiophagus hannah* is?

1. Write a sentence using the word *venomous*. Include context clues to help a reader figure out the meaning of the word.

   My lyrics are venomous or poisonous.

2. Write a sentence using the word *aggressive*. Include context clues to help a reader figure out the meaning of the word.

   I am agressive if you step on my toes, because I will fight anyone who disrespects me.

Apply   **Directions** Read the passage below. Then answer the questions that follow it.

Keep Your Head
by Dewey Gram

Concussions are common. And for kid athletes, they're a special threat. Here's why.

When pro quarterback Steve Young of the San Francisco 49ers took a hard hit to the head against the Arizona Cardinals, he was taken out of the game, and kept out. Reason: Doctors are learning that repeated concussions, even mild ones, are a much more serious medical problem than people once believed.

Concussions are injuries to your brain caused by thumps to your head. They are a special threat to kids. According to new studies that appeared in *The Journal of the American Medical Association* in September 1999, teenagers who take two or more significant hits to the head can suffer long-term damage to their thinking abilities.

Dumbing Down

Their memories, attention spans and planning abilities also were impaired, especially among kids who already had learning disabilities. There were 393 college football players in the study. The one in five of them who had suffered multiple concussions had continuous headache, sleep and concentration problems. They also scored lower on pencil and paper tests.

Concussions are common. Nearly 63,000 athletes competing in 10 high-school sports suffer mild concussions each year, almost two-thirds of them in football.

"This is a major public health issue," says Dr. Michael Collins, lead author of one study.

What is most important to know, says neurologist Dr. Vernon Williams at the Kerlan-Jobe sports clinic in Los Angeles, is that "Athletes are four to six times more likely to have a second concussion after a first."

Where Dangers Lie

A concussion isn't just getting knocked out, says Dr. Collins. It is any alteration in mental function caused by a significant blow to the head.

Concussions occur not just in the so-called "gladiator" or "collision" sports like football and hockey, but also in noncollision, nonhelmet sports like soccer, which has about the same concussion rate as hockey.

In soccer, the main danger is players' knocking heads or hitting the ground or goalpost, more than heading the ball.

Always report any hard thump to the head.

"Athletes see mild concussions simply as part of the game," says Dr. Williams, "and won't report it to the trainer. They don't want to appear weak."

Play Smart

"There is no such thing as a minor concussion," says concussion expert Dr. James P. Kelly. He also argues the injury shouldn't be trivialized by calling it "a ding to the head," or "getting your bell rung."

To reduce the harm caused by head injuries in sports, Dr. Williams advocates educating coaches, players and parents about the seriousness of multiple mild concussions. He also recommends continuing to improve protective head gear, and further strengthening the penalties for dangerous practices like "spearing" (head-on tackling), roughing the quarterback, and head shots in hockey.

Steve Young is getting the message. "I'm much more sober about it than ever before," he said after his Arizona concussion. "I will see my buddy [a neurosurgeon] and I will deal with it as realistically as I can."

1. In paragraph 2, what happened to Steve Young? What word in the paragraph tells you about the condition that resulted from this?

   Steve Young received a concussion while playing football. It says he took
   a hard hit to the head.

2. The definition of concussion is given in paragraph 3. What is it? Name one type of accident that might cause a concussion.

   Car accident

3. In paragraph 3, the author mentions new studies in *The Journal of the American Medical Association*. In this context, what must the word *studies* mean?

   Statistics

4. Paraphrase, or put in your own words, what Dr. Williams says in paragraph 7. Based on the context, what do you think a neurologist is?

   Someone who studies neurons and nerves in the body. Dr. Williams says
   once you have a concussion you are 4 to 6 more times

5. What examples does the author give of "gladiator" or "collision" sports? How would you define the terms?

   _____

   _____

Assessment Practice

Directions Answer the questions based on the selection you just read.

1. **Read this sentence from the selection.**

   > It is any alteration in mental function caused by a significant blow to the head.

   What is the meaning of the word *alteration*?

   A   occurrence

   B   change

   C   importance

   D   increase

2. **Read this sentence from the selection.**

   > He also argues the injury shouldn't be trivialized by calling it "a ding to the head," or "getting your bell rung."

   What is the meaning of the word *trivialized*?

   A   made more important than it is

   B   given medical treatment

   C   ignored

   D   minimized

3. **Read this sentence from the selection.**

   > Steve Young is getting the message. "I'm much more sober about it than ever before," he said after his Arizona concussion. "I will see my buddy [a neurosurgeon] and I will deal with it as realistically as I can."

   What context clue best explains the meaning of *sober* in this paragraph?

   A   realistically

   B   message

   C   see my buddy

   D   deal with

4. **Read these sentences from the selection.**

   > To reduce the harm caused by head injuries in sports, Dr. Williams advocates educating coaches, players and parents about the seriousness of multiple mild concussions. He also recommends continuing to improve protective head gear, and further strengthening the penalties for dangerous practices like "spearing" (head-on tackling), roughing the quarterback, and head shots in hockey.

   In this paragraph, what is a synonym that best helps you figure out the meaning of the word *advocates*?

   A   improve

   B   educating

   C   recommends

   D   strengthening

5. **Read this sentence from the selection.**

   > Their memories, attention spans and planning abilities also were impaired, especially among kids who already had learning disabilities.

   What is the meaning of the word *impaired*?

   A   diminished

   B   disabled

   C   destroyed

   D   demonstrated

Focus on California Content Standards

Lesson 5   **Understand Connotation and Denotation**

Reading Vocabulary 9.1.2 Distinguish between the denotative and connotative meanings of words and interpret the connotative power of words.

When you read, you respond to words in two ways. First, you respond to their literal meaning, or **denotation**. Second, you respond to the feelings and associations words bring to mind. This emotional impression is a word's **connotation**.

For example, look at the synonyms *cheap* and *thrifty*. Both words can refer to someone who is careful about spending money. However, the word *cheap* brings to mind someone who is selfish and penny-pinching. The word *thrifty*, on the other hand, brings to mind someone who is careful and responsible. If someone doesn't offer to buy you dinner, you might think of him or her as *cheap*. If you don't offer to buy someone else dinner, you might think of yourself as *thrifty*. Certainly, you would not have a chance of having dinner bought for you by someone who is *stingy*, another synonym with a similar denotation but a different connotation.

Look at the words *stubborn* and *determined*. Both denote persistence and perseverance. However, *stubborn* provokes negative associations, suggesting that the person is too bull-headed and unable to listen to reason. *Determined* inspires more positive feelings, suggesting that a person is strong-minded, firm, and resolute. You would want to negotiate with a determined person; you would not want to deal with a person who is stubborn.

These shades of meaning in words make a great deal of difference in how you perceive things. When you read, think about why the author has chosen certain words. What purpose did the author have in choosing a particular word rather than another word with the same denotation but different connotations?

Guided Reading Instruction

Directions Read the following passage. Use the questions in the margin to guide your reading. Then answer the questions that follow.

from **The Sphinx**
by Edgar Allan Poe

1 During the dread reign of cholera in New York, I had accepted the invitation of a relative to spend a fortnight with him in the retirement of his *cottage orné* on the banks of the Hudson. **2** We had here around us all the ordinary means of summer amusement; and what with rambling in the woods, sketching, boating, fishing, bathing, music, and books, we should have passed the time pleasantly enough, but for the fearful intelligence which reached us every morning from the populous city. Not a day elapsed which did not bring us news of the decease of some acquaintance. Then, as the fatality increased, we learned to expect daily the loss of some friend. **3** At length we trembled at the approach of every messenger. The very air from the South seemed to us redolent with death. That palsying thought, indeed, took entire possession of my soul. I could neither speak, think, nor dream of anything else. My host was of a less excitable temperament, and, although greatly depressed in spirits, exerted himself to sustain my own. His richly philosophical intellect was not at any time affected by unrealities. To the substances of terror he was sufficiently alive, but of its shadows he had no apprehension.

4 His endeavors to arouse me from the condition of abnormal gloom into which I had fallen, were frustrated, in great measure, by certain volumes which I had found in his library. These were of a character to force into germination whatever seeds of hereditary superstition lay latent in my bosom. **5** I had been reading these books without his knowledge, and thus he was often at a loss to account for the forcible impressions which had been made upon my fancy.

A favorite topic with me was the popular belief in omens—a belief which, at this one epoch of my life, I was almost seriously disposed to defend. **6** On this subject we had long and animated discussions; he maintaining the utter groundlessness of faith in such matters, I contending that a popular sentiment arising with absolute spontaneity—that is to say, without apparent traces of suggestion—had in itself the unmistakable elements of truth, and was entitled to much respect.

The fact is, that soon after my arrival at the cottage there had occurred to myself an incident so entirely inexplicable, and which had in it so much of the portentous character, that I might well have been excused for regarding it as an omen. **7** It appalled, and at the same time so confounded and bewildered me, that many days elapsed before I could make up my mind to communicate the circumstance to my friend.

Guided Questions

1 Circle the word *dread*. What impression does it create?

Dread implies fear

2 Circle the word *rambling*. How would your response be different if the author had used the word *walking* instead?

rambling is for enjoyment, and walking is for a purpose

3 Circle the word *trembled*. How would the selection be changed if the author had used the word *quivered* instead? What difference would it make if *trembled* were replaced with *shuddered*?

Quivering is positive and shuttering is negative

4 Circle the word *gloom*. Think of four antonyms for it.

5 Circle the word *fancy*. Think of three synonyms for it.

Dream, imagination, fantasy

6 Circle the word *spontaneity*. Think of a synonym for this word with a negative connotation.

7 Circle the word *appalled*. Does this word have positive or negative connotations? Think of five antonyms for *appalled*.

1. List three synonyms for *redolent*, one with a positive connotation, one with a neutral connotation, and one with a negative connotation. You may use a dictionary or thesaurus to help you.

   Scent, stench, aroma

2. Look at the word *terror*. Does the word have positive or negative connotations? List three antonyms for the word. You may use a dictionary or thesaurus to help you.

   fear, horror, panic.

3. Rewrite the following by replacing the underlined words with either synonyms or antonyms with positive connotations to paint a cheerful picture.

   > The very air from the South seemed to us <u>redolent</u> with <u>death</u>. That <u>palsying</u> thought, indeed, took entire possession of my soul. I could neither speak, think, nor dream of anything else. My host was of a less excitable temperament, and although greatly <u>depressed</u> in spirits, exerted himself to sustain my own. His highly philosophical intellect was not at any time affected by unrealities. To the substances of <u>terror</u> he was sufficiently alive, but of its <u>shadows</u> he had <u>no apprehension</u>.

   The very air from the South seemed to us scented with a life. The freeing thought, indeed, took entire possession of my soul. I could neither speak, think, nor dream of anything else. My host was of a less excitable temperament, and although greatly excited in spirits, exerted himself to sustain my own. His highly philosophical intellect was not at any time affected by unrealities. To the substances of fear he was sufficiently alive, but of its shade he had no understanding.

Apply

Directions As you read the following humorous account of a visit to modern China think about why the author chose certain words. Then answer the questions that follow the passage.

from At War with Grandma

by Ashley Palmer

Grandmothers and food. For better or for worse, there is an undeniable connection between the two. Your grandmother may have tempted you with homemade apple pie that magically appeared from her oven as you walked in the door. Or perhaps you dreaded grandma's mystery casserole, developed from a recipe she dug up from the Dark Ages. You may have had a grandma who lovingly indulged you with the sweets forbidden by your own parents. Or maybe she was the one who most despaired of your picky eating habits by nagging, "Your mother loved this when she was your age, why won't you eat it?" While living in Japan, I found that this connection between grandmothers and food not only exists cross-culturally, but also, in my case, extended to include a surrogate Japanese grandmother.

I was introduced to Kobayashi-san by my university advisor, who lived in the same village. When we met, I was approaching the end of a year living in Nagano Prefecture, researching Japanese rural lifestyles. My advisor had arranged for me to work with Kobayashi-san several days a week, helping out at her home, where she cultivated and sold bonsai and other plants.

It wasn't only the connection with food that made Kobayashi-san seem grandmotherly. Neither was it merely her age. At seventy-five, she puttered around her gardens from dawn to dusk, her bent frame moving up and down the rows of plants, muttering to herself constantly. She immediately gave up on the difficult pronunciation of my name, and adopted the more familiar nickname, "Ah-chan." She also didn't hesitate to put me to work, weeding, stacking newspapers, washing dishes. But what most made her a grandmother in my mind was that telltale combination of being simultaneously concerned, critical, frank, and affectionate. One minute she would scold me for refusing to wear a hat in the sun, and the next minute she would insist I was working too hard. Unlike many Japanese, who initially hide behind a wall of social formality, Kobayashi-san was surprisingly forward with me, and seemed unfazed by our cultural and linguistic differences. Being so far from home and my own two wonderful grandmothers, I found her acceptance of me endearing.

It all started rather innocently. There was a steady stream of people flowing in and out of her home. Some were customers, but most were local people, looking for conversation, gossip, or just a friendly face. Keeping with the custom in Japan, she religiously served tea and snacks to all the visitors who joined her at the big table. It was there, on my first day, that she asked me, "Do you like Japanese food?" I replied promptly in the affirmative. It could have been that I answered too confidently, or she may have just wanted to have a little fun. But, looking back to that day, I swear there was a gleam in her eye when she responded, "Oh, really?"

I do love Japanese food. Moreover, I felt that during the previous ten months I had developed an appreciation for the cuisine that had been lacking during my prior experiences living in Japan. Raw fish so fresh and soft it melts in your mouth. The simplicity of cold soba noodles slurped on a summer afternoon. However, I had never claimed to love every type of Japanese food. I knew of differences between mainstream Japanese cuisine and local country specialties, having once been offered candied grasshoppers on a research trip to the same village. But this time it wasn't the food itself that took me by surprise, but rather the spirit in which Kobayashi-san offered it.

Kobayashi-san prided herself on having a variety of snacks to offer her guests, and on that first day she deliberately arranged several bowls of cookies, crackers, and pickles around my place. As I reached for a mild-looking rice cracker, she intercepted my hand mid-reach and pushed something else into it. "I bet you've never tried this before. I don't know if you'll like it, but you should try it!" she challenged. I cast a longing glance in the direction of my rice cracker and opened my hand to reveal a much more menacing seafood snack. It was a dried fish, the chewy kind meant to be consumed whole—bones, tail, and head. I gnawed on it tentatively and, finding the taste bearable, I politely responded, "It's good, really!" Kobayashi-san threw back her head and laughed, her eyes crinkling up until they almost disappeared into the wrinkles on her face.

1. Circle the word *Grandma* in the title. What impression does this word create? How is this word different than *grandmother*?

$$\begin{array}{r} 24 \\ \times\ 5 \\ \hline 120 \end{array}$$

Grandma shows familiarity and a good relationship. Grandmother

2. Circle the word *homemade* in paragraph 1. What connotations are associated with this word? Are the connotations positive or negative?

~~Homemade~~ Homemade has a positive connotation suggesting that something is good, made with love, and thoughtful.

3. Circle the word *indulged* in paragraph 1. What connotations are associated with the word? Write three antonyms for the word.

To make yourself feel good. Treating yourself to. Seperate. Distance, Stray

4. Circle the word *nagging* in paragraph 1. Look it up in the dictionary. What does it mean? Why do you think the author chose this word instead of the synonym *harassing*?

Nagging insinuates that there is a reason for someone's bickering. Harassing does not suggest there is a reason for it.

5. Circle the word *puttered* in paragraph 3. Look it up in the dictionary. What does it mean? Why do you think the author chose this word?

Move around aimlessly.

6. Circle the word *scold* in paragraph 3. List as many synonyms for the word as you can. Then list as many antonyms that you can think of for the word.

lecture, hassle, reprimand, chastize.

Assessment Practice

Directions Answer the questions based on the selection you just read.

1. **Read this sentence from the selection.**

   > Your grandmother may have tempted you with homemade apple pie that magically appeared from her oven as you walked in the door.

   Why did the narrator choose the word *tempted* instead of the synonym lured?

   A   The author wanted to show how difficult grandmothers can be at times.

   B   The author wanted to show that children love their grandmothers for their pies.

   C   The author wanted to create the impression of generous grandmothers.

   D   The author wanted to describe the flavor of apple pie.

2. **Read this sentence from the selection.**

   > Or perhaps you dreaded grandma's mystery casserole, developed from a recipe she dug up from the Dark Ages.

   Which of the following items carries the closest connotation to *dreaded*?

   A   shrank from

   B   were afraid of

   C   didn't look forward

   D   were embarrassed by

3. **Read this sentence from the selection.**

   > I cast a longing glance in the direction of my rice cracker and opened my hand to reveal a much more menacing seafood snack.

   Which synonym for *menacing* best captures the narrator's feelings about the seafood snack?

   A   sparkling

   B   harsh

   C   groomed

   D   unearthly

4. **Read this sentence from the selection.**

   > At seventy-five, she puttered around her gardens from dawn to dusk, her bent frame moving up and down the rows of plants, muttering to herself constantly.

   In paragraph 3, the narrator uses the word muttering to describe grandmother's complaining ways. Which synonym below would best suggest a more irritated frame of mind?

   A   grumbling

   B   murmuring

   C   mumbling

   D   whispering

5. **Read this sentence from the selection.**

   > I knew of differences between mainstream Japanese cuisine and local country specialties, having once been offered candied grasshopper on a research trip to the same village.

   What is the author suggesting by using the word *cuisine*?

   A   She is suggesting that the Japanese like spicy food.

   B   She is suggesting that Japanese food can be fine.

   C   She is suggesting that Japanese food is similar to French cuisine.

   D   She is suggesting that she does not like Japanese food.

The following article makes some surprising predictions for the future. Read the article and answer questions 1 through 10.

The last thirty years of the nineteenth century are called the Gilded Age. This was a time of industrial and economic innovation that produced glittering wealth for some and poverty and over-crowded living conditions for others.

The Birth of Big Business
By Peter Barnes

In the spring of 1865, the bloody Civil War came to an end. It had nearly destroyed the nation. But it had also created opportunities. The war meant almost instant wealth for the men who manufactured arms, clothing, and supplies for the opposing armies.

After the war, many of these businessmen competed for new opportunities to invest their wealth and make money. The United States was expanding rapidly. Many fortunes were made on railroads. Railways opened up access to the West and new areas for farming, ranching, and land development.

Railroads were extremely expensive to construct. They required large amounts of labor and materials. A businessman could build a factory, such as an oil refinery, for about fifty thousand dollars. But it sometimes took twenty thousand dollars to create just one mile of railroad track.

To help raise the necessary money, or capital, railroad companies sold stock. The stockholder, or investor, then became a partial owner of the company. Anyone—farmers, shopkeepers, teachers—could own tiny shares, or stocks, of an enormous company. The financial district in New York, located on and around Wall Street, played an important role in the growth of big business during this period.

Industries, such as steel and coal, exploded as railroads moved goods quickly from New York to California. Factories popped up across the country, mass-producing items such as sewing machines, hand soap, and bags of flour.

The growing businesses benefited from new manufacturing techniques. Powerful machines performed tasks five to ten times faster than humans had ever been able to before. Some factories ran twenty-four hours a day and seven days a week to deliver maximum production. James Buchanan "Buck" Duke's factories produced 500,000 cigarettes a day using the tobacco-rolling machines invented by James Bonsack. These quickly outproduced the skilled worker's ability to hand-roll three thousand cigarettes a day. The Pillsbury family of Minneapolis used modern steel rollers and shucking machines to turn wheat into barrels of white four.

Some of these companies grew into corporations, with thousands of investors and employees. Finding it impractical to bring that many people together for business meetings, elected boards of directors began to make management decisions. Employees were separated into departments where they worked at specific jobs, such as bookkeeping, purchasing, engineering, and payroll.

Fierce competition led many businesses to increase efficiency. For example, the Chicago meat-packer Gustavus Swift built his own railroad cars, wagons, and warehouses to transport and store his beef. Workers for the Singer Company supplied replacement parts, made repairs, and taught classes on the use of their new sewing machines.

Creative advertising increased sales. Buck Duke, for instance, placed pictures of actresses and athletes on all his cigarette packs. People soon became familiar with products that were advertised heavily and refused to purchase lesser-known brands. All of this led to the first trademark being issued by the U.S. Patent Office in 1870.

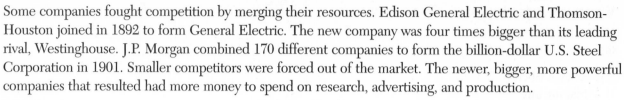

Some companies fought competition by merging their resources. Edison General Electric and Thomson-Houston joined in 1892 to form General Electric. The new company was four times bigger than its leading rival, Westinghouse. J.P. Morgan combined 170 different companies to form the billion-dollar U.S. Steel Corporation in 1901. Smaller competitors were forced out of the market. The newer, bigger, more powerful companies that resulted had more money to spend on research, advertising, and production.

The most famous of these new companies was the Standard Oil Trust, created in 1882. Under this legal agreement, John D. Rockefeller and his partners gained control over more than four-fifths of the nation's oil refining business. With its competition greatly reduced until the early 1900s, Standard Oil enjoyed a monopoly for a short time.

By the late 1880s, however, Americans were complaining about trusts and monopolies. Many citizens thought it was unfair for giant corporations to force smaller companies out of business. The Sherman Antitrust Act of 1890 was created "to protect trade and commerce against unlawful restraints and monopolies." But the law's vagueness left interpretation up to the courts. The courts tended to side with big businesses. The act was only moderately successful at stopping the expansion of certain industries.

Wealthy industrialists and entrepreneurs defended themselves against their critics. Steelmaker Andrew Carnegie argued that competition brought quality goods at cheap prices to all Americans. Railroad tycoon Cornelius Vanderbilt claimed that the millions he had earned were "worth three times as much to the people of the United Stated." Such businessmen felt that pooling their resources was a natural way to succeed in the business world.

Can you imagine the United States today without giant corporations such as Coca-Cola, General Motors, and Nike? These companies all were influenced by the ideas and hard work of the Gilded Age industrialists. Critics such as Henry D. Lloyd thought modern corporations would cause the "wiping out of the middle classes" and the "destruction of liberty." But American industries continue to grow in the twenty-first century.

       Measuring Up® to the California Content Standards

1. **Why were businessmen so eager to invest their money and compete for new opportunities after the Civil War ended?**

A They wished to prevent poorer people from making any money.

B They wanted to further the scientific advances made during the war.

C They wished to prevent any further wars.

D They wanted to replace the income they lost when the war ended.

2. **Read this sentence from the selection.**

> A businessman could build a factory, such as an oil refinery, for about fifty thousand dollars.

A *refinery* **must be—**

A a place where oil is sold.

B a place where oil is purified.

C a device for removing particles from oil.

D a place where people buy oil.

3. **Read this sentence from the selection.**

> To help raise the necessary money, or capital, railroad companies sold stock.

Which item below best helps you figure out the meaning of *capital?*

A stock

B necessary

C money

D companies

4. **Read this sentence from the selection.**

> Factories popped up across the country, mass-producing items such as sewing machines, hand soap, and bags of flour.

Which of the words below is based on the same root as *factories?*

A inventories

B deface

C manufacture

D torque

5. **Read this sentence from the article.**

> Industries, such as steel and coal, exploded as railroads moved goods quickly from New York to California.

In this sentence, what does the word *exploded* **suggest about the industries?**

A They blew up.

B They multiplied quickly.

C They had labor problems.

D They used gas as a fuel.

6. **Read these sentences from the selection.**

> The Sherman Antitrust Act of 1890 was created "to protect trade and commerce against unlawful restraints and monopolies." But the law's vagueness left interpretation up to the courts. The courts tended to side with big businesses.

What does the context suggest that *vagueness* **means?**

A lack of fairness

B lack of precision

C poor word choices

D over-optimism

7. **Read these sentences from the selection.**

> Wealthy industrialists and entrepreneurs defended themselves against their critics. Steelmaker Andrew Carnegie argued that competition brought quality goods at cheap prices to all Americans.

An *entrepreneur* **is a person who—**

A   argues that competition brings quality goods at lower prices.

B   undertakes to bring the prices of goods down.

C   has inherited wealth from his or her family.

D   undertakes the risks of setting up and operating a business.

8. **Read this sentence from the selection.**

> With its competition greatly reduced until the early 1900s, Standard Oil enjoyed a monopoly for a short time.

A *monopoly* **must refer to—**

A   control over a particular market.

B   control by a small group of companies.

C   control by many companies.

D   control by the government.

9. **Why do you think this era was called "the Gilded Age?"**

A   The word *gilded* suggests that rich people wore a lot of gold jewelry.

B   The word *gilded* suggests that rich people liked to display their wealth.

C   The word *gilded* suggests that most people worked very hard to earn a living.

D   The word *gilded* suggests that the times occurred after a period of warfare.

10. **Read this sentence from the selection.**

> Such businessmen felt that pooling their resources was a natural way to succeed in the business world.

The expression *pooling their resources* **means—**

A   working separately.

B   building a swimming pool.

C   investing in raw materials.

D   joining assets.

Reading Informational Materials 8.2.1 Compare and contrast the features and elements of consumer materials to gain meaning from documents (e.g., warranties, contracts, product information, instruction manuals).

A consumer is a person who buys products. There is a great deal of information that helps consumers make decisions about what products to buy and how to use them. For example, consumer reports and product information sheets help buyers decide which product is the best, and instruction manuals help consumers assemble and use products. Warranties tell consumers what they can do if the product they bought doesn't work, and contracts tell them their legal obligations.

You don't read most **consumer documents** for pleasure. Instead, you read it to find out something. Because of this, writers assume that readers aren't going to linger over the text but want to find the information they need quickly. Therefore, consumer documents often contain **structural features** that help you identify at a glance the information you need. These features include:

- **headings**—the words above a section of the text that tell you what that section is about;

- **numbers**—the numbers in steps or lists that tell you the order in which to do things;

- **bullets**—black dots before items in lists that help you identify each separate item;

- **graphics**—illustrations, charts, graphs, and diagrams that present information visually;

- **special type treatment**—**boldface**, *italic*, and colored type that highlight headings and special information;

- **table of contents**—the list at the front of a book or manual that tells you what appears in the book;

- **indexes**—the alphabetical lists at the end of books or manuals that tell you what topics and subtopics appear in the book;

- **glossaries**—lists of special words and terms used in the book and their definitions;

- **works cited**—list of works consulted to research a topic and write a text;

- **bibliographies**—lists of other books to read about a topic.

Guided Reading Instruction

Directions Read the following passage. Use the questions in the margin to guide your reading. Then answer the questions that follow.

Refrigerators: Comparing the Types
Adapted from ConsumerReports.org

ConsumerReports.org® [SEARCH] Advanced

Our Mission since 1936: Test, Inform, Protect. We accept no ads.

[HOME] | A to Z Index | Privacy | Security

For Subscriber [LOGIN] | Appliances | Autos | Electronics | Computers | More Ratings | Consumer Advice

Guided Questions

1 Pick where you want the freezer. Then pick depth. If you want the built-in look, see "**Designer" fridges**.

1 How does the document tell you that there is a link to another Web site?

2 **TOP-FREEZER MODELS**

Generally least expensive and in a range of sizes, they're economical to run and offer a lot of storage space for their dimensions. Some have stylish curved doors with smooth, stainless-look surfaces.

Best for small spaces, and people looking for value above all.

2 Based on the heading, why would you read the information in this section?

3 On the **downside**, they're not generally full-featured. **You must bend for frequently used items** in the fridge. **Doors swing wide**.

Price range, about $450 to $1,200.

Cost to run, about $36 to $44 a year.

3 What is the purpose of the boldface type?

BOTTOM-FREEZER MODELS

More expensive than top-freezer types, they also have less usable freezer space. But they put things you use most at eye level.

Best for: people who don't like to bend for frequently used items.

On the downside, not generally as full-featured as side-by-side models. You must bend or squat for items at the back of the deep freezer drawers.

4 **Price range**, about $700 to $1,800.

Cost to run, about $42 to $46 a year.

4 Would this refrigerator be a possible purchase by someone who wanted to spend about $1000? Why or why not?

SIDE-BY-SIDE MODELS

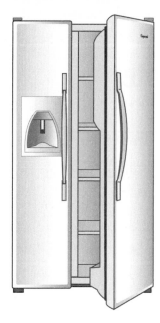

More expensive to buy and run, they have more features. They're large on the outside but not very efficient with space inside.

5 **Best for spaces** where you can't have a wide-swinging door. For households wanting a custom look, some models take cabinet-matching panels, or offer a stainless or stainless-look finish.

On the downside, no room for wide items like pizza boxes. Moving items within the narrow space can be tedious.

Price range, about $800 to $2,400.

Cost to run, about $49 to $60 a year.

5 What is the key benefit of this type of refrigerator?

---

1. Consumer 1 wants the most inexpensive refrigerator on the market. Which model should he buy? Why?

   He should get the top freezer model.

2. Consumer 2 has just remodeled her kitchen and wants a refrigerator that fits in. Which model should she buy? Why?

   She should get the side-by-side model for enclosed spaces.

3. Consumer 3 wants the things he uses most often at eye level where he can see them. Which model should he buy? Why?

   The bottom freezer model is better since the top is used most often.

4. Consumer 4 throws a pizza party once a week for her kids. There are always leftovers. She has a small kitchen and doesn't want a refrigerator that takes up too much space. She's on a budget and doesn't want to spend more than she has to. Which refrigerator should she buy? Why?

   She should use the Bottom-freezer model so they can throw the leftovers in the Bottom-freezer; it's also affordable.

Apply **Directions** Read the document below from a Web site explaining how to do different tasks. Then answer the questions that follow it.

eHow to Assemble a Scooter
by Sally Ann Barnes

Sometimes you can save five to ten dollars by putting your new scooter together at home instead of having the store do it for you.

The Things You'll Need

bike grease
bike helmet
combination wrench set
electric motorized scooter
gas motorized scooter
kick scooter
rags
scooter carry bag
scooter carry strap

Steps:

1. Read all of the instructions provided by the manufacturer before starting to assemble the scooter.

2. Check the size of the tools needed for the nuts and bolts before you begin. (Are they in metric or U.S. units?)

3. Use a good gear grease and have lots of shop rags or paper towels close by to keep your hands clean.

4. Lay out the larger pieces by steps—such as the footboard, handle bar, and wheels.

5. Keep the gear section and its bolts together and to one side of your work area.

6. Place the nuts and bolts for the assembly of the larger pieces next to your tools, within easy reach.

7. Place the handlebar in position and bolt into place according to the manufacturer's instructions.

8. Assemble the wheels and axles if necessary.

9. Bolt the axle into the base of the scooter at the specified location.

10. Assemble gears and brakes.

11. Affix the gear and brake box to the handlebars and to the base according to the diagram provided by the company.

12. Test the gears and brakes for tension, and adjust if needed.

13. Grease any joints.

14. Attach any stickers or decals provided.

Measuring Up® to the California Content Standards

Tips

- If your scooter is motorized, you will need to mount the motor according to the instructions provided and service the motor as instructed.
- Always test the brakes and gears before riding the scooter.
- Periodically, check the axles for grease, the tension on the brake, and the gears to correct any problems.

More Resources

Related eHows:

- Buy a Scooter
- Choose a Kick Scooter
- Choose a Motorized Scooter
- Ride a Kick Scooter
- Ride a Motorized Scooter

Project Details:

Skill Advisory: Moderately Challenging

---

1. What type of information do you find in the box that begins this document?

Things you will need.

2. The two headings in the main part of the text introduce sections that provide different types of information. What type of information is included under each of these headings?

The two headings are Steps', and Tips'.

3. How are the steps organized? What feature makes them easy to follow?

The y are organized chronologically. In order from what should be done.

4. According to the tips, what three things should you check for periodically?

You should check the joints, wheels, and axels.

5. Look at the box labeled More Resources. According to the rating, how difficult is it to assemble a scooter?

It is moderately challenging.

Assessment Practice

Directions Answer the questions based on the selection you just read.

1. According to the first five steps, why is it important to have a lot of shop rags or paper towels available when you assemble a scooter?

   A   You might need to use metric tools.

   B   You will be using grease for the gears.

   C   The instruction manual for the manufacturer says to do this.

   D   Shop rags and paper towels are inexpensive.

2. Which of the following steps is it NOT necessary for you to do?

   A   9. Bolt the axle into the base of the scooter at the specified location.

   B   7. Place the handlebar in position and bolt into place according to the manufacturer's instructions.

   C   11. Affix the gear and brake box to the handlebars and to the base according to the diagram provided by the company.

   D   14. Attach any stickers or decals provided.

3. If you are assembling a motorized scooter—

   A   you would find all the information you need in this set of instructions.

   B   you would need to change the order of the steps.

   C   you would need to follow the instructions provided by the manufacturer.

   D   you would not need as many shop rags and paper towels.

4. If you wanted an electric motorized scooter, all of the related eHows would be of interest EXCEPT—

   A   Buy a Scooter.

   B   Choose a Motorized Scooter.

   C   Ride a Motorized Scooter.

   D   Choose a Kick Scooter.

5. Which of the following steps should you do before you start to assemble your scooter?

   A   Affix the gear and brake box.

   B   Check the size of the tools you will need.

   C   Place the handlebar in position.

   D   Test the tension of the gears and brakes.

Focus on California Content Standards

Lesson 7 Analyze Structure of Functional Documents

Reading Informational Materials 9.2.1 Analyze the structure and format of functional workplace documents, including the graphics and headers, and explain how authors use the features to achieve their purposes.

As a student, you may have a part-time job. Or you may be thinking about when you graduate from high school or college and get a job. To get a job, you will have to write a cover letter and resumé and fill out an application. At work, you will read many documents designed to give you information and help you get the job done. These **workplace documents** include:

- procedure manuals

- job applications

- memos

- guides to health benefits

- e-mail messages and notices kept on the servers

- organizational charts

- instructions for operating machinery

Like consumer documents, workplace documents are designed to help you get the information fast. They may contain titles, headings, diagrams, charts, as well as numbered lists and bullets, all of which serve to help you locate and understand the important elements in the text.

Guided Reading Instruction

Directions Read the passage below. Use the questions in the margin to guide your reading. Then answer the questions that follow.

Tips for Success—The Resume
from Work Smart
www.worksmart.ca.gov.tips-resume.html

1 **Preparing to Write Resume Tips   Resume Types
Cover Letter   Action Words Internet Sources**

2 A resume is a brief, written summary of your skills and experience. It is an overview of who you are and a tool to present yourself to employers. The goal of a well-written resume is to gain a job interview. Job interviews may lead to employment!

Employers and personnel managers are very busy and tend to rapidly review resumes. Therefore, your resume must quickly catch the employer's attention. Writing a brief, to-the-point description of your experience and skills can do this. Tell the truth on your resume. Write your resume to describe how your skills will meet the employer's needs.

When applying for a job, read the job advertisement or announcement very carefully. Then customize your resume by writing up your skills to describe and match what the employer is looking for. It is helpful to describe your experience and skills by using some of the same words the employer used in the job advertisement.

Read each of the WorkSmart resume sections for helpful suggestions, before getting started on writing your resume.

3 **Preparing to Write Your Resume**

Writing a resume requires a little time and planning. However, it is well worth the effort. It is a good idea to begin by writing a master resume. Having an attractive resume on hand that stresses your strongest skills, better prepares you to attend job fairs and respond to a large number of jobs advertised in newspapers and on the Internet.

Get organized! Before beginning to write your resume:

1. Gather information on your past employment: names and addresses, and dates of employment.
2. Gather information for personal references: names and addresses.
3. Research information on the employer. (See "**Research the Employer**" under "**How to Find a Job**.")
4. Select a quiet area to gather your thoughts and begin working on your resume.
5. Decide what type of resume suits you best: chronological, functional, or automated. (See "**Resume Types**.")

Guided Questions

A table of contents.

1 What does the information at the top of this document provide?

2 What information is provided in the first paragraph?

A dictionary definition of a resume.

3 Based on the heading, what information do you think you will find in this section?

Tips on how to write your resume.

4 **Resume Tips**

1. Make your resume short (one page, if possible, two pages at most).
2. Use white or ivory paper.
3. Type your resume on a computer, when possible. (If you do not have access to a computer, visit your local Job Service office, One-Stop Career Center, or local public library for help.)
4. Use action words to describe your work skills. (See "**Action Words**.")
5. Stress skills, knowledge, and abilities that fulfill the job requirements.
6. Be specific about accomplishments, but do not stretch the truth.
7. Provide information about career goals.
8. Make the layout of the resume attractive.
9. Emphasize most recent jobs.
10. Proofread it for grammar, punctuation, and spelling errors.
11. If possible, have someone else check your resume for errors.
12. Save references and personal data for the interview.
13. Avoid including your date of birth.
14. Avoid stating salary information or the reason for leaving the last job.
15. When you look at your resume, ask yourself, "Would I interview this person?"
16. Keep your resume current.
17. Finally, prepare a cover letter to introduce your resume. (See "**Cover Letter**.")

4 How is the information in this section different from the information on the preceding page?

This page is tips and the page before is instructions.

1. According to the points under Resume Tips, what should you do if you do not have a computer?

   Visit a local Job Service Office, One-Stop Career Center, or local public library for help.

2. In the points made under Preparing to Write Your Resume, why do you think it is important to research information about the employer?

   It is important so that you know what your employer likes and dislikes.

3. Which point tells you whether or not you should exaggerate your accomplishments?

   Resume Tips tells you not to stretch the truth.

4. What section on this Web site would help you write more emphatically?

   Resume tips would help someone write more emphatically.

Apply

Directions You might read a document like this if you worked in a publishing house or for a literary agent. Read the document carefully. Then answer the questions that follow it.

COPYRIGHT YOUR WORK
by Sheree Bykofsky and Paul Fargis

A copyright officially registers your original creations and protects them against unauthorized performance, reproduction, distribution, and adaptation by others. Literary, musical, dramatic, and artistic expressions, as well as certain intellectual works, can be copyrighted. Facts, ideas, and methods cannot. In addition, works in the public domain cannot be copyrighted. Public domain refers either to works created before copyright laws existed (such as ancient plays), or works whose copyrights have expired or been forfeited.

All works, whether published or not, are eligible for copyright registration with the Library of Congress. Publishers will frequently take care of copyrighting and register works on behalf of the author in the author's name. Registration is not necessary for a work to be considered copyrighted, though. A work is copyrighted as soon as it is created, and registration merely establishes a formal record of your creation. Still, you may be entitled to infringement damages only if your work has been registered correctly.

Formally copyrighting a work is quick and simple if you know exactly how to go about it. Here's how to register.

Ask for and fill out the proper forms. There are several different forms to choose from when registering a copyright. The proper form depends on the nature of the work to be registered. Pick the appropriate form:

• **Form PA**	for performing arts (plays, choreography)
• **Form VA**	for visual arts (painting, sculpture)
• **Form S**	for sound recordings
• **Form SE**	serials (a written work that appears in seperate parts, such as a continuing magazine piece)

To receive the proper form, call the Copyright Office at 202-707-9100, or write to Copyright Office, Publications Section LM-455, Library of Congress, Washington, DC 20559. If you have further questions about forms or other matters, you can call the Copyright Information Line at 202-707-3000.

When you receive the correct form, fill out all necessary information by typing or printing legibly in black pen. Along with the form, you will need to send in a copy of your work and a fee.

Deposit a copy of your work. For published material, send in two copies of your work after it has been published. For unpublished works, send in only one copy. For works too large to send in, such as a large sculpture, send in identifying material like a photograph of the work and sample pages. The Library of Congress will keep a copy of your work on file as proof of your authorship.

Pay the registration fee. Copyright applications cost $20 to file. Make out a check or money order to the Register of Copyrights. Mail the check along with the proper form and copies of your work to:

> Copyright Office
> Library of Congress
> Washington, DC 20559

Allow from one to three months for the copyright office to process your application, although registration becomes effective as soon as it is received. You will be sent a formal certificate of registration for your records.

Copyrights for new works created after 1978, remain in effect for the life of the author plus 50 years and do not need to be renewed. Works published before 1978 have a copyright that lasts 75 years. If the work was published before 1964, the copyright needs to be renewed by the author or the author's estate when the first copyright term (28 years) expires; after 1964, renewal is automatic.

Special Copyrights

- **Works for hire.** A piece of writing is deemed work for hire if the entity commissioning it owns all title and copyright to the text; for example, when a publishing company or journal buys text or illustrations directly from a writer or artist. Work-for-hire copyrights remain in effect for 75 years after publication or 100 years from creation, whichever is shorter.

- **Journal articles.** Usually, the owner of the journal publication will control the copyright. The author is granted the right to reprint the article without permission, as long as a proper credit line also appears.

- **Magazine articles.** Usually, the magazine will copyright the entire contents of an issue but the author will retain copyright to his or her specific work.

- **Revised editions.** Any new materials added to a work must be copyrighted. Compilations of public domain text, such as anthologies of 17th-century poetry, are copyrightable with respect to their organization and contents, though the source text itself cannot be registered and remains in the public domain.

- **Electronic formats.** If you are authoring a text that may go on-line, protect your rights to copyright. As new electronic database and CD-ROM outlets for printed materials expand, authors must be vigilant in safeguarding their proprietary rights to reproduced texts.

1. What is the purpose of the boxed information?

   The boxed informaition is a key or legend.

2. Find the section with the heading "Deposit a copy of your work." When should you send in a photograph instead of the complete work?

   When the complete work is too large to send in.

3. How is the address of the Copyright Office made easy to find?

   It is seperated by indentions and spacing.

4. How many different types of special copyrights are there? How do you know this?

   There are five different types of copyright, the document lists them all.

5. What reason might you have for reading this document?

   To learn how to copyright your work.

Assessment Practice

Directions Answer the questions based on the selection you just read.

1. **According to the information in the box, you would use Form VA if you had—**

   A   written an article that appears over a series of issues of a magazine.

   B   written a play that is being performed at your local theater.

   C   created a painting that is on display in your local art gallery.

   D   written and recorded the music for a class song.

2. **According to the information under "Special Copyrights," a "work for hire" is—**

   A   writing for a specific purpose that someone is paid to do.

   B   a company that buys text or illustrations.

   C   the date when a work is copyrighted.

   D   a person who writes for a publishing company.

3. **According to the information under "Special Copyrights," which of these statements is NOT true?**

   A   You can copyright your work, even if it appears only in electronic format.

   B   You cannot copyright a public domain text.

   C   The author of a journal article can reprint the article without permission.

   D   Work-for-hire copyrights can last for as long as 100 years.

4. **According to the two paragraphs, the purpose of a copyright is to—**

   A   protect a person's ideas and methods.

   B   protect the rights of the person who created a certain work.

   C   protect only writers of literature.

   D   make sure any literary work can be used freely.

5. **In order to get a copyright, you must do all of the following EXCEPT—**

   A   fill out a form.

   B   send in money.

   C   send in a copy of the work.

   D   call the Copyright Office.

Focus on California Content Standards

Lesson 8 Generate Relevant Questions

Reading Informational Materials 9.2.3 Generate relevant questions about readings on issues that can be researched.

When you do **research**, you find out more about a topic. To do this, you construct questions to guide you. For example, imagine you read an article about how computers have changed animated movies. The article gets you so interested in the topic that you want to find out more. A good place to start your research is with good questions.

Good questions are related to the topic. They deal with an aspect of the topic that is significant enough to warrant research. There should be enough material—books, articles, diaries, etc.—available so that you can find the answers you need.

Good questions are NOT:

- **Too idiosyncratic or personal**
  This means that the question appeals to you but maybe not to a wider audience. Here is an example of a question that is too idiosyncratic.

  Would I make a good computer animator?

- **Too broad**
  This means that the question is too large or covers too much material to be covered in one research paper. Here is an example of a question that is too broad.

  What is the history of animation?

- **Too narrow**
  This means that the question deals with too small an aspect of the topic for a research paper. Often it can be answered with only a word or two or perhaps a short paragraph. Here is an example of a question that is too narrow.

  Who was the first person to use a computer to animate a movie?

There are several categories of research questions:

Definition	What is computer animation?
How It Works	How does a computer help someone animate a film?
How It Has Changed	How has the process of computer animation changed over the last ten years?
Advantages and Disadvantages	What are the advantages and disadvantages of computer animation?
Cause and Effect	What effect have computers had on animation?
Comparison and Contrast	What are the disadvantages and advantages of computer animation?

Guided Reading Instruction

Directions Read the following passage. Use the questions in the margin to guide your reading. Then answer the questions that follow.

1 Is the Monster in the Loch a Myth? Not Nessie-sarily!
Patricia Thomas

Sunlight dances down the blue expanse of Loch Ness. A light breeze stirs the water where Castle Urquhart guards the curve of the bay. It is a fine, calm day to launch a boat or cast a line. Or is it?

2 For centuries, debate has raged over whether a huge, unknown creature inhabits this mysterious loch—largest, longest, and deepest of three lakes threading Scotland's wildly beautiful Great Glen.

3 Vikings may have been first to ask the question. Their mythology tells of "water horses" in Scotland's lochs. The first written account of a lake creature dates back to the sixth century when, says an ancient Latin text, a swimmer was killed by a frightful beast near the loch's north end. St. Columba, on hearing of the attack, rowed out and scolded the monster so severely that never since has it been known to repeat such a misdeed.

Rumors and whisperings of a "horrible great beastie" continued, century after century. But they were spoken in hushed tones and not often when strangers were about. In the 1930s, however, word of the Loch Ness Monster began to spread. Nessie made a big splash in 1934 when Robert Gould, a respected scientific writer, published a book called *The Loch Ness Monster and Others*.

4 Residents and visitors to the loch began coming forward with stories of sightings, some from earlier times. An elderly gentleman wrote to Gould, recalling that about 1871 he saw something "like an upturned boat . . . wriggling and churning up water." In a startling land encounter, a London couple driving home from a holiday in 1933 saw an enormous, black "prehistoric animal" loom in from of them, then shuffle into the loch.

Stories grew more dramatic, descriptions more specific. The classic image of Nessie with long neck, multiple bumps, and long tail emerged.

Guided Questions

1 What question does this article address?

2 Why is the fact that the loch is the "largest, longest, and deepest of the three lochs" important?

3 What questions do you have based on the information in this paragraph?

4 What questions do you have based on the information in this paragraph?

5 The first photo of Nessie was snapped by a workman who watched "an object of considerable dimensions" rise out of the dark loch. His photo is believed to be authentic, but it is too blurry to prove anything. A clearer (but, it turns out, much less authentic) shot of Nessie labeled "the surgeon's picture" was produced by Robert Wilson, a London doctor. Although years later the photo was proven to be a hoax, it remains the best known likeness of Nessie.

Hoaxes (and, possibly, hallucinations) aside, the case for a real life Nessie continued to grow. Researchers began using modern tools to find an answer to the riddle. In the 1970s, a team of scientists used sonar to track two objects, 20 to 30 feet long, and photographed them with an underwater camera. A photo showed what looked like a big flipper with a bulky, rough-textured body.

6 Although debate still rages, emphasis seems to have shifted from trying to prove whether Nessie exists to determining what she could be. Crytozoologists suggest it might be a primitive snakelike whale called a zeuglondon, a long-necked seal, or a school of giant eels. Prevailing opinion, however, favors the idea that Nessie is a plesiosaur, a descendant of dinosaurs long thought extinct but somehow able to survive in the deep loch. Undoubtedly, of course, Nessie is not alone. To have survived for so many centuries, she must be part of a breeding family. In fact, more than one creature has been seen at once—though such sightings are rare.

7 The mystery is far from solved. No one theory fits all data. Scientists even argue about what is actually "data." No body or body parts identified with the monster have ever been found. And ancient myth may be, after all, simply myth.

But some photos and films do appear to be authentic. Reported Nessie sightings now number more than 3,000—and counting.

8 Arthurian legend tells of Sir Launcelot's quest to the north, where he slew a great water dragon. Perhaps there is more truth to those old tales than we imagine after all.

5 What is the problem with the workman's photo? What is the problem with the doctor's photo?

6 What does this shift in emphasis suggest?

7 Based on what you have read so far, what is one piece of data that might be argued about?

8 The author suggests that Sir Launcelot's dragon might be what?

Directions Evaluate each research question below. If the question can be effectively developed into a research topic, write Yes next to it. Write No next to any question that is too broad, too narrow, or too personal to be developed into an effective research topic.

1. What evidence supports the existence of the Loch Ness monster and what evidence supports the idea that it doesn't exist?

_____

2. How does a person feel when he or she stands in the dark and sees a strange creature rise out of the water?

_____

3. What are the fifty greatest hoaxes in history?

_____

4. Is the photo snapped by the workman authentic?

_____

5. What effect have stories about the Loch Ness monster had on the tourist industry in Scotland?

_____

Apply   **Directions**   Read the passage below. Then follow the instructions after it.

Sssh! Don't Mention His Name

by Dean Durber

The lights are going down. Inside, all is dark and quiet. If you listen closely, you can hear the sound of footsteps walking across the stage. The curtain begins to rise. And we welcome you to the wonderful world of theater, home to the many characters of Mr. William Shakespeare.

"Look! I can see one now. It's Mac. . . ."

Sssh! Don't mention his name.

Don't walk under a ladder. Don't place new shoes on a table. Don't cross a person on the stairs. These are just some of the many superstitions people believe. If you break the rules, it could bring bad luck. If you speak the name of "Macbeth" inside a theater, something awful could happen to the show.

Do you believe this?

Shakespeare's play Macbeth is a tale of greed. We see three ugly witches huddled around their smoldering cauldron, speaking prophecies.

"All hail Macbeth! You shall be King."

How can this be? Macbeth is not next in line to the throne. King Duncan already has two sons. Surely, Malcolm, the eldest son, will be the man to take over after the death of his father. Are the witches speaking the truth?

Macbeth and his wife, Lady Macbeth, have a secret, cunning plan. In the middle of the night, when all are asleep, Macbeth sneaks into the bedroom of King Duncan and murders him with a knife. In the morning, he pretends to know nothing about this awful deed, and wakes the castle with his cries and tears.

To hide the crime, Macbeth kills two guards and covers their hands in blood. They will get the blame for the death of their King. Duncan's sons fear for their lives and flee from the kingdom, leaving many to wonder if these two young men had a hand in the cruel murder of their father. Only Macbeth remains behind to sit on the throne of Scotland with his lovely lady beside him.

Try as they might, the royal couple are unable to wash away the blood of the murders. Look how the lady rubs at her hands.

Her shame drives her mad, and soon she too is dead. Macbeth is left alone to ponder the words of those wise, ugly witches.

"You will be King, until Birnam [BURN-um] Wood comes to Dunsinane [DONE-sin-ane] Castle."

Is Macbeth safe? Birnam Wood looks far away from his castle. But as he looks into the distance, he sees the return of Malcolm, son of Duncan. The soldiers carry green branches in their hands as they approach. Macbeth's brief reign ends. Soon the crown of Scotland will rest again on the head of the rightful ruler.

Now let us turn from William Shakespeare's play to the pages of history, where we find quite a different tale.

In 11th-century Scotland, it was rare for the throne of a kingdom to pass to a direct descendent of a decreased king. Usually, the crown would go to a nephew or cousin, whoever seemed to be the strongest contender within the family group. This led to many murders of kings by those who were eager to take over the throne too early. In fact, between 943 and 1040, seven of the nine kings of Scotland were killed by their successors.

Malcolm II, who reigned from 1005 until 1034, was keen to change this law. He wanted his grandson Duncan to take the throne after his death. He managed to kill off many members of his family who might have blocked this plan, but he forgot about one person—Gruoch (GRE-ok), the wife of Macbeth Macfinlay. Gruoch had previously been married to the grandson of Malcolm II. According to the old law, this double family connection gave Macbeth more claims to the throne than Duncan. From the viewpoint of those living at the time, Duncan was the villain and Macbeth was the true king.

After the murder of Duncan in 1040, Macbeth ruled as king of Scotland for 17 years. The length of this reign proved his popularity. In 1050, he even went on a trip to Rome, showing he had no concerns about problems occurring at home during his absence. But when Malcolm III, Duncan's son, finally returned from England, his real troubles began. Macbeth was defeated in battle in 1057 and laid to rest in Iona, the burial place for true kings, not criminals.

So, who was the real king of Scotland? Was it Duncan? Or was it that man tiptoeing across the stage, the one they call Mac. . . . Sssh! It might bring you bad luck.

Directions The article you just read provides a lot of information about the real-life Macbeth and the character presented in Shakespeare's famous play. Generate questions for further research on this topic using the prompts below.

1. Definition

   What is Macbeth about?

2. How It Works:

   How were the kings of Scottland chosen in Macbeth's time?

3. Comparison and Contrast:

   How is Macbeth similar and different than Duncan?

4. Cause and Effect:

   What caused Macbeth to kill his family?

5. A question of your choice:

Why is Macbeth's name bad luck if said in a theatre?

Assessment Practice   **Directions** Answer the questions based on the selection you just read.

1. **Which question could MOST effectively be developed into a research paper?**

   A What did the witches say to Macbeth in the play?

   B How can woods walk or move?

   C Why is Shakespeare's *Macbeth* considered "unlucky"?

   D What was Lady Macbeth's real name?

2. **Which question could MOST effectively be developed into a research paper?**

   A In the play, why did Macbeth kill the two guards?

   B How does Lady Macbeth in Shakespeare compare with Gruoch?

   C Why shouldn't you put new shoes on the table?

   D How do superstitions affect my behavior?

3. **Which question could MOST effectively be developed into a research paper?**

   A What kings ruled Scotland during the eleventh century?

   B How were kings chosen in eleventh-century Scotland?

   C What is the meaning of the term "direct descendent"?

   D What is the history of the kings of Scotland?

4. **Which question could MOST effectively be developed into a research paper?**

   A What was the role of law in eleventh-century Scotland?

   B What is the history of law?

   C What law did Malcolm II want to change?

   D When did Malcolm II reign?

5. **Which question could MOST effectively be developed into a research paper?**

   A How did the reign of Macbeth compare with the reign of Duncan III?

   B Who was the ruler of England at the time of Macbeth?

   C When did Shakespeare write Macbeth?

   D Who are the rulers buried at Iona and what are their stories?

Focus on California Content Standards

Lesson 9 Synthesize and Paraphrase

Reading Informational Materials 9.2.4 Synthesize the content from several sources or works by a single author dealing with a single issue; paraphrase the ideas and connect them to other sources and related topics to demonstrate comprehension.

When you **synthesize** information, you connect or combine it. Sometimes, you make connections between one part of a text and another. Sometimes, you make connections between two or more different texts about the same topic. For example, if you used material from two different biographies of the same person to write a paper about that person, you might be synthesizing information from two sources.

In order to synthesize information, you look for different types of relationships. For example, as you read you notice:

- how things are alike and how they are different

- the causes of events and the results of actions

- the order in which events happen

- the way the parts relate to the whole

When you **paraphrase**, you restate the information in a text or passage in your own words, usually to show that you understand it or to clarify its meaning. For example, read the sentences below:

> He didn't know it then, but his fate was sealed from the day he stepped aboard the ship. Never again would he be able to tend the land as a farmer; his heart was lost to the sea.

You could paraphrase this sentence, or put it in your own words, as follows:

> Signing aboard the ship changed his life. He could never again be farmer. He was now a sailor who loved the sea.

When you **summarize**, you provide the most important ideas and details in a text in a condensed form, leaving out unimportant details. You have to identify clearly the **main idea**, the most important idea in a text. Then you include only the most important **supporting details**, the facts, examples, statistics, and concepts that back up the main idea.

For example, read this paragraph about teachers:

> Teachers juggle many tasks. They often teach more than one subject. This means that they have to prepare a variety of lessons, which can be quite time consuming. They must communicate with all kinds of kids from many different backgrounds with all kinds of different interests. Sometimes, they take classes on field trips to places like museums and restored villages.

The first sentence of the paragraph states the main idea that: "Teachers juggle many tasks." The rest of the paragraph lists details describing the tasks. A summary of this paragraph might be: Teachers juggle many tasks including preparing lessons for various subjects, communicating with a variety of kids, and going on field trips.

Guided Reading Instruction

Directions Read the following passage. Use the questions in the margin to guide your reading. Then answer the questions that follow.

A Little Girl from Illinois
by Bonnie Geisert

1 Laura Jane Addams was born on September 6, 1860, in Cedarville, Illinois, the youngest of five children. Known as Jennie in her hometown, she was small, frail, and pigeon-toed. Those traits, plus a slightly curved spine that forced her to carry her head to one side, caused Jane to see herself as an ugly duckling.

1 What is the most significant idea you learn about Jane in this paragraph?

2 Her mother, Sarah, died when Jane was just two years old. A note in her mother's obituary seemed to offer a sign of Jane's future. It said that Sarah had "a heart ever alive to the wants of the poor." Of the Addamses' nine children, only four lived to adulthood.

2 Paraphrase the comment that Jane's mother makes. Put it in your own words.

Jane's father, John, was one of the most influential people in her life. A respected businessman, he owned a flour mill and a lumber mill. He also had investments in banking and insurance. John was politically active too, serving as an Illinois state senator for sixteen years. Jane wanted to be like him in every way: "I centered upon him all that careful imitation which a little girl ordinarily gives to her mother's ways and habits," she later wrote in her autobiography.

On the way to church, Jane would walk beside her Uncle James Addams because she did not want strangers to "know that my handsome father owned this homely little girl." Her father drove that idea from her mind one day by a show of "public recognition." **3** Meeting Jane after leaving work at his bank, "he lifted his high and shining silk hat and made me an imposing bow."

3 Why did Jane's father do this?

Jane gained a strong sense of morality from her Quaker father. He helped establish two churches in Cedarville and taught a Bible class. **4** One night, Jane could not sleep because she had told a lie. Afraid that she or her father would die before she confessed, Jane crept down to her father's bedroom. After she blurted out her offense, his response comforted her. He simply said he was glad that she felt "too bad to go to sleep" after telling a lie.

4 What can you assume about Jane based on this incident?

5 Jane was six years old when she realized that not all children enjoyed the privileges she did. On a trip with her father to a mill near a very poor section of Freeport, Illinois, Jane was surprised by the poverty. She then vowed to her father that when she grew up, she would live in a large house, not "built among the other large houses, but right in the midst of horrid little houses like these." And one Sunday, Jane showed her father her beautiful new coat. According to Jane, John Addams pointed out that the coat was "so much prettier than any cloak the other little girls in the Sunday school had." He then advised Jane to wear her old coat. It would keep her just as warm as the new one and not make the other girls feel sad at their lack of luxuries.

5 Connect the information in this paragraph to what Jane's mother had said about her earlier.

When Jane was seven, John Addams married Anna Haldeman, a strong-willed, well-educated widow. The marriage gave Jane two stepbrothers, one of whom, George, became her constant playmate.

6 Jane's stepmother saw to the children's education. The family would gather regularly to read aloud from novels and plays, with Jane and George sometimes taking the parts in plays.

When she was seventeen, Jane left home for college. Her carefree and happy childhood would lay the foundation for the path she would pursue in life. Remembering her own upbringing would help her as she tried to improve the lives of children growing up in the Illinois city of Chicago.

Guided Questions

6 What does this information tell you about Jane's new family life?

1. How do you think that Jane's family influenced her?

   Confidence and ethics. were influenced as well as self-esteem

2. What two details support the conclusion that Jane would "improve the lives of children growing up in the Illinois city of Chicago"?

   She wanted a house in the midst of poverty

3. Based on this article, what type of person do you think Jane Addams was?

   An ethical, confident person.

4. Circle the statement below that provides the BEST summary of this article.

   a. Laura Jane Addams was a small, frail, ungainly child who lost her mother when she was young. From an early age she showed concern for the needs of the poor. From her father she developed a strong sense of morality and responsibility. She vowed that when she grew up, she would live with those less privileged than she. Her childhood provided the foundation for her life's work.

   b. Laura Jane Addams was born in Cedarville, Illinois. She was a frail, ungainly child. Her mother died when she was two. Her father remarried. Her new mother was a strong-willed woman. As a result of the marriage she gained two stepbrothers. One of them became her constant playmate. Jane's family life was very happy and taught her some important values.

Apply   **Directions**   Read the passage below. Then answer the questions that follow it.

The House That Jane Built

by Shawn Hoffelt

In 1877, seventeen-year-old Jane Addams entered Rockford Seminary in Rockford, Illinois. At that time, Rockford graduates received certificates instead of college degrees. Determined to obtain a genuine degree, Addams took advanced courses. She received her college diploma when Rockford was accredited one year after Addams finished her studies there.

After college, Addams traveled in Europe with Ellen Gates Starr. Starr and Addams had become close friends while they were both at Rockford. When she saw the dreadful conditions in which people lived in the slums of London, England, Addams's life commitment to social services began to take shape. She was horrified as she observed the sale of decaying fruits and vegetables to the poor.

Addams became inspired by the progressive work being done at Toynbee Hall, the world's first settlement house, located in an impoverished section of London. While visiting there, she observed college-educated people living in the community and helping to improve the lives of those in need.

Addams realized that America had its share of poverty-stricken areas. In her home state of Illinois, the city of Chicago had large numbers of immigrants who lived in overcrowded and dirty conditions.

Addams became convinced that in order to help the poor, she must know them first. She told Starr her ideas. She wanted to establish a residence in which privileged young women would live and work among the poor of Chicago. Starr was enthusiastic, and the two women decided to turn Addams's idea into a reality.

Addams and Starr searched Chicago for a big house that would suit their needs. They found a rundown mansion in a poor area of the city. With its spacious rooms, fine woodwork, and many fireplaces, the house had potential. All it needed was some cleaning and painting.

Built by Charles J. Hull, a Chicago pioneer, the house was located in an immigrant neighborhood. The community was lean on resources but rich in spirit and culture. In September 1889, Addams and Starr moved into Hull-House, Chicago's first settlement house.

Addams knew that immigrants faced many difficulties. Few spoke English or understood American ways. They were unable to get work at anything but the most menial jobs. Entire families, including children, worked for pennies a day in factories. Few homes had indoor water or plumbing.

Addams and Starr began by helping wherever they were needed. They washed newborn babies, tended to the sick, and prepared the dead for burial. Addams worked alongside the people in the community and gradually earned their respect. Both Addams and Starr gained recognition for their hard work and dedication.

Volunteers began to offer their services to Hull-House. Programs that fit the needs of the community were launched. Classes to teach immigrants the English language and to assist the unemployed in their job searches were considered especially important. There were social activities for the elderly, as well as concerts and art shows at Hull-House. A kindergarten and a playground were organized. Eventually, twelve new buildings were added to Hull-House, including a theater, a gymnasium, a music school, a cafeteria, and a library.

Hull-House became a place of hope. It offered its neighbors respect, support, and opportunity. And Addams came to realize that the work at Hull-House was as important to its volunteers as it was to the people of the community. In the years that followed, the settlement house movement spread across the United States. Cities throughout America modeled their settlement houses after Hull-House. Jane Addams became known as "Our Nation's Defender of the Poor."

1. Based on the description of Jane Addams in the first paragraph, how would you describe her personality?

Determined and hard working.

2. What can you tell about the poor in Chicago at this time?

3. What types of services did the immigrants need?

Classes to learn english, places to live, and childcare.

4. In your own words, tell what the volunteers were like.

5. Summarize the information you learned about settlement houses from this article.

Assessment Practice **Directions** Answer the questions based on the selection you just read.

1. In "The House That Jane Built," paragraph 1 allows the reader to understand that—

   A Jane Addams was the youngest student at the Rockford Seminary.

   B Rockford Seminary was among the finest colleges in Illinois at that time.

   C few women attended college in the late 19th century.

   D Jane Addams was a determined and ambitious woman.

2. What detail from "The House That Jane Built" shows that by helping others, we help ourselves?

   A Hull-House was as important to its volunteers as it was to the people of the community.

   B Eventually, twelve new buildings were added to Hull-House, including a theater, a gymnasium, a music school, a cafeteria, and a library.

   C Volunteers began to offer their services to Hull-House.

   D It offered its neighbors respect, support, and opportunity.

3. Which of the following BEST summarizes the information in "The House That Jane Built"?

   A Seventeen-year-old Jane Addams attended Rockford Seminary. Unlike students who attended before her, she obtained a genuine college degree, not just a certificate. She moved to Chicago, Illinois, where she bought an old house in a poor neighborhood. She became very popular with her neighbors and offered programs to help them. Today she is known as "Our Nation's Defender of the Poor."

   B Jane Addams studied the work being done at Toynbee Hall in London. She was very impressed and wanted to do the same kind of work back home in America. She bought an old house in a well-to-do section of Chicago. There she put together a group of volunteers. They encouraged the poor to flee their old neighborhoods and join them at Hull-House, where they could lead a better life.

   C After receiving her college degree, Jane Addams traveled to Europe where she was inspired by the work being done at Toynbee Hall. She returned to America determined to help the poor by establishing a residence in which well-to-do young women could live and work with the poor. At Hull-House, Addams and her friend Starr developed programs to fit the needs of the community. America's first settlement house was a success and the movement spread across the country.

   D Jane Addams established the first settlement house in the world. She located it in an impoverished neighborhood in Chicago in her home state of Illinois. She chose Chicago because of the large number of immigrants living there. Hull-House was a run-down mansion with spacious rooms. It provided the space that her and her volunteers needed. Hull-House offered programs to fit the needs of the community. It was very successful.

4. **Which statement from "A Little Girl from Illinois" shows the strongest connection to the title of "The House That Jane Built"?**

   A On the way to church, Jane would walk beside her Uncle James Addams because she did not want strangers to "know that my handsome father owned this homely little girl."

   B Jane was six years old when she realized that not all children enjoyed the privileges she did.

   C She then vowed to her father that when she grew up, she would live in a large house, not "built among other large houses, but right in the midst of horrid little houses like these."

   D When Jane was seven, John Addams married Anna Halderman, a strong-willed, well-educated widow.

5. **"A Little Girl from Illinois" deals with Jane's childhood, while "The House That Jane Built"—**

   A concentrates on her time at Rockford Seminary.

   B concentrates on her accomplishments as an adult.

   C deals only with the time she spent in Europe.

   D deals only with the establishment of Hull-House.

Focus on California Content Standards

Lesson 10   Analyze, Evaluate, and Elaborate

Reading Informational Materials 9.2.5 Extend ideas presented in primary or secondary sources through original analysis, evaluation, and elaboration.

Critical thinking involves analyzing, evaluating, and elaborating. When you **analyze**, you break down the information in a source to examine the individual ideas. When you **evaluate**, you make a judgment about the ideas in a source. When you **elaborate**, you state those ideas in detail and add your own ideas.

To use the material you find in different sources for your own purposes, you make inferences, draw conclusions, and make predictions.

An **inference** is an educated guess based on evidence in the text and what you already know about the topic. For example, imagine it's your birthday. When you get home from school you see a balloon peeking up behind the couch in the living room and someone is hiding behind the curtains, giggling. By connecting this information with what you already know, you would probably infer that you are about to have a surprise birthday party.

You draw a **conclusion** when you add up all the evidence available. In some ways, drawing a conclusion involves thinking like a detective. For example, suppose you read that there was a fire at a factory. You discover that traces of gasoline were found, that the owner had a lot of insurance for the building, and that the owner needed money. By adding up the evidence, you conclude that arson was involved.

A **prediction** is a guess based on evidence about what will happen. You often make predictions when you read and then check to see if your prediction is correct as you read on. For example, imagine you are reading a mystery about a detective in pursuit of a master criminal. When the detective receives a piece of information, she gets all excited and says, "Aha, now everything has fallen into place." Based on the evidence, you predict that she will find the criminal. Then you read on to see if your prediction was right. If she doesn't find the criminal, you revise or change your prediction based on the new evidence.

It is also important to understand how an author supports his or her ideas in a text and to determine how an author organizes information. Understanding the support for ideas means first finding the **main idea**, or most important idea in a passage, and then identifying the **details** the author uses to back up or support this idea.

Determining the way the author **organizes** information involves identifying the **structure** of the text and seeing how it affects the text. For example, text may be organized to show

- cause and effect;
- comparison and contrast;
- time order;
- order of importance.

Guided Reading Instruction

Directions Read the following passage. Use the questions in the margin to guide your reading. Then answer the questions that follow.

Daily Life:
Making the Most of Everything
by Jane A. Beem

1 Daily life was a challenge for the ancient cliff dwellers. They built their pueblos in high alcoves that the water had eroded and carved out of cliffs. Living in the alcoves kept the ground-level land open for farming. The alcoves also sheltered the people from the wind, rain, and snow. In some areas, homes built high enough on the cliffs were protected even from flooding. The Puebloan cliff homes stayed shady and cool in the summer, when the sun was low.

1 Based on the information in this paragraph, what conclusion can you draw about how the ancient Puebloans supported themselves? Underline the detail that tells you this.

They were farmers

2 The cliff-dwelling Puebloans farmed corn, beans, and squash. These ancient people understood gardening methods. They loosened the soil with heavy stone hoes. They planted corn deep enough so birds could not steal the seeds. Their irrigation processes helped ensure the crops had water. In some dry areas, such as Mesa Verde, the Puebloans practiced dry farming by developing seeds that were drought resistant.

2 What details support the idea that "These ancient peoples understood gardening methods"?

They lived in cliff dwellings that are ideal places for gar.

3 To supplement their farming, the cliff dwellers gathered wild plants. They were able to make use of every part of the plants. For example, the yucca plant could be roasted or left raw for its flowers and fruits to be eaten. Its stalks were brewed to make a sweet, hot drink. Soap was made from the yucca's roots. The long, stringy leaf fibers, twisted into strong cords, were woven into baskets and sandals. And the sharp spines at the ends of the yucca leaves were employed as needles or awls.

3 What inference do you make about the ancient Puebloans based on the information in this paragraph?

They were houses that were in the side of the mountain.

Besides farming and gathering, some of the other daily activities of the Puebloans included hunting, visiting, and exploring. The men and boys hunted mostly mule, deer, and rabbit. In some areas it was bighorn sheep, elk, and birds. As with the wild plants, the Puebloans also used most parts of the wild game they caught. The animal skins became pouches, moccasins, and blankets. The bones were turned into tools, dice, earrings, and whistles. The sinews (tendons) made excellent bowstrings. The fat became seasoning or ointment. The meat was stewed, roasted, baked, or dried and eaten. The Pueblo people actually spent much of each day preparing what they had farmed, gathered, or hunted.

4 The ancient Puebloans also were skilled craftsmen. They used materials they found in their surroundings—stone, mud, and water—to build their pueblos. They created magnificent masonry structures from ordinary resources.

4 Underline the main idea of this paragraph.

The Pueblo people combined water and clay from the ground to form pottery. Cinders, sand, and crushed rock were added to prevent cracking. Then designs were painted on the pottery using paints from plant life and shredded yucca leaf fibers as paintbrush bristles.

5 The ancient Puebloans made beautiful things. They often traded some of their craftwork, such as turquoise jewelry, for shells from California or colorful

5 What evidence supports the idea that other people found the work of the ancient Puebloans beautiful?

parrot feathers from Mexico. Sometimes their trading was direct, such as for cotton at Mesa Verde. Trading for other items, such as shells, probably was indirect, as they traded with different groups that traveled to and from California.

How have we learned about these people who left no written record? The dry desert climate preserved many artifacts in the trash heaps of the ancient cliff dwelling sites. Sifting through these trash heaps, archaeologists have found items that help them reconstruct the daily lives of the cliff dwellers. At Chaco Canyon, New Mexico, for instance, turquoise pendants and clay pottery were found in perfect condition. Pictographs on the cliffs reveal stories, as do the decorations on pottery. In addition, the customs and oral traditions of modern Pueblo people help piece together the story of their ancient ancestors. The Hopis in northern Arizona, the Rio Grande Pueblos in northern New Mexico, and the Zunis in western New Mexico are just some of the descendants of the Puebloan cliff dwellers.

1. Where did the ancient cliff dwellers build their houses? Why did they choose this site?

   They built their houses in the sides of cliffs for agricultural and
   environmental reasons.

2. Besides farming and gathering, what were some of the daily activities of the Puebloans?

   They hunted and crafted structures and pots.

3. How did the Puebloans use the animals they hunted?

   They used them for food, seasoning, bowstrings, and ointmant.
   They also made tools, dice, earrings, whistles, and pouches.

4. How can sifting through trash help people learn about the ancient Puebloans?

   _____

   _____

   _____

5. Explain the connection between the title of this article and the author's purpose.

   _____

   _____

Apply   **Directions** Read the passage below. Then answer the questions that follow it.

from GRANT AND LEE: A STUDY IN CONTRAST
by Bruce Catton

When Ulysses S. Grant and Robert E. Lee met in the parlor of a modest house at Appomattox Court House, Virginia, on April 9, 1865, to work out the terms for the surrender of Lee's Army of Northern Virginia, a great chapter in American life came to a close, and a great new chapter began.

These men were bringing the Civil War to its virtual finish. To be sure, other armies had yet to surrender, and for a few days the fugitive Confederate government would struggle desperately and vainly, trying to find some way to go on living now that its chief support was gone. But in effect it was all over when Grant and Lee signed the papers. And the little room where they wrote out the terms was the scene of one of the poignant, dramatic contrasts in American history.

They were two strong men, these oddly different generals, and they represented the strengths of two conflicting currents that, through them, had come into final collision.

Back of Robert E. Lee was the notion that the old aristocratic concept might somehow survive and be dominant in American life.

Lee was tidewater Virginia, and in his background were family, culture, and tradition . . . the age of chivalry transplanted to a New World which was making its own legends and its own myths. He embodied a way of life that had come down through the age of knighthood and the English country squire. America was a land that was beginning all over again, dedicated to nothing much more complicated than the rather hazy belief that all men had equal rights and should have an equal chance in the world. In such a land Lee stood for the feeling that it was somehow of advantage to human society to have a pronounced inequality in the social structure. There should be a leisure class, backed by ownership of land; in turn, society itself should be keyed to the land as the chief source of wealth and influence. It would bring forth (according to this ideal) a class of men with a strong sense of obligation to the community; men who lived not to gain advantage for themselves, but to meet the solemn obligations which had been laid on them by the very fact that they were privileged. From them the country would get its leadership; to them it could look for the higher values—of thought, of conduct, of personal deportment—to give it strength and virtue.

Lee embodied the noblest elements of this aristocratic ideal. Through him, the landed nobility justified itself. For four years, the Southern states had fought a desperate war to uphold the ideals for which Lee stood. In the end, it almost seemed as if the Confederacy fought for Lee; as if he himself was the Confederacy . . . the best thing that the way of life for which the Confederacy stood could ever have to offer. He had passed into legend before Appomattox. Thousands of tired, underfed, poorly clothed Confederate soldiers, long since past the simple enthusiasm of the early days of the struggle, somehow considered Lee the symbol of everything for which they had been willing to die. But they could not quite put this feeling into words. If the Lost Cause, sanctified by so much heroism and so many deaths, had a living justification, its justification was General Lee.

Grant, the son of a tanner on the Western frontier, was everything Lee was not. He had come up the hard way and embodied nothing in particular except the eternal toughness and sinewy fiber of the men who grew up beyond the mountains. He was one of a body of men who owed reverence and obeisance to no one, who were self-reliant to a fault, who cared hardly anything for the past but who had a sharp eye for the future.

These frontier men were the precise opposites of the tidewater aristocrats. Back of them, in the great surge that had taken people over the Alleghenies and into the opening Western country, there was a deep, implicit dissatisfaction with a past that had settled into grooves. They stood for democracy, not from any reasoned conclusion about the proper ordering of human society, but simply because they had grown up in the middle of democracy and knew how it worked. Their society might have privileges, but they would be privileges each man had won for himself. Forms and patterns meant nothing. No man was born to anything, except perhaps to a chance to show how far he could rise. Life was competition.

Yet along with this feeling had come a deep sense of belonging to a national community. The Westerner who developed a farm, opened a shop, or set up in business as a trader, could hope to prosper only as his own community prospered—and his community ran from the Atlantic to the Pacific and from Canada down to Mexico. If the land was settled, with towns and highways and accessible markets, he could better himself. He saw his fate in terms of the nation's own destiny. As its horizons expanded, so did his. He had, in other words, an acute dollars-and-cents stake in the continued growth and development of his country.

And that, perhaps, is where the contrast between Grant and Lee becomes most striking. The Virginia aristocrat, inevitably, saw himself in relation to his own region. He lived in a static society which could endure almost anything except change. Instinctively, his first loyalty would go to the locality in which that society existed. He would fight to the limit of endurance to defend it, because in defending it he was defending everything that gave his own life its deepest meaning.

The Westerner, on the other hand, would fight with an equal tenacity for the broader concept of society. He fought so because everything he lived by was tied to growth, expansion, and a constantly widening horizon. What he lived by would survive or fall with the nation itself. He could not possibly stand by unmoved in the face of an attempt to destroy the Union. He would combat it with everything he had, because he could only see it as an effort to cut the ground out from under his feet.

So Grant and Lee were in complete contrast, representing two diametrically opposed elements in American life. Grant was the modern man emerging; beyond him, ready to come on the stage, was the great age of steel and machinery, of crowded cities and a restless burgeoning vitality. Lee might have ridden down from the old age of chivalry, lance in hand, silken banner fluttering over his head. Each man was the perfect champion of his cause, drawing both his strengths and his weaknesses from the people he led.

1. Based on the title of this article, what do you immediately know about its organization?

   It is in compare & contrast format.

2. In paragraph 1, what does the author mean when he writes that "a great chapter in American life came to a close"? What is the new chapter that began?

   The new chapter was the age

3. What two different ideals were represented in Grant and Lee?

Grant was a rough and tough liberal that was moral and Lee
was a conservative

4. Compare and contrast Lee and Grant's view of privilege.

Lee believed that you would be what your parents were, Grant
believed you should make your own destiny.

5. Based on the information in this article, why does it make sense that Lee fought for the South, not for the United States?

Lee fought to save what he knew and lived

Assessment Practice

Directions Answer the questions based on the selection you just read.

1. The author contrasts the "age of chivalry" with a nation "making its own legends and its own myths" to show that—

   A no one in the United States believed in chivalry.

   B Lee was out of touch with how the United States was moving.

   C Grant was a finer person than Lee.

   D Lee belonged to a class of men who felt a strong obligation to the community.

2. Based on the information in this article, all of the details about Lee are accurate EXCEPT that—

   A he was a Virginia aristocrat.

   B he valued family, culture, and tradition.

   C he looked to the future.

   D he disliked change.

3. Which statement below best expresses how Lee and Grant were alike?

   A They were two strong men, these oddly different generals, and they represented the strengths of two conflicting currents that, through them, had come into final collision.

   B They stood for democracy, not from any reasoned conclusion about the proper ordering of human society, but simply because they had grown up in the middle of democracy and knew how it worked.

   C And that, perhaps, is where the contrast between Grant and Lee becomes most striking.

   D Each man was the perfect champion of his cause, drawing both his strengths and his weaknesses from the people he led.

4. The author states that the Westerner saw his fate in terms of the nation's own destiny to explain why—

   A Westerners are self-reliant.

   B Grant aligned himself with the Union.

   C Lee supported the South and its ideals.

   D people in the West became good business people.

5. Based on information in this document, which statement explaining why Confederate soldiers went on fighting for their lost cause is accurate?

   A They all planned to be aristocrats themselves.

   B They knew Lee was a better soldier than Grant.

   C They wanted to be heroes.

   D They believed in the way of life that Lee represented.

Focus on California Content Standards

Lesson 11   **Critique Functional Documents**

Reading Informational Materials 9.2.7 Critique the logic of functional documents by examining the sequence of information and procedures in anticipation of possible reader misunderstandings.

Written instructions, travel brochures, advertisements, policy guidelines—all these are types of **functional documents**. The purpose of this type of text is very specific. It is to give you information that helps you function, or learn how to do things, in the real world. For example, if you wanted to go camping in a state park, you would read rules and regulations for doing this. If you wanted to get a learner's permit, you would read information telling you how to apply for one and then get an application and fill it out. If you wanted to learn how to operate a motor scooter, you would read the user's manual.

Some examples of functional documents are

> user's manuals
> directions for experiments
> cookbooks
> product information
> information booklets
> procedure memos
> health insurance documents
> guides for getting permits

Usually, functional documents are **organized** in ways that make the information clear and easy to understand. For example, the instructions on how to perform the Heimlich maneuver are probably organized in time order to show what step to do first, what step to do second, and so on. Documents also usually contain **text features** such as headings, special type, and bullets that make the information accessible.

When you read a functional document, look to see how **complete** the information is. Does it answer all of your questions? If not, what questions are left unanswered and where can you find the information to these questions? Think about the **amount** of information. Ask yourself which topic the document provides the most information about and which the least.

Look at the **support** the author provides. Does the author use facts and details? Does the author include personal experiences? Does the author use quotations from experts in the field?

Guided Reading Instruction

Directions Read the following passage. Use the questions in the margin to guide your reading. Then answer the questions that follow.

How to Get Started with Your Family Tree
by Kimberly Powell
http://genealogy.about.com

You have a little knowledge about your family history, a few old photos and documents and a consuming curiosity. Here are some basic steps to start you on your family tree adventure!

1

Difficulty: Average
Time Required: Varies

2 **Here's How:**

1. Gather together everything you have—papers, photos, documents, etc.

2. Interview the relatives. Start with Mom and Dad and then move on from there. Ask for stories, not just names and dates!

3. Write down everything you have learned from your family.

4. Choose which surname you want to work on first.

5. Explore the Internet. It is a great place for information and leads. Just don't expect to find your entire family tree online!

6. Visit your local Family History Center where you can access the world's largest collection of genealogical information.

7. Look at the records of your ancestors including wills; birth, marriage, and death records; land deeds; etc.

8. Organize your new information—take notes, make photocopies, etc. Make sure you save and date everything!

9. Visit the place where your family lived—look at cemeteries, courthouses, churches, etc. for information.

10. Make sure you continue to document everything, including taking pictures. You never know when you might need it.

3 11. When you have gone as far as you can go, step back and take a break—then go to Step #4 and choose a new ancestor to start searching for.

12. Remember to have fun!

Tips:

1. Ask your family members if there is a genealogy book or other records within your family. This could give you a wonderful head start!

2. Keep copies of everything you find in your search. It may not seem important now, but it probably will be in the future.

4 3. Make sure that you keep in mind possible alternate spellings of your surname as you are researching.

Guided Questions

1 What is the purpose of this information?
To help readers make their family tree.

2 How are these steps organized?
Chronologically

3 Why should you go back to Step #4 at this point?
To make a new branch of the family tree.

4 Why would this step be helpful?

More How To's from Your Guide to Genealogy

5 **Related Resources**

- One Stop Guide to Beginner's Genealogy
- Free Family Tree Charts and Forms
- Search for Your Surname
- How to Interview a Relative
- Genealogy A–Z

Guided Questions

5 Which resource would you use if you were going to talk to your great aunt and uncle in order to get information about your father?

1. Look at Step 2. Why is it important to ask for stories and not just facts?

Then you'll have more info to fill your tree with.

2. What are four sources of information about your family?

family, internet, books, and documents.

3. What is a genealogy book? Why would locating one that someone in your family had prepared be helpful?

A book with refrences, dates, and birth certificates.

4. Based on this document, do you think you would be able to start researching your family tree? Why or why not?

No because I don't have enough info on my family.

Apply **Directions** Read the passage below. Then answer the questions that follow it.

Animals in Disaster
www.fema.gov/pdf/areyouready/animals.pdf

Disaster disrupts and affects everything in its path, including pets, livestock, and wildlife. The following section provides general guidelines for handling animals in emergencies and disaster situations.

Pets in disaster

Pets need to be included in your household disaster plan since they depend on you for their safety and well being. It is important to consider and prepare for your pets before disaster strikes. Consider the following preparedness measures:

1. If you must evacuate, do not leave pets behind—there is a chance they may not survive, or get lost before you return.

2. With the exception of service animals, pets are not typically permitted in emergency shelters for health reasons.

3. Find out before a disaster which local hotels and motels allow pets and where pet boarding facilities are located. Be sure to include some outside your local area in case local facilities have closed.

4. Know that most boarding facilities require veterinarian records to prove vaccinations are current.

5. Only some animal shelters will provide care for pets during emergency and disaster situations. They should be used as a last resort. Use friends and family or keep them with you.

6. Be sure your pet has proper identification tags securely fastened to the collar. A current photo of your pet will assist identification should it become necessary.

7. Make sure you have a secure pet carrier or leash for your pet—they may need to be restrained during tense emergency situations.

8. Assemble a disaster kit for your pet. Include pet food, water, medications, veterinary records, little box, can opener, food dishes, first aid kit, other supplies that may not be available at a later time, and an information sheet with pet's name and such things as behavior problems. Provide the kit to whomever assumes responsibility for your pet during a disaster.

9. Call your local emergency management office or animal shelter for further information.

Large animals in disaster

If you have large animals, such as horses or cattle on your property, be sure to prepare before a disaster.

1. Evacuate animals whenever possible. Map out primary and secondary routes in advance.

2. Evacuation destinations should be prepared with, or ready to obtain, food, water, veterinary care, and handling equipment.

3. Vehicles and trailers needed for transporting and supporting each type of animal should be available along with experienced handlers and drivers. It is best to allow animals a chance to become accustomed to vehicular travel so they are less frightened and easier to move.

4. In case evacuation is not possible, animal owners must decide whether to move large animals to shelter or turn them outside. This decision should be based on the disaster type, quality and location of shelter, and the risks of turning them outside.

5. All animals should have some form of identification.

Wildlife in disaster

Disaster and life threatening situations will exacerbate the unpredictable nature of wild animals. To protect yourself and your household, learn how to deal with wildlife.

1. Be cautious approaching wild animals during emergency situations. Do not corner them. Wild animals will likely feel threatened and may endanger themselves by dashing off into floodwaters, fire, etc.

2. If wild animals are trapped or no natural food source is available, you can leave food appropriate to individual animals (i.e., animals could become trapped on an "island" after seeking high ground as floodwaters rise).

3. Wild animals such as snakes, opossums, and raccoons often seek refuge from floodwaters on upper levels of homes and have been known to remain after water recedes. If you encounter animals in this situation—open a window or other escape route and the animal will likely leave on its own. Do not attempt to capture or handle the animal. Should the animal stay, call your local animal control office or animal shelter.

4. If you see an injured or stranded animal, do not approach or attempt to help. Call your local emergency department for specific help and instructions.

5. Animal carcasses can present serious health risks. Contact your local emergency management office or health department for specific help and instructions.

Animals after disaster

Wild or stray domestic animals can pose a danger during or after many types of disaster. Remember, most animals are disoriented and displaced. too. Do not corner an animal. If an animal must be removed, contact your local animal control authorities.

If any animal bites you, seek immediate medical attention. If a snake bites you, try to accurately identify the type of snake so that, if poisonous, the correct anti-venom can be administered. Do not cut the wound or attempt to suck the venom out.

Certain animals may carry rabies. Although the virus is rare, care should be taken to avoid contact with stray animals and rodents. Health departments can provide information on the types of animals that carry rabies in your area.

Rats may also be a problem during and after many types of disaster. Be sure to secure all food supplies and contact your local animal control authorities to remove any animal carcasses in the vicinity.

Contact your local emergency manager for more information on animals in disaster. The Humane Society of the United States can be reached at: 2100 L Street, NW, Washington, D.C., 20037, Attn: Disaster Services Program or by phone at 202-452-1100 or online at **www.hsus.org/disaster**.

1. Would you find this article useful if your primary concern was caring for children during a disaster? Why or why not?

_____

_____

2. If you were searching for this article on the Internet, what website would you go to?

3. If you didn't find the information in this article that answers your specific questions, what resources could you go to?

_____

_____

4. What should you do to prepare horses for the possibility of being evacuated in a truck?

_____

_____

Directions Answer the questions based on the selection you just read.

1. **This document provides the MOST information about—**

   A   what to do to protect your pets before disaster strikes.

   B   what to do with wild animals during a disaster.

   C   how to protect horses and cattle during a disaster.

   D   how to treat animals after a disaster.

2. **Before a disaster, you should do all of the following things EXCEPT—**

   A   find out which hotels and motels allow pets.

   B   get your pet's veterinarian records in order.

   C   prepare a disaster kit.

   D   leave your pet behind to await your return.

3. **This document MOSTLY includes—**

   A   anecdotes or stories.

   B   practical steps.

   C   statistics.

   D   quotations from veterinarians.

4. **If you encounter a wild animal trapped in your home after a disaster, you should—**

   A   try to capture it.

   B   open a window or other escape route.

   C   leave food out for it.

   D   chase it until it leaves.

5. **The information under "Animals after disaster" is organized to—**

   A   provide reasons to stay away from animals.

   B   show the effects of a disaster on animals.

   C   compare and contrast animals before and after a disaster.

   D   show the most important and then the least important information.

Focus on California Content Standards

Lesson 12 Evaluate an Argument or Defense

Reading Informational Materials 9.2.8 Evaluate the credibility of an author's argument or defense of a claim by critiquing the relationship between generalizations and evidence, the comprehensiveness of evidence, and the way in which the author's intent affects the structure and tone of the text (e.g., in professional journals, editorials, political speeches, primary source material).

An **argument** is a defense of a position or claim. The author presents evidence to get you to accept his or her **premise**, or **viewpoint**. The evidence may consist of facts, reasons, data, or even valid opinions. A **fact** is a statement that can be proved true. An **opinion** is a judgment or personal evaluation. A **valid opinion** is a judgment backed up by facts.

When you read an argument, look for the **main points** that the writer makes. Examine the evidence that **supports** these points. Watch for broad generalizations, or sweeping statements. For example:

Generalization: All people love freedom and value liberty.

Generalization: Kids of all ages can't resist a circus.

Then decide for yourself whether or not it supports the author's claim.

Look at the **purpose** of the text. In an argument, the purpose usually will be to persuade, although it may be simply to inform. Question whether the author uses persuasive techniques that appeal to reason or that are designed to stir the emotions. Make sure the persuasive techniques are fair, and not biased, or slanted. Examine the writer's tone, or the attitude toward the subject that comes through the writing style. Is it objective or highly subjective? Is it professional and matter-of-fact or sarcastic and biting?

**Guided
Reading
Instruction**

Directions Read the following passage. Use the questions in the margin to guide your reading. Then answer the questions that follow.

Guided Questions

**1 A Tribute to Eleanor Roosevelt:
Address to the First Anniversary Luncheon
of the Eleanor Roosevelt Memorial Foundation**
by Mrs. Lyndon Baines (Lady Bird) Johnson
Former First Lady, United States of America
April 9, 1964

For me, it is a great privilege to come here today and participate in this anniversary occasion.

I met Eleanor Roosevelt first in print and admired her. I met her later in person and loved her. As she did to many very young and very timid Congressional wives, she extended her hand and hospitality to me . . . and Washington was warmer.

I saw her last when she came to my home on February 12, 1962, the day the Commission on the Status of Women was organized under her chairmanship and her inspiration. She was 78. **2** I have often thought how much she made those years count for her country.

Nobody, said Marcus Aurelius, is either the better or the worse for being praised. We are engaged in an idle ceremony, which would have brought no comfort to Eleanor Roosevelt, if we come here merely to praise her great qualities and achievements. She does not need our praise.

All of us are familiar with people who are the partisans of departed virtue, but are afraid to defend an unpopular truth today. Mrs. Roosevelt never stood with this timid company. Her conscience was her counselor, and she followed its commands with unfaltering courage. Nor did she really understand what people meant when they praised her for taking so many risks. She would have taken the greatest risk of all if she had remained silent in the presence of wrong. She would have risked the integrity of her soul. **3** A rabbi of the Jewish community in Berlin under the Hitler regime once said: "The most important thing I learned is that bigotry and hatred are not the most urgent problems. The most urgent, the most disgraceful, the most shameful, and the most tragic problem—is silence."

Eleanor Roosevelt taught us that sometimes silence is the greatest sin.
Do you remember what Dr. Samuel Johnson said about courage? "Unless a man has that virtue, he has no security for preserving any other." **4** Mrs. Roosevelt knew what those words meant. She lived their meaning every day of her life. Courage sustained by compassion—that was the watchword of her entire career.

Always she thought not of abstract rights, but of living wrongs.
I watched her at close range one day when she spent two hours helping the 75th Congressional Club give a benefit luncheon to buy a wheelchair for a crippled boy.

1 What is the purpose of this speech?

2 What opinion does Mrs. Johnson present here?

3 Why does Mrs. Johnson include this statement from the rabbi?

4 How does this detail help to persuade the listener to view Eleanor Roosevelt in a positive way?

Only one person was involved. Where else do you start, but with one person?

She thought of the suffering individual, not of a theoretical principle. She saw an unemployed father, and so she helped him. She saw a neglected Negro child, and so she educated him. She saw dictators hurling the world into war, and so she worked unflinchingly for peace. She saw the United Nations divided by the conflict of ideology and power, and so she became the prophet of the Universal Declaration of Human Rights. Are we ready to fight similar battles against new foes in our own day? If not, our grief is an empty thing, and the spirit of Eleanor Roosevelt is not among us. **5**

5 How does the information in the next paragraph support the premise introduced in the previous paragraphs?

President Wilson used to say that some people in Washington grow in office, while others merely swell. Mrs. Roosevelt steadily grew under the compulsions and inspirations of her great office. But, it is perhaps the ultimate tribute to Mrs. Roosevelt that she reached true greatness after the shock of her bereavement when she went bravely forward in a new career as a spokesman for America and a servant of world peace. In the White House she was the First Lady in the land, but after the White House she became, as Ambassador Stevenson has reminded us, the First Lady in the world. Great was her goodness, and it was her goodness that made her so great. **6**

6 What is the purpose of this paragraph?

Let us today earnestly resolve to build the true foundation for Eleanor Roosevelt's memory—to pluck out prejudice from our lives, to remove fear and hate where it exists, and to create a world unafraid to work out its destiny in peace. Eleanor Roosevelt has already made her own splendid and incomparable contribution to that foundation. Let us go and do likewise, within the measure of our faith and the limits of our ability. **7** Let Eleanor Roosevelt teach us all how to turn the arts of compassion into the victories of democracy.

7 What does this sentence ask of the listener?

1. In your own words, what view of Eleanor Roosevelt did Lady Bird Johnson's argue in her address?

_____

_____

2. What detail about the life of Eleanor Roosevelt leads up to the conclusion: "Great was her goodness, and it was her goodness that made her so great"?

_____

_____

3. How do you feel about Eleanor Roosevelt after reading this address?

_____

_____

_____

4. Look at the following political cartoon. Who is the figure in the car? What impression do you form of her.

_____

_____

5. The woman walking down the road is a symbol of what?

_____

_____

6. What is the message of this cartoon?

_____

_____

Apply **Directions** Read the passage below. Then answer the questions that follow it.

First Lady Barbara Bush delivers the commencement address at Wellesley College, June 1, 1990.

Thank you, President Keohane, Mrs. Gorbachev, trustees, faculty, parents, Julie Porter, Christine Bicknell, and, of course, the Class of 1990.

I am thrilled to be with you today, and very excited, as I know you must all be, that Mrs. Gorbachev could join us. This is an exciting time in Washington, D.C. But I am so glad to be here. I knew coming to Wellesley would be fun, but I never dreamed it would be this much fun! [Laughter.]

More than ten years ago, when I was invited here to talk about our experiences in the People's Republic of China, I was struck by both the natural beauty of your campus and the spirit of this place.

Wellesley, you see, is not just a place, but an idea, an experiment in excellence in which diversity is not just tolerated, but is embraced.

The essence of this spirit was captured in a moving speech about tolerance, given last year by the student body president of one of your sister colleges. She related the story by Robert Fulghum about a young pastor who, finding himself in charge of some very energetic children, hits upon a game called "Giants, Wizards and Dwarfs." "You have to decide now," the pastor instructed the children, "which you are: a giant, a wizard or a dwarf?"

At that, a small girl tugging at his pants leg asked, "But where do the mermaids stand?"

The pastor told her there are no mermaids. "Oh, yes there are," she said. "I am a mermaid."

Now this little girl knew what she was, and she was not about to give up on either her identity or the game. She intended to take her place, wherever mermaids fit into the scheme of things. Where do mermaids stand—all those who are different—those who do not fit the boxes and the pigeonholes?

"Answer that question," wrote Fulghum, "and you can build a school, a nation, or a whole world."

As that very wise young woman said, "Diversity, like anything worth having, requires effort." Effort to learn about and respect difference, to be compassionate with one another, to cherish our own identity and to accept unconditionally the same in others.

You should all be very proud that this is the Wellesley spirit.

Now I know your first choice today was Alice Walker, known for *The Color Purple*. And guess how I know? [Bush glances at administration officials.] Instead you got me—known for the color of my hair! [Laughter.] Alice Walker's book has a special resonance here. At Wellesley, each class is known by a special color: For four years the class of '90 has worn the color purple. Today you meet on Severance Green to say goodbye to all of that, to begin a new and very personal journey to search for your own true colors.

In the world that awaits you beyond the shores of Lake Waban, no one can say what your true colors will be. But this I do know: You have a first-class education from a first-class school. And so you need not, probably cannot, live a "paint-by-numbers" life. Decisions are not irrevocable. Choices do come back. As you set off from Wellesley, I hope that many of you will consider making three very special choices.

The first is to believe in something larger than yourself—to get involved in some of the big ideas of your time. I chose literacy because I honestly believe that if more people could read, write and comprehend, we would be that much closer to solving so many of the problems plaguing our society. Early on, I made another choice which I hope you will make as well. Whether you are talking about education, career or service, you are talking about life — and life must have joy.

It's supposed to be fun! [Applause.]

One of the reasons I made the most important decision of my life, to marry George Bush, is because he made me laugh.

It's true, sometimes we've laughed through our tears, but that shared laughter has been one of our strongest bonds. Find the joy in life, because as Ferris Bueller said on his day off , "Life moves pretty fast. Ya' don't stop and look around once in a while, ya' gonna miss it!" [Cheers and applause.]

I won't tell George that you applauded Ferris more than you applauded him! [Laughter.]

The third choice that must not be missed is to cherish your human connections, your relationships with friends and family. For several years, you've had impressed upon you the importance to your career of dedication and hard work. This is true, but as important as your obligations as a doctor, lawyer or business leader will be, you are a human being first and those human connections—with spouses, with children, with friends—are the most important investments you will ever make.

At the end of your life, you will never regret not having passed one more test, not winning one more verdict or not closing one more deal. You will regret time not spent with a husband, a friend, a child or a parent.

We are in a transitional period right now—fascinating and exhilarating times—learning to adjust to the changes and the choices we men and women are facing.

As an example, I remember what a friend said, on hearing her husband complain to his buddies that he had to babysit. Quickly setting him straight, my friend told her husband that when it's your own kids, it's not called babysitting! [Applause.]

Maybe we should adjust faster, maybe slower. But whatever the era, whatever the times, one thing will never change: Fathers and mothers, if you have children, they must come first. You must read to your children, you must hug your children, you must love your children. Your success as a family, our success as a society, depends not on what happens at the White House, but on what happens inside your house.

For over fifty years, it was said that the winner of Wellesley's annual hoop race would be the first to get married. Now, they say the winner will be the first to become a CEO. Both of those stereotypes show too little tolerance for those who want to know where the mermaids stand.

So I want to offer you today a new legend: The winner of the hoop race will be the first to realize her dream, not society's dream, her own personal dream. Who knows? Somewhere out in this audience may even be someone who will one day follow in my footsteps, and preside over the White House as the President's spouse. I wish him well! [Cheers and applause.]

The controversy ends here. But our conversation is only beginning. And a worthwhile conversation it has been. So as you leave Wellesley today, take with you deep thanks for the courtesy and the honor you have shared with Mrs. Gorbachev and me.

Thank you. God bless you.

And may your future be worthy of your dreams. [Applause.]

1. Mrs. Bush starts her address by trying to get the listeners on her side. How does she appeal to her listeners' emotions in paragraph 11 which begins with the words "You should all be . . ." ?

_____

_____

2. In the next paragraph, how does Mrs. Bush use humor to get her listeners on her side?

_____

_____

3. In *The Color Purple*, Alice Walker uses purple as a symbol for pride. How does this symbol relate to the ideas Mrs. Bush has presented so far? Why does she then say that the students are about to search for their own true colors?

_____

_____

4. What premise, or important idea, does Mrs. Bush present in paragraph 13, which begins with the words "In the world that awaits you . . ."?

_____

_____

5. Mrs. Bush continues her argument by making three points about how to lead a fulfilling life as an individual. What two points does she make in paragraph 14, which begins with the words "The first is . . . "?

_____

_____

6. In paragraph 18, which begins with the words "It's true . . . ," what kind of example does Mrs. Bush use to help persuade her audience?

_____

_____

7. What third point does Mrs. Bush use in paragraph 20 to support her premise? This paragraph begins with the words "The third choice . . . "

_____

_____

8. In paragraph 25, which begins with the words "For over fifty years," how does Mrs. Bush tie the story of the hoop dance to her original premise?

_____

_____

9. Look at the cartoon below. How does it connect to the premise of the speech?

_____

10. Why is the cartoon humorous?

_____

_____

Measuring Up® to the California Content Standards

Assessment Practice **Directions** Answer the questions based on the selection you just read.

1. Mrs. Bush tells the story of the little girl playing "Giants, Wizards, and Dwarfs" in order to support the idea that—

   A having a role model is important.

   B diversity must be embraced.

   C Robert Fulghum is a good storyteller.

   D mermaids are a better choice than giants, wizards, or dwarfs.

2. Mrs. Bush uses symbols to support which idea below?

   A It is important to have pride in yourself.

   B It is important to have a sense of humor.

   C It is important to learn how to be a writer.

   D It is important to love your family.

3. Barbara Bush supports the idea that laughter is important by—

   A presenting a quote from a humorous movie.

   B making a humorous reference to her husband.

   C talking about the importance of marriage.

   D intentionally using bad grammar.

4. How does Mrs. Bush suggest that dedication to career is not of foremost importance?

   A She shows the importance of investments.

   B She arouses emotions by discussing how people will feel at the time of their death.

   C She attacks people who think otherwise and calls them foolish.

   D She gives examples of people who were unhappy as doctors, lawyers, or business leaders.

5. Which statement BEST expresses the premise of the cartoon?

   A It is impossible to find out who you really are.

   B People who try to find out who they really are foolish.

   C It is the search or the journey that is important.

   D Everyone gets lost sometimes.

The following article describes the events that inspired the Iditarod. Read the article and answer questions 1 through 10.

THE IDITAROD: COMMEMORATING THE 1925 EMERGENCY DELIVERY OF DIPHTHERIA SERUM TO NOME, ALASKA

The Iditarod is run each year to commemorate the emergency delivery in 1925 of diphtheria antitoxin to Nome, Alaska. Nome in 1925 had changed from a booming, boisterous turn-of-the-century gold-rush camp into a small, quiet town of about 1,500 people. It was fifteen years since the end of the gold rush, but Nome remained an important settlement on the Seward Peninsula.

The First Signs of an Epidemic

It was a normal mid-January afternoon in Nome. Doctor Curtis Welch, physician and director of the U.S. Public Health Service, was doing paperwork in his office at the Merchants and Miners Bank of Alaska building. An Eskimo man came into the office asking the doctor to come quickly, his two children were very sick. Dr. Welch raced to the Sand Spit Eskimo settlement, west of the Snake River on the fringes of Nome.

The children's temperatures were dangerously high, and their breathing was labored and shallow. Dr. Welch asked the mother how the children had become ill and what their symptoms had been. She replied that they had been sick for about three days. She thought it was a bad cold because their throats had become red and sore. Dr. Welch tried to examine their throats, but they could not open their mouths far enough for him to do so. He tried to comfort the mother and then returned to his office.

Dr. Welch had wished many times that he had access to a good laboratory where he could send specimens for analysis. It was very strange. Children don't die of sore throats, but the two Eskimo children were dying. At one point he considered diphtheria but it was highly unlikely. He hadn't seen a case in northern Alaska in twenty years. Despite the doctor's efforts the Eskimo children died the following day.

A few days later, on January 21, Dr. Welch was called to the home of a white family to examine their six-year-old son. The child had been sick for two days with a sore throat. Dr. Welch examined the boy's throat and recognized immediately the dirty white patches of the diphtheria membrane. The doctor realized the terrible implications of this diagnosis. Diphtheria, left unchecked, would spread with devastating speed.

Dr. Welch met at once with Nome's mayor and city council. He told them of the imminent epidemic and stressed that some way must be found to get the diphtheria antitoxin to Nome within two weeks. The serum would check the spread of the disease and would help those already infected. His main concern was with the native population that had little or no immunity to white man's diseases. A flu epidemic in 1919 had wiped out entire Eskimo villages.

There was widespread relief when it was discovered that the Alaska Railroad Hospital in Anchorage had 300,000 units of the life-saving serum. It was not much, but it would be enough to stem the tide of the epidemic. It was decided to transport the serum by train from Anchorage to Nenana, a town on the Tanana River 220 miles north of Anchorage, and then by a relay of dog teams over the 674 miles between Nenana and Nome. This epic relay was carried out by a diverse group of twenty mushers: Eskimo, Russian-Eskimo, Norwegian, Irish and Indians. These men had stamina and toughness in common, and all shared the special understanding and working partnership with their sled dogs that would be the key to the success of the venture.

On January 27, 1925, "Wild Bill" Shannon and his dog team set out from Nenana, Alaska on the first leg of the relay to Nome.

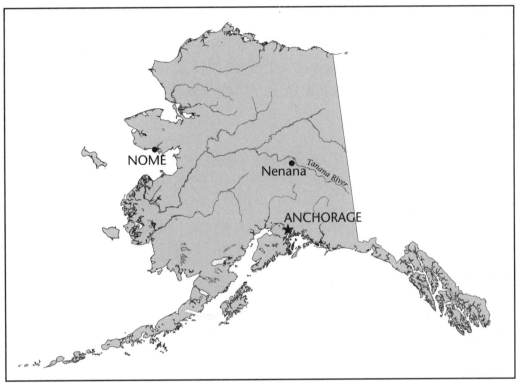

The Alaska Railroad Hospital in Anchorage had 300,000 units of the antitoxin.

The last leg reached Nome on Monday, February 2 at 5:30 in the morning. Dr. Welch was awakened by a persistent knocking on his front door. When he opened it he found an exhausted Gunnar Kaasen, the musher of the final leg of the relay. Kaasen handed him a twenty pound, fur-and-canvas-covered package containing the 300,000 units of serum. In the street were his thirteen dogs harnessed to a sled, their heads and bushy tails hanging almost to the ground. They had covered the last fifty-three miles of the epic relay in seven and a half hours. These dogs and the teams that proceded them, had traversed 674 ice-and-snow covered miles in less than five days. They delivered to Dr. Welch the life-saving serum that within a week would break the back of the diphtheria epidemic.

Almost forgotten is the fact that five days later a second batch of serum arrived in Seward, Alaska. It was shipped in record time by train to Nenana and again relayed by dog teams as far as Unalakeleet (a little over 200 miles from Nome). Many of the original mushers were in the second run.

In 1966–67 Dorothy Page and Joe Redington Sr. organized the first Iditarod Trail Dog Sled Race to commemorate the serum relay. In 1973 the race was expanded to its present course.

More Facts About the Iditarod Trail Sled Dog Race

First Iditarod Trail Sled Dog Race (1967)

Winner: Dick Wilmarth, Red 9 Devil, AK, in 20 days, 49 minutes, 41 seconds.

1996 Winner: Jeff King, Denali Park, AK, in 9 days, 5 hours, 43 minutes, 13 seconds.

First Woman Winner: Libby Riddles, Teller, AK, in 18 days, 20 minutes, 17 seconds in 1985.

Fastest Running: Martin Buser, Big Lake, Alaska, in 8 days, 22 two hours, 46 minutes and 2 seconds in 2002.

Most Wins: Rick Swenson, Two Rivers, AK, with five wins.

Most Wins by Woman Musher: Susan Butcher, Manley, AK, with four wins.

Links to Related Web Sites

- The Official Iditarod Web site
- Dogsled.com: This Web site provides viewers intimate, intense, interactive action—the next best thing to being a competitor.

 1. **Which question could MOST effectively be developed into a research paper?**

A What is the exact location of Nome, Alaska?

B Who was Dr. Curtis Welch?

C What were the causes and effects of the flu epidemic in 1919?

D What is the present course of the Idiatrod dog sled race?

2. **What reason led Dr. Welch to conclude that diphtheria was unlikely?**

A Most children don't die of sore throats and two children had died.

B He hadn't seen a case of diphtheria in northern Alaska in twenty years.

C He found dirty white patches in the boy's throat.

D One child had been sick with a sore throat for two days.

3. **According to the map, the reader can tell that the problem was to get the serum—**

A from Nome to Anchorage.

B from Anchorage to Nenana.

C from Nenana to the Tanana River.

D from Anchorage to Nome.

 4. **Which of the following BEST summarizes the information in the article?**

A After Dr. Welch identified an outbreak of diphtheria, people organized to get the serum needed to check its spread from Anchorage to Nome in two weeks time.

B The first Idiatrod dog sled race occurred when it was necessary to get a serum to children in Anchorage, Alaska.

C An outbreak of diphtheria could wipe out many people, so Dr. Welch asked the mayor and city council for help.

D Without the brave dog sled teams the serum would never have gotten to the children who needed it.

5. **How is the information in paragraphs 1–7 mostly organized?**

A by comparing and contrasting the symptoms of sore throat and diphtheria

B by showing the sequence of events leading up to the epic relay

C by showing the effects of diphtheria and the need for the serum

D by providing evidence proving that Dr. Welch was a caring physician

6. **Which of the following would be a useful source for evaluating the information in this article?**

A the Official Iditarod Web site

B a listing of winners of the race

C a Web site showing what the relay race is like today

D a book about winners of the relay race

 7. **Based on the information in this article, the reader can tell that the author believes that the people who delivered the serum were—**

A crude and rough.

B hardy and heroic.

C reckless and dangerous.

D just ordinary, everyday people.

8. **Which of the following statements best supports the argument that the dogs that pulled the sleds were remarkable?**

A In the street were his thirteen dogs harnessed to a sled, their heads and bushy tails hanging almost to the ground.

B On January 27, 1925, "Wild Bill" Shannon and his dog team set out from Nenana, Alaska on the first leg of the relay to Nome.

C These dogs and the teams that proceeded them, had traversed 674 ice-and-snow covered miles in less than five days.

D In 1966-67 Dorothy Page and Joe Redington Sr. organized the first Iditarod Trail Dog Sled Race to commemorate the serum relay.

9. **The boxed feature tells MOSTLY about—**

A winners of the Iditarod.

B the original race.

C related Websites.

D the fastest runner.

 10. **Dr. Welch persuaded the mayor and city council to help by—**

A using reason.

B citing authorities.

C using broad generalizations.

D offering a prize of money.

Reading Literature 9.3.1 Articulate the relationship between the expressed purposes and the characteristics of different forms of dramatic literature (e.g., comedy, tragedy, drama, dramatic monologue).

Dramatic literature is literature that is meant to be acted out or performed for an audience. Actors take the parts of the characters in the play. They may perform on the stage, in a movie or on television, or in an audio production on tape or CD. Dramatic literature is also called **drama**.

Comedy is one type of dramatic literature. In a comedy, characters face certain obstacles that they try to overcome. Often, but not always, their attempts to overcome these obstacles are humorous. Today, we often use the word *comedy* to refer to stories that make us laugh. However, a comedy does not have to be funny, but it *does* have to end happily.

Tragedy is the opposite of comedy. In a tragedy, the main character faces a problem that brings about his or her downfall—and often death. This cause of the problem may be a character flaw to which the main character is blind. It may also be the result of powerful forces beyond the character's control or understanding. Usually, a tragedy deals with serious issues, such as the effects of pride or a terrible crime committed in the past. Unlike a comedy, a tragedy always ends unhappily for the main character.

A **dramatic monologue** is a long speech by one character. In it, the character reveals a lot about himself or herself. You learn the speaker's inner thoughts and feelings. If the speech is part of a longer play, it is called a **soliloquy**. Dramatic monologues have often been written as poetry, but many modern ones are in prose.

Guided Reading Instruction

Directions Read the following passage. Use the questions in the margin to guide your reading. Then answer the questions that follow.

Julie
by Roger Karshner

Guided Questions

1 Kerry, this is—like this is like kinda real hard for me to say, you know. But . . . but we've been going steady now for almost five months, okay? **2** (*Pause.*) How many? (*Pause.*)

Okay, four. Like I was saying—we've been going steady for almost four months and it's really neat and all that and you're a nice guy and I really like you a lot. Okay? (*Pause.*)

Yes, sure, I know you like me, too. I know that. But, let me finish. Like we've been seeing each other and nobody else all the time, okay? After school every day and every weekend and everything. We're always together. Always.

3 What I mean is . . . what I'm trying to say here is . . . is that maybe we're tying ourselves down too much at our age and that it really isn't fair for someone

1 To whom is Julie speaking? What is her purpose?

2 What do the pauses indicate?

3 How does Julie feel at this point? How do you know?

like you who is real cute and who would probably like to date a bunch of other girls to feel obligated to just one person, you know. And to be super honest, sometimes I'd like to be alone and be able to mess around with Jane and Esther and stuff.

What I'm trying to say, is that maybe we should think about not going steady anymore. Now I know what you're going to say, okay! But don't get the idea that

I'm trying to . . . **4** (*She is interrupted by Kerry.*) What? (*Pause.*) You what? (*Pause.*) It's okay with you? Just like that, it's okay with you? I mean, I barely get it out of my mouth and it's all right with you. Wow! Ah ha! I get it! Kathryn Anderson, right?

(*Break for his response.*) Don't give me that. (*Pause.*) Oh yeah, sure, that's your story! Here I just kind of hint that maybe we shouldn't see each other so much and right away you want to break it off. (*Pause.*)

Oh no, huh uh. Don't go trying to smooth it over. I don't believe this! I don't . . . (*She is interrupted.*)

5 You do? No you don't. (*Pause.*) You do? No. (*Pause.*) No you don't, you're just saying that. Do you really? (*Pause.*) Honest? (*Pause.*) You really like me that much? No kidding, Kerry? (*Pause.*) Sure, of course I like you. You kidding? More than anything. You're the coolest guy in school. (*Pause.*)

6 Break up? Who said anything about breaking up? All I was saying is that maybe you felt tied down, that's all. I was just giving you a way out, okay? Hey! I mean, gee whiz, I was just thinking of you, that's all, you know. (*Pause.*)

Sure I want to keep going steady. You kidding? (*Pause.*) You do? (*Pause.*) Me too.

(*Reaction.*) There's the bell! I'll meet you out front like always, okay? **7** And about Katy Anderson . . . my dad says everything her father owns is on paper.

4 How does Julie feel when her boyfriend tells her breaking up is all right with him?

5 What do you think Julie's boyfriend has just said?

6 Is Julie being completely honest here? Explain.

7 Why do you think Julie says this?

1. How did the playwright's choice of language make Julie seem like an actual teenager? Give one example to support your answer.

   _____

   _____

2. If you were casting this role, or looking for an actress to play the part of Julie, what three qualities would you mention about her?

   _____

   _____

3. Find the section that begins with the words in parentheses "Break for his response." Write the words you think Kerry says.

   _____

   _____

4. Do you think that Kerry really wanted to break up with Terry? Explain your response.

   _____

   _____

Apply   **Directions** Read the passage below. Then answer the questions that follow it.

Jeff

by Roger Karshner

I don't think I ever really knew my father. Not really. I mean, not where it counts, that is, down deep. It always seemed like there was this distance between us, you know.

He was always so busy all of the time. And all I can remember about him when I was little was that he always seemed to either be coming or going. He was like this roomer who lived with us and ate with us and slept upstairs. We never spent much time together, just the two of us. And when we were together, like there was nothing happening, ya know? Seemed like nobody ever had time. Or made time. Or cared, maybe, I guess. I don't know. But I sure know how I feel now, now that he's dead. I really miss him a lot. And I wish he was still around so we could sit down and share things. And talk about things we never got into when he was alive. I mean, real things. Things from in here. (*He pounds his fist to his chest.*)

I've got all this love inside for him that never got out. Why didn't I ever tell him how I felt? Why? Why didn't I open up? Why is it so hard to get stuff out in the open? I mean like, love. Why is it so scary? (*He pauses, then looks up and addresses his remarks heavenward.*)

I love you, Dad. I love you more than anything. And I'm sorry I never told you so, and that you never ever told me. I wish you were here so I could put my arms around you and hold you tight and tell you all the things I always wanted to say but never did. Like how much I respected you and how I thought you were a really neat guy and the best father in the whole world and how you were something special. And I'd tell ya I love ya.

I love ya, Dad. I *love* ya!

1. In the first paragraph, what is Jeff's problem? Put it in your own words.

   _____

   _____

2. What is one reason for the distance between Jeff and his father?

   _____

   _____

3. What does Jeff mean when he says that he would like to talk to his father about real things?

   _____

   _____

4. Do you agree with Jeff that it is hard to get things out in the open? Why or why not?

   _____

   _____

5. Do you think that many teenagers feel the way that Jeff feels? Why or why not?

   _____

   _____

   _____

Assessment Practice

Directions Answer the questions based on the selection you just read.

1. The reader knows that this is a dramatic monologue because—

    A Jeff seems like a typical teenager.

    B Jeff is the only speaker in this passage.

    C Jeff's father has died and Jeff misses him.

    D Jeff is troubled by his feelings.

2. The word that best describes how Jeff feels in the second paragraph is—

    A pleased.

    B regretful.

    C angry.

    D sympathetic.

3. At the end of this monologue, Jeff addresses his comments heavenward because—

    A he doesn't want anyone else to overhear his comments.

    B he is protesting the fact that his father is dead.

    C he is trying to get his father to tell him that he loves him.

    D he wants to tell his father things he couldn't tell him while he was living.

4. Like most dramatic monologues, this one—

    A reveals a lot about the character who is speaking.

    B is very short.

    C is written in verse.

    D tells a lot about relationships between children and parents.

5. Why does Jeff compare his father to a roomer?

    A to show that he paid for the house

    B to suggest that he spent a lot of time at home

    C to indicate that he seemed like a stranger

    D to reveal that fact that there was no love between them

Reading Literature 9.3.3 Analyze interactions between main and subordinate characters in a literary text (e.g., internal and external conflicts, motivations, relationships, influences) and explain the way those interactions affect the plot.

Reading Literature 9.3.4 Determine characters' traits by what the characters say about themselves in narration, dialogue, dramatic monologue, and soliloquy.

Characters are the different people in the story. The **main character**—the character who is at the center of the story—is the **protagonist**. Often another character opposes the protagonist in some way. This opponent is called the **antagonist**.

Characters affect the **plot**, or pattern of action of a story. Often the plot centers on the **conflict** the protagonist faces. The conflict may be between the protagonist and the antagonist. For example, in a western, the sheriff might struggle to save the town from an outlaw who is trying to take it over. The conflict may be between the protagonist and a force of nature. For example, a woman caught in a hurricane might struggle against the fierce wind to survive. Or a conflict may be within the mind of the protagonist. For example, a boy who must take an airplane across the country might struggle against his fear of flying.

Some characters are developed in rich detail, with many aspects of their personalities portrayed. Other characters—especially in very short works such as fables—are presented in clear, simple outline without much complexity.

Authors can use **direct characterization** or **indirect characterization** to reveal a character's traits and to put flesh and bones on a character's skeleton. In direct characterization, the author tells you directly what a character is like. For example:

> Dr. Hastings was the most difficult villain the great detective had ever come up against. He was an evil person. He was born into a family of hardened criminals who would sooner spend five years in jail than do a day of honest work. Of his entire family, Dr. Hastings was the meanest, through and through.

With indirect characterization, the writer presents evidence and the reader must draw inferences about the characters. Examples of character evidence include:

- How the character looks and dresses
- What the characters says
- What the character thinks
- How the character behaves toward others
- What others say and think about the character

For example:

> "He has a brilliant mind," said the great detective, Simon Manchester, as he and his assistant waited inside the bank vault, "but he has one major weakness. He is too proud, and in the end his pride will lead to his capture."

"Listen," said Louis Greenway. "I think I hear someone fiddling with the lock."

They both looked toward the vault door as it inched open. In walked the massive figure of Dr. Hastings.

"I didn't want to disappoint you," Hastings said with mock cordiality. "This time, however, I think you will find that you are caught in your own trap." With that remark, he laughed, reset the lock, and slammed the vault door behind him.

Just like real people, characters reveal a lot about themselves through what they say. Pay special attention to the character's own words in narration, dialogue, dramatic monologue and soliloquy.

Guided Reading Instruction

Directions Read the following passage. Use the questions in the margin to guide your reading. Then answer the questions that follow.

from **Aunt Dan and Lemon**
by Wallace Shawn

In this dramatic monologue, Aunt Dan, a young woman who has taught at Oxford, tells Lemon, the daughter of her best friends, about respect.

Guided Questions

1 Now Lemon, I have to tell you something very important about myself. And there aren't many things I'm sure about myself, but this is something I can honestly say with absolute confidence, and it's something that I think is very important. It is that I never—no matter how annoyed or angry I may be—I *never, ever shout at a waiter*. And as a matter of fact, I never shout at a porter or a clerk in a bank or anybody else who is in a weaker position in society that me. Now this is very, very important. I will never even use a *tone of voice* with a person like that which I wouldn't use with you or your father or anyone else.

1 What important thing does Aunt Dan tell Lemon about herself? What does this detail suggest to you about her?

2 You see, there are a lot of people today who will simply *shout* if they're angry at a waiter, but if they happen to be angry at some powerful person like their boss or a government official, well then they'll *very respectfully disagree*. Now to me that's a terrible thing, a horrible thing. First of all, because I think it's cowardly. But mainly because it shows that these people don't recognize the value and importance of all those different jobs in society! They think a waiter is *less important* than a president. They look down on waiters! They don't admire what they do! They don't even notice whether someone is a good waiter or a bad waiter! They act as if we could sort of all afford to have no respect for waiters now, or secretaries, or maids, or building superintendents, because somehow we've reached a point where we can really do *without* these people.

2 Underline the words that show the important truth that Aunt Dan thinks people who shout at waiters miss.

3 Well, maybe there's some kind of fantasy in these people's minds that we're already living in some society of the future in which these incredible robots are going to be doing all the work, and every actual citizen will be some kind of concert pianist or a sculptor or a president or something. But I mean, where are all these robots, actually? Have you ever seen one? Have they even been invented? Maybe they *will* be. But they're not here *now*.

3 What is the purpose of Aunt Dan's argument in this paragraph?

Copying is illegal.
Measuring Up® to the California Content Standards

4 The way things are *now*, everybody just can't be a president. I mean—I mean, if there's no one around to cook the president's lunch, he's going to have to cook it himself. Do you know what I'm saying? But if no one has put any food in his kitchen, he's going to have to go out and buy it himself. And if no one is waiting in the shop to sell it, he's going to have to go out into the countryside and *grow* it himself, and, you know, that's going to be a full-time job. I mean, he's going to have to resign as president in order to grow that food. It's as simple as that.

4 Think about Aunt Dan's words in this paragraph. How do you think she feels as she says them?

5 If every shop clerk or maid or farmer were to quit their job today and try to be a painter or a nuclear physicist, then within about two weeks everyone in society, even people who used to be painters or nuclear physicists, would be out in the woods foraging for berries and roots. Society would completely break down. Because regular work is not one tiny fraction less necessary today than it ever was. And yet we're in this crazy situation that people have gotten it into their heads that regular work is somehow unimportant—it's somehow worth nothing. So now almost everyone who isn't at least a Minister of Foreign Affairs feels that there's something wrong with what they do—they feel ashamed of it.

5 According to Aunt Dan, why is regular work important?

1. What is the purpose of the opening of the monologue?

_____

_____

2. In paragraph 2, why does Aunt Dan think that people who shout at a waiter but "respectfully disagree" with someone in a higher position are cowardly?

_____

_____

3. What is Aunt Dan's opinion of people who think they can get along without waiters, "or secretaries, or maids, or building superintendents"?

_____

_____

_____

_____

4. Aunt Dan is a professor. If she lost her job and had to work as a waiter, how do you think she would feel? Explain.

_____

_____

5. Based on what Aunt Dan says, what impression do you form of her?

_____

_____

Apply **Directions** Read the passage below. Then answer the questions that follow it.

from Carrot for a Chestnut
by Dick Francis

Chick stood and sweated with the carrot in his hand. His head seemed to be floating, and he couldn't feel his feet on the ground, and the pulse thudded massively in his ear. A clammy green pain shivered in his gut.

Treachery was making him sick.

The time: fifty minutes before sunrise. The morning: cold. The raw, swirling wind was clearing its throat for a fiercer blow, and a heavy layer of nimbostratus was fighting every inch of the way against the hint of light. In the neat box stalls round the stable yard, the dozing horses struck a random hoof against a wooden wall, rattled a tethering chain, sneezed the hay dust out of a moist, black nostril.

Chick was late. Two hours late. He'd been told to give the carrot to the lanky chestnut at four o'clock in the morning, but at four o'clock in the morning, it had been pouring with rain—hard, slanting rain that soaked a man to the skin in one minute flat, and Chick had reckoned it would be too difficult explaining away a soaking at four o'clock in the morning. Chick had reckoned it would be better to wait until the rain stopped; it couldn't make any difference. Four o'clock, six o'clock, what the heck. Chick always knew better than anyone else.

Chick was a thin, disgruntled nineteen-year-old who always felt the world owed him more than he got. He had been a bad–tempered, argumentative child and an aggressively rebellious adolescent. The resulting snarling habit of mind was precisely what was now hindering his success as an adult. Not that Chick would have agreed, of course. Chick never agreed with anyone if he could help it. Always knew better, did Chick.

He was unprepared for the severity of the physical symptoms of fear. His usual attitude toward any form of authority was scorn (and authority had not so far actually belted him one across his sulky mouth). Horses had never scared him, because he had been born to the saddle and had grown up mastering everything on four legs with conspicuous ease. He believed in his heart that no one could really ride better than he could. He was wrong.

1. Which details in the first paragraph suggest how Chick is feeling?

_____

_____

2. What was Chick supposed to do at four o'clock in the morning? Why did he wait until later?

_____

_____

3. In the fourth paragraph, which begins with the words, "Chick was late," what does the author tell you directly about Chick's character?

_____

_____

4. In the fifth paragraph, what do you learn directly about how Chick looks? Find four adjectives that describe his personality.

_____

_____

5. Why was Chick unprepared for the way he now feels?

_____

_____

Assessment Practice

Directions Answer the questions based on the selection you just read.

1. **How does Chick usually react to people in authority?**

   A   He gets along well with them.

   B   He gets into violent arguments with them.

   C   He feels contempt for them.

   D   He is frightened of them.

2. **From the view into Chick's mind in the first two paragraphs, what do you learn about Chick?**

   A   Chick has always been a sickly child.

   B   Chick ate a carrot that made him sick.

   C   Chick is about to do something treacherous.

   D   Chick is afraid of horses.

3. **Which of the following statements by the author shows that Chick is arrogant?**

   A   He'd been told to give the carrot to the lanky chestnut at four o'clock in the morning . . .

   B   . . . it had been pouring rain—hard, slanting rain that soaked a man to the skin in one minute flat . . .

   C   Chick had reckoned it would be better to wait until the rain stopped . . .

   D   Chick always knew better than anyone else.

4. **The words *disgruntled, bad-tempered, argumentative,* and *aggressively rebellious* suggest that Chick is—**

   A   someone who would not be afraid of horses.

   B   someone likely to get his way.

   C   someone likely to get in trouble.

   D   someone who is like most kids his age.

5. **Which item below reveals a positive trait for Chick?**

   A   never agreed with anyone if he could help it

   B   believes no one could ride better than he could

   C   experiences the physical symptoms of fear

   D   scorned any form of authority

Focus on California Content Standards

Lesson 15 Understand Theme

Reading Literature 9.3.5 Compare works that express a universal theme and provide evidence to support the ideas expressed in each work.

Theme is a general observation about life or human nature expressed through a work of literature. A theme is an idea that goes beyond a simple recounting of what the characters are like and what happens to them. Instead, it provides insight into the human condition.

For example, you may read an exciting story about people trying to escape from Nazi Germany. The plot tells about the steps they take to leave Germany, their close encounters with the enemy, and their final escape. However, during the course of seeing what happens to them, you come to understand how strong the power of hope can be. Without hope, they would not have tried to escape and most likely would have perished. Based on your understanding of the characters and the plot, you form a generalization about life. You interpret the theme of the story as something like this: *Hope gives people courage to face and survive even the darkest times.*

Theme can often be detected through an author's use of symbols. A **symbol** is an object that stands for an idea. For example, a rose is a symbol of beauty or love which most people in Western culture readily understand. A withered rose is a symbol of beauty or love that has faded. A rose with thorns is a symbol of beauty or love that is surrounded by painful obstacles.

Some themes are **universal**. This means that you can find them in the literature of many different cultures and from many different times.

The same or similar theme can be treated in different kinds of literature. For example, one writer might choose to write a poem about the healing power of love, while another chooses to write a short story about the same subject.

Guided Reading Instruction

Directions Read the following passage. Use the questions in the margin to guide your reading. Then answer the questions that follow.

The Atlas Moth
by Ethel Pochocki

1 the sensible mind
attuned to usefulness
cannot comprehend
such senseless beauty,
such a waste of flamboyance
unharnessed by purpose

2 it cannot see the point
of a life obscured
in sunless heat
and silent dripping trees,
so brief that everything
is first and only
and full of wonder,
3 no comparison of sunsets,
no growing old with your mate,
no pride in offspring,
no hoarding for winter,
no last supper
4 (would there be, perhaps, an afternoon nostalgia
for the morning's maiden flight?)
in a different place,
the Atlas moth might be a god
or patron saint of carpet weavers
5 or hang in a proper frame
on a rich man's wall,
homage would be given,
but in this forest
which will never become familiar,
it lives and dies unnoticed. **6**

Tolstoy said the world
would be saved by beauty.
7 He did not specify
the terms. **8**

Guided Questions

1 What kind of mind is "the sensible mind"? What does it value highly? What does it not understand?

2 Whose life is being discussed here?

3 Describe the chief characteristics of the moth's life.

4 How is the moth's life unlike human life?

5 Why might the moth be considered a god or a saint in some other culture?

6 Why is the statement "it lives and dies unnoticed" ironic in the context of this poem?

7 What do you think that Tolstoi meant?

8 What do you think the poet means by her final sentence?

1. What does the Atlas Moth symbolize in this poem? Explain your answer.

_____

_____

2. What do you think sunset symbolizes in line 14?

_____

_____

3. What is Tolstoy's opinion of the importance of beauty? Write the two lines that express this opinion on the line below.

_____

4. How does the final sentence suggest that the poet may have a "sensible mind"?

_____

_____

5. Interpret the theme of "The Atlas Moth," providing evidence from the poem to support your interpretation.

_____

_____

_____

_____

Directions Read the passage below. Then answer the questions that follow it.

A Tale of Love

A Mexican Folktale
translated and edited by Anthony John Campos

It was that time when the swallows return. They leave on the feast day of San José and come back on the feast day of San Juan. They say that many cross the ocean but few return, because they are eaten by the Moors.

They waste no time, once on land, but begin immediately to gather mud and build their nests. Most of them choose the eaves of houses and barns, but one young and especially pretty swallow chose the belfry of a little church.

In the churchyard there was a large mesquite tree where a pitacochi came and sang every day. One morning, when the swallow stuck her neck out to hear better, he noticed her and began to sing as he had never sung before. It was truly love at first sight.

From then on the two birds spent every moment together. In the mornings, they would circle low around the village and then fly away into the countryside. And in the evenings, they would rest on the branches of the mesquite and he would serenade her. Indeed, the little swallow made a wonderful summer for the pitacochi.

Time flew by and the green leaves turned to gold. One day, as they sat on a branch of the mesquite, the pitacochi noticed how sad the swallow's eyes were and how she bent her head.

"What's the matter?" the pitacochi asked. "Why are you so sad?"

The little swallow was silent for a moment, then looked up at him. "The time for us to leave is almost here and I wish I didn't have to go. It will hurt me to leave you," she said, bending her head down again.

"That's right," said the pitacochi. "I'm so in love that I had forgotten you have to leave." The pitacochi tried to comfort her. "You can stay here with me. I'll take care of you."

The swallow looked at him again. "We must all go away together," she told him. "If I stay here, I will surely die."

"Then I'll go with you," said the pitacochi.

Though his decision made the little swallow happy, she still tried to change his mind. "You'll never make it,' she said. "We have to fly clear across the ocean and you're too heavy." But despite all her pleading, the pitacochi was determined to go with her.

Swallows always carry two small twigs in their beaks, when they fly over the sea, so they can rest on the waves when they become tired. And so, when the feast day of San José arrived, the swallow had two little twigs ready for the pitacochi. When they reached the edge of the sea, they stopped on a cliff top to rest, and once more the swallow tried to persuade the pitacochi to change his mind.

"It's best for you to remain here," she said. "If you should have to turn back, I'll never stop worrying about you."

In the distance the flock made crooked little lines against the blue horizon.

"You wait here," said the swallow, "and if God grants, I'll return and we'll be together again."

The pitacochi looked out at the mighty sea. "We'd better catch up with the rest," he said.

The land kept sinking deeper each time the swallow turned around, "Drop your twigs in the water," she would tell the pitacochi when she noticed him getting tired. They would stop to rest for a while and then start up again. But after many tries, the pitacochi lost all hope.

"You're right," he cried. "I cannot make it. I'm not good for anything. I wish I were dead." He tried to make the swallow catch up with the flock.

"We're not too far out yet," he said. "You must go on."

"No," said the swallow. "If I let you go back alone, I will surely die of grief."

The two birds slowly made their way back to shore. When they were on the cliff top once again, they began to weep. "Wait for me," the swallow told the pitacochi, "and pray to God that I can return."

They embraced each other for the last time and the little swallow spread her wings and took off "Adios," she called as she swooped out toward the sea.

The pitacochi stood on the cliff watching, with tears rolling from his eyes, until he could no longer see the fading form of his love.

Summer came once more and it was time again for the swallows to return. When they arrived, they began as usual to build their nests in the eaves of houses and barns. The pitacochi waited and waited for the little swallow to return. But he was still sitting alone in the mesquite tree when the stars came out that evening.

And so it was every summer until one day, he waited no more.

1. At the beginning of this tale, how do the swallow and the pitacochi show their love for one another?

_____

_____

2. Once autumn comes, why does the swallow grow sad?

_____

_____

3. When the swallow tells him that the swallows must all go away together, how does the pitacochi show his love for her?

_____

_____

4. On the trip across the sea, why does the pitacochi lose all hope?

_____

_____

5. Does the tale show love to be mostly a painful thing or mostly a joyous thing? Does it show love to be worthwhile or not? Explain.

_____

_____

_____

Assessment Practice

Directions Answer the questions based on the selection you just read.

1. The ocean voyage that the swallow must take in paragraph 9 symbolizes—

   A travel by water across great distances.

   B the love of the swallow and the pitacochi.

   C obstacles that life puts in the way of true love.

   D the migration of birds in the spring.

2. The theme of this folktale concerns—

   A the hazards of life in the wild.

   B the destruction of the natural environment.

   C the fickleness of both bird love and human love.

   D the fragile, doomed nature of true love.

3. Because this is a folktale, truths about human life are represented by—

   A the love and affection between two birds.

   B the feast day of San José.

   C the cruelty of people toward birds.

   D the separation of two human characters.

4. In the first paragraph, the most important detail you learn about the swallows is that—

   A they leave on the feast day of San José.

   B they return on the feast day of San Juan.

   C they fly across the ocean.

   D few return from their journey.

5. The fact that the swallow makes her home in a church belfry suggests—

   A the sacredness of the characters and their love.

   B that these characters are really not birds but people.

   C that many bird species dwell near human sites.

   D that this particular bird is a little "batty."

Lesson 16   **Trace Time and Sequence**

Reading Literature 9.3.3 Analyze interactions between main and subordinate characters in a literary text (e.g., internal and external conflicts, motivations, relationships, influences) and explain the way those interactions affect the plot.

Reading Literature 9.3.6 Analyze and trace an author's development of time and sequence, including the use of complex literary devices (e.g., foreshadowing, flashbacks).

The plot of a work of fiction is the series of linked events that make up the story. Plot usually develops through the following stages.

Stage of the Plot	What Happens In It
Exposition (Basic Situation)	The main character (or characters) and central conflict are introduced. Essential background information is given.
Rising Action	The character first tries to deal with the conflict, unsuccessfully. Each attempt leads to further **complications**.
Turning Point	The character's efforts begins to lead him or her toward resolving the conflict.
Climax (Crisis)	The high point of tension occurs. This is the point where the character will either succeed or fail.
Resolution (Dénouement; Outcome)	The conflict is resolved as a result of the character's successful or unsuccessful effort to deal with the problem.

Most stories are told in **chronological order**. This means that the author starts with the event that happens first, moves on to the event that happens next, and continues this way until reaching the end of the story.

However, sometimes writers play with time. They rearrange the sequence or order of events. The two most common techniques for rearranging time are flashbacks and foreshadowing.

A **flashback** is a look at a past event. The author will halt the action temporarily in order to look back at an event that happened at an earlier time. You see flashbacks a lot in movies. The screen turns dark and then a new scene fills the screen showing something that happened before the main events. Flashbacks provide important information. Often they explain why a character is doing something now or what motivates this character.

Foreshadowing is providing hints at what will happen in the future. Early in the story, something may be mentioned casually that turns out to be very important.

Guided Reading Instruction

Directions Read the following passage. Use the questions in the margin to guide your reading. Then answer the questions that follow.

from **That's Ghosts for You**
by Susan Price

Guided Questions

1   This is a ghost story from England, the country of ghosts. It happened in the early years of the last century, in the 1920s, in the town of Oldbury in Warwickshire. **2** In those days Warwickshire policemen had black uniforms. Their black helmets had black badges, and their black jackets had black buttons. Even their whistles, on black chains, were black.

Why do I tell you this? What do you care about the uniforms of Warwickshire policemen? Because it's important to the story that you know this—though you won't know why until the end.

It's a true story. My father heard it from a man named Bill, who taught him his trade of repairing electrical motors. "I saw a ghost once," Bill said. "When I was about your age, about fourteen."

"Of course, my father wanted to hear about the ghost. Bill told him the story many times, and later Dad told it to me.

3   It happened on a winter's night when a burned-out motor was brought back into the works. The factory it came from wanted it back as soon as possible, so Jim McAamnie was given the job of working through the night to rewind the coils. And Jim's apprentice, who would be helping him, was Bill.

They worked all day, stripping the burned coils from the motor and cleaning it up. At about six they went home with the other men to have their tea, but Jim took the works' keys with him so he could let himself and Bill back in that evening.

So it was getting on for seven o'clock when Bill walked back to work by himself in the dark. Now we're so used to street lamps and lights in houses, bright headlights and brilliantly lit shop windows, that we forget how very dark it is at night when there's no moon and only the faintest spattering of stars.

The works was on the edge of Oldbury, where a long road led out into the country, and there weren't any streetlights. No houses, either, only factories, and they were locked and empty, with no lights. No cars on the road. You saw more horses and carts in those days than cars.

4   So Bill was walking down this long, dark road all by himself, with nobody else in sight or hearing. And naturally his mind ran on ghosts, as it often does at such times.

5   There was a strong wind that night, too, and a lot of the ghost stories he knew had storms and strong winds in them. The wind screamed and thrashed the branches of trees, and the noise made him think of ghostly horses that screamed as they pulled ghost coaches.

6   And there was a gypsy girl, it was said, who'd drowned herself in a pool not far away. Her ghost roamed around the pool, hair and clothes dripping wet.

1 Underline the two important facts the narrator reveals in the first sentence.

2 How many times does the narrator mention the color black?

3 This paragraph represents a flashback. To what time or events does the story flash back?

4 Why did Bill's mind turn to thinking about ghosts?

5 How would you characterize Bill based on his reactions?

6 Why do you think the story of the gypsy girl who drowned herself could be significant?

Sometimes she screamed too—he jumped at the next howl of wind. He tried to tell himself that the pool was too far away. She wouldn't bother coming this far. But who knew what a ghost might do?

7   At the entry to the works' yard, Bill stopped. From the other end of the entry came a regular banging, clapping noise. He couldn't think what it was, but his imagination showed him a huge, hulking brute of a man—or possibly some kind of goblin—crouching in the yard, banging on a big club on the wall while it waited for Bill. When he came, it would raise the club high and . . .

Footsteps echoed in the entry, and Bill nearly ran away. A shape loomed from the darkness, and his heart lurched while his heels left the pavement with shock.

"That you, Bill?" said the shape. It was Jim, his hands in his pockets. "What's up?"

8   "Nothing," Bill said with relief. He felt quite unafraid now that he was with Jim and happily followed him through the entry, a low, arched tunnel of brick that smelled of dank, green water. Their feet splashed in puddles, and their footsteps echoed from the roof. Ahead of them that banging and clapping went on—but now, because he was with Jim, Bill knew it was only the door of their workshop blowing in the wind, banging to and fro.

The entry opened into a dark yard. The ground underfoot was rough, with half-buried bricks and broken cobblestones, and the only light came, dimly, from the doorway of the workshop. A gust of wind, a bang as the door slammed into its frame, and the light vanished. A moment later it reappeared as the door blew open and crashed against the wall.

They went in, and Jim stayed by the door for a moment to make sure it was shut against the wind.

9   It was a long, chilly building, full of darkness. The warmth seeped out through holes in the brickwork and gaps round the doors and windows, and piercing drafts blew about, snapping at the ears and ankles. The only light was at the far end of the shop, over the motor they were repairing. From the deep shadows overhead hung loops of oily rope and chain, dangling from the crane tracks. To either side iron shelves, loaded with drums of wire, emerged from the dark. There were faint shapes of tool racks and workbenches, vises and lathes. The whole place smelled of oil, with an underlying metallic tang, and whiffs of varnish. The smells grew stronger as Bill neared the motor, because the air was warmer there, softened by the old stove.

"There's some tea on the stove," Jim said, coming up behind him. The old enamel teapot sat on top of the stove most of the time.

"I had a bellyful at home," Bill said. "Let's get on."

7 The narrator suggests that the banging is just that—banging. But what does Bill imagine it to be?

8 What effect does Jim have on Bill?

9 Underline the details in this paragraph that are likely to make Bill feel uneasy.

1. At the beginning of the story, why does the narrator tell about the uniforms worn by the policemen?

_____

_____

2. The narrator provides details that contrast the two time periods. When is this story being told? How were streets at night different in Bill's day? What effect do you think this might have on the plot of the story?

_____

_____

3. Read the events below. Write 1 by the event that happens at the earliest time, 2 by the event that happens second, 3 by the event that happens next, and 4 by the event that happens at the latest time.

_____ Bill goes back to work by himself in the evening.
_____ Bill tells the story to the narrator's father
_____ A gypsy girl drowns in a pool.
_____ The narrator tells the story.

4. Based on the clues in this part of the story, do you think Bill will see a real ghost or not? Explain your response.

_____

_____

_____

Apply   **Directions** Read the passage below. Then answer the questions that follow it.

from **That's Ghosts for You** (continued)
by Susan Price

They had to replace the motor's burned-out coils with new coils of wire. Jim threaded the wire through the slots in the motor, and Bill "drew the wire through." That is, he took the wire and ran backward down the length of the shop, holding it in front of him and pulling it tight. He had to keep it as straight as he could so it wouldn't kink. When the wire was pulled tight, he went back to Jim, who threaded it through again and shaped the coil.

They went at it for hours. Again and again Bill ran backward from the little circle of light and the warmth of the stove into the chill darkness at the other end of the shop. His footsteps brought muffled echoes from the brick walls and the corrugated iron roof in the gloom above. When he reached the far end of the shop by the door, he was in darkness and could hear the wind biffing against the door and walls. Chilled by freezing drafts, he looked up the length of the shop and, far away, saw Jim stooping over the motor in the little circle of light, like someone on a lit stage in a dark, empty theater.

Then back up the shop he'd run, and with every step it would be warmer and lighter until he was back by the stove with Jim.

The wind outside never stopped rattling the door. Every now and again, it blew the door off its latch and slammed it into its frame and crashed against the wall. Strong, cold currents of air rushed through the shop. Jim would say, "Go and shut that door."

         Measuring Up® to the California Content Standards

Bill would run to the door and fight to pull it shut against the wind, which struck cold against the seat on his face and neck, making him shiver. Heaving the door shut, he firmly pressed the latch into place.

But the door blew open again. Why did it keep blowing open? Was it being opened by something other than the wind? Once that thought had occurred to Bill, it plagued him, just as thoughts of the gypsy girl's ghost had plagued him earlier.

That coldness that passed him by, prickling his skin—was it a draft, or was it a ghost? The darkness behind him that he ran into backward—was it empty? If he looked over his shoulder, what would he see? He snatched his head round, only to glimpse the shadowy racks of wire and tools.

"Don't twist the wire," Jim said.

The door end of the shop seemed lonely and dangerous—a long way from the light and from Jim, and much too close to the ill-fitting door and the dark, cold, windy night. Bill started to stop short of the door so he could run back to the light sooner. He tried not to—he would never have admitted being afraid to Jim—but it was as if his body had a mind of its own. "Far enough," his feet said. "It's too scary down here. Run back!"

"You're not pulling it tight enough," Jim said and waved his hand to send him farther back.

So Bill ran farther back into the dark by the rattling door. It sounded as if someone were trying to open the door and couldn't—as if cold, stiff fingers couldn't quite manage the latch. His skin crawled ~~~~ under his clothes. He was tensed for the touch of a wet, freezing hand that he was sure was coming. With relief he went racing back to the circle of light.

Bill had a moment's rest, standing in the warmth and light while Jim shaped the coils. While he was standing there, the wind blew the door open again. It crashed against the wall and let in a strong gust of cold air.

"Go and see if you can't make that door stop shut," Jim said. His voice was muffled in all the space and silence of the big empty shop. "I'm sick to death of it."

Bill wanted to say, "Why don't you go and shut it?" But he was the boy, and Jim was the man. And Bill couldn't admit that he was afraid. So he started walking, slowly, down the length of the shop toward the racketing, banging door.

He was within a couple of feet of the door when he saw it. The door had blown open again, making a frame of darkness. At the center of that frame, hanging in midair, was a head. A face. A deathly white face, without a body, staring at him.

Bill's every joint locked. He couldn't run away; he couldn't move. His eyes stayed open and fixed on the thing outside the door. Somewhere deep inside him, his heart picked up speed.

The face was round, he saw, putty and rounded as well as white. Like a face that had been under water a long time, he thought. Drowned.

From a long way behind him, from where it was light and warm, Jim shouted, "Are you going to shut the door?"

Bill's answer was a dry little cough in his throat. "Ack. Ack."

Still the face hung there, glowering. And then it moved. Toward him. Drifting, floating, it bobbed nearer, as though blown by the wind or carried along by water. All the time it stared at him.

Bill's locked knees melted and sagged. With them wobbling beneath him, he turned and ran for the other end of the shop, for Jim and light and warmth. Looking back over his shoulder, he saw that the face was closer still, almost at the door. It was going to drift right through the doorway, into the shop. It was coming to get him!

As Bill neared the circle of yellowish light, Jim's head jerked up in surprise, and Jim's stare locked on to something behind him. So Jim could see it, too! It was real and it was close behind him! Bill leaped the last few feet to Jim and hid behind his back.

Jim said, "Evening, Officer. Anything we can do for you?"

Another voice said, "Just looked in to see why the light was on. What's up with the lad?"

"Dunno," Jim said. "We'm just rewinding these coils, fix this up for the morning. You want a cup of tea?"

Bill looked out from behind Jim to see a big policeman, with a black badge on a black helmet and black buttons on a black coat. Nothing at all to catch the light.

"What's up?" the policeman said to Bill.

The only part of the policeman that caught the light had been his pale, pudgy face between the high, black collar of his uniform and his black helmet.

"I thought you was the gypsy girl!" Bill said.

"I am on me day's off," said the policeman. "But I don't bring me tambourine on duty."

My father used to tell this story when we were scared of ghosts. He used to say to us what Bill had said to him. "That's ghosts for you," Bill said.

1. Why is it significant that Bill has to run to the end of the shop to draw the wire through?

_____

_____

2. What does Bill think is going on when the door keeps blowing open?

_____

_____

3. Why can't Bill move when he sees the head in the doorway?

_____

_____

4. Explain why the way the policeman is dressed is significant. How was this detail foreshadowed in the first part of the story?

_____

_____

5. What does Bill mean when he says, "That's ghosts for you"?

_____

_____

Assessment Practice

Directions Answer the questions based on the selection you just read.

1. **It is important for the reader to know what Warwickshire policemen wore in the 1920s because it explains why—**

   A Jim recognized the officer.

   B Bill thought he saw a ghost.

   C the officer did not blow a whistle.

   D the gypsy girl appeared with a man's face.

2. **When Bill sees the puffy face, why does he think "drowned"?**

   A The shop is by a river.

   B He has seen someone drowned before.

   C The face is round.

   D He has been thinking of the gypsy girl.

3. **The last paragraph of this story represents—**

   A a flashback to the past.

   B a return to the present.

   C a foreshadowing of events to come.

   D a hint that Bill will see another ghost.

4. **Why is Bill frightened by the appearance of the policeman?**

   A He is young and impressionable.

   B He has a guilty secret.

   C The policeman is carrying a tambourine.

   D The policeman is a ghost.

5. **How is Jim's reaction to the slapping door different from Bill's?**

   A Unlike Bill, he is terrified by the noise.

   B Unlike Bill, he knows a policeman is waiting outside.

   C Unlike Bill, he is simply irritated by the noise.

   D Unlike Bill, he doesn't hear the noise.

Reading Literature 9.3.7 Recognize and understand the significance of various literary devices, including figurative language, imagery, allegory, and symbolism, and explain their appeal.

Figurative language consists of expressions whose poetic meaning goes beyond the literal meaning of the words. Figurative language is most often found in **figurative comparisons**—comparisons between two essentially unlike things, which deepen the reader's understanding of both. The major types of figurative comparison are:

Type of Comparision	Definition	Example
simile	Two things are compared using linking words such as *like*, *as*, or *resembling*	Bill is as prompt as a clock—a clock that hasn't been wound in a while.
metaphor	Two things are compared without using linking words	Time is a bottomless well, into which we peer without ever seeing anything there.
personification	Human traits are attributed to something nonhuman	The wooden creature on the cuckoo clock seemed to take pleasure in jarring its listeners awake.

An **analogy** is another type of comparison, but it is not necessarily figurative. An analogy seeks to explain something by comparing it to something else. For example:

> In the kitchen, Anita has the skills of a surgeon. She slices and dices every vegetable with precision as though her professional reputation depended on it.

Thinking of Anita in terms of a surgeon helps you appreciate her skill and mastery.

Guided Reading Instruction

Directions Read the poem. Use the questions in the margin to guide your reading. Then answer the questions that follow.

Watch Repair
by Charles Simic

A small wheel
Incandescent,
Shivering like
A pinned butterfly. **1**

Hands
Pointing in all directions:
The crossroads
One enters
In a nightmare. **2**

Higher than anyone
Number 12 presides
3 Like a beekeeper
Over the swarming honeycomb
Of the open watch.

—Other wheels
That could fit
Inside a raindrop,

Tools
That must be splinters
Of arctic starlight . . .

Tiny golden mills
Grinding invisible
Coffee beans. **4**

When the coffee's boiling,
Cautiously,
So it doesn't burn us, **5**

We raise it
To the lips
Of the nearest
Ear. **6**

Guided Questions

1 How is the main wheel inside a watch like a pinned butterfly?

2 How can the hands of a clock be compared to a nightmarish crossroad?

3 Find both a simile and a metaphor in this line and the next.

4 What is the connection between a watch and a coffee grinder?

5 Metaphorically, how can time "burn us"?

6 Analyze the personification: What does "We raise it/ To the lips/ Of the nearest/ ear" mean, with regard to the watch and the coffee grinder?

1. Which figurative comparison did you find the most effective? Explain your response.

_____

_____

_____

2. Do the figurative comparisons in this poem adhere to an overall pattern, or are they unrelated to one another? Explain.

_____

_____

_____

_____

_____

Apply   **Directions** Read the following passages. Then answer the questions that follow each.

Cast Up

by Lawrence Ferlinghetti

Cast up

    the heart flops over

        gasping 'Love'

a foolish fish which tries to draw

    its breath from flesh of air

And no one there to hear its death

        among the sad bushes

where the world rushes by

        in a blather of asphalt and delay

The Night Has a Thousand Eyes
by Francis William Bourdillon

The night has a thousand eyes,
    And the day but one;
Yet the light of the bright world dies
    With the dying sun.

The mind has a thousand eyes,
    And the heart but one;
Yet the light of a whole life dies
    When love is done.

1. Look at the first five lines of "Cast Up." To what is the heart being compared? What kind of figurative language is used to make the comparison?

   _____

   _____

2. How are these compared things alike? What impression does the poet make with this comparison?

   _____

   _____

3. Look at the first two lines of "The Night Has a Thousand Eyes." The comparison is suggested instead of clearly stated. What are the "thousand eyes"? What is the "one eye" of day?

   _____

   _____

4. Look at the third and fourth lines. What is the poet saying about night and day?

   _____

   _____

5. Look at the next stanza. What comparison does the poet make in the first two lines?

   _____

   _____

6. In the final lines of the second poem, what conclusion does the poet express?

   _____

   _____

Assessment Practice

Directions Answer the questions based on the selections you just read.

1. **What idea is expressed in the first three lines of the poem "Cast Up"?**

   A Fishing is like searching for your true love.

   B Once you capture someone's heart, that person is at your mercy.

   C A person needs love to live.

   D Love can be a destructive force.

2. **Which of the following lines uses personification to create a melancholy effect?**

   A a foolish fish which tries to draw/its breath from flesh of air

   B And no one there to hear its death/among the sad bushes

   C The night has a thousand eyes/And the day but one

   D The mind has a thousand eyes/And the heart but one

3. **How is a fish dying in the bushes like an unloved person?**

   A Everyone notices.

   B Both smell bad.

   C They need water.

   D No one notices.

4. **When the poet says that "the mind has a thousand eyes," he is suggesting—**

   A the heart focuses only on what it loves.

   B the mind cries a thousand tears.

   C the mind sees all and knows all.

   D the mind sees and thinks many things.

5. **How are the sun and love alike?**

   A Both are hot and passionate.

   B Life dies without them.

   C The moon is their enemy.

   D They rest at night.

Focus on California Content Standards

Lesson 18 Understand Symbolism and Allegory

Reading Literature 9.3.7 Recognize and understand the significance of various literary devices, including figurative language, imagery, allegory, and symbolism, and explain their appeal.

Two **literary devices** that help writers reveal the theme of their work are **symbolism** and **allegory**. Symbolism is the use of people, places, or things to stand for ideas and concepts. For example, in ancient legends, a man's hair was often used as a symbol of his strength: If his hair was cut, he lost his power.

Often, a writer creates symbols that can be understood only from the context of the story. However, some symbols are public. In other words, they are understood and shared by an entire culture. Examples of **public symbols** include:

Symbol	Stands For
flag	nation
eagle	United States
Uncle Sam	United States
golden poppy	California
fleur-de-lys	France

Allegory is a special type of story in which all the characters represent qualities and types. Often, in an allegory, characters do not have names. You read about The Man, The Woman, and The King, for example. Or, they have names that tell the quality they represent. For example, characters might be called Charity, Hope, and Honor. These characters are not well rounded or like people in real life. Instead, they represent this single trait. Many fables and folktales are allegorical. If you've read Aesop's famous fable of the grasshopper and ant, for example, you recognize that these characters stand for two very different approaches to life.

Guided Reading Instruction

Directions Read the following passage. Use the questions in the margin to guide your reading. Then answer the questions that follow.

The King and the Shirt
by Leo Tolstoy

A king once fell ill.

1 "I will give half my kingdom to the man who can cure me," he said. All his wise men gathered together to decide how the king could be cured. But no one knew. Only one of the wise men said what he thought would cure the king.

2 "If you can find a happy man, take his shirt, put it on the king—and the king will be cured."

3 The king sent his emissaries to search for a happy man. They traveled far and wide throughout his whole kingdom, but they could not find a happy man. There was no one who was completely satisfied: if a man was rich he was ailing; if he was healthy he was poor; if he was rich and healthy he had a bad wife; or if he had children they were bad—everyone had something to complain of.

Finally, late one night, the king's son was passing by a poor little hut and he heard someone say:

4 "Now, God be praised, I have finished my work, I have eaten my fill, and I can lie down and sleep! What more could I want?"

The king's son rejoiced and gave orders that the man's shirt be taken and carried to the king, and that the man be given as much money as he wanted.

5 The emissaries went in to take off the man's shirt, but the happy man was so poor that he had no shirt.

Guided Questions

1 What is the king's problem?

2 What solution does the wise man suggest?

3 What significant detail do you learn in the paragraph?

4 How is this man different from the others?

5 Why are the emissaries unable to bring the king a happy man's shirt?

1. In this tale, the king has no name. What do you think he might represent?

_____

_____

2. What do you think might be the nature of the king's illness?

_____

_____

3. What is significant about where the shirt must come from? What do you think it represents?

_____

_____

4. How are the king and everyone the emissaries meet, except the last man, alike?

_____

_____

5. What is the story saying about the relationship between wealth and happiness? Support your response with details from the text.

_____

_____

Apply   **Directions**   Read the story below. Then answer the questions that follow it.

The Waterfall of White Hair
a tale from China
retold by Josephine Evetts-Secker

Once upon a time in China there lived a girl with the longest hair you have ever seen. It was shining and black and reached past her ankles. She had to tie it up so that it didn't drag along the ground. Everyone called her Long Hair.

Long Hair lived with her mother, who was old and weak, so the girl had to take care of her, doing all the housework and feeding the pigs. Since there was no stream nearby, she had to fetch water from far away, along with all the other villagers. Each morning as she trudged along with the heavy water jar, she thought how strange it was that there were no streams rushing down from Lofty Mountain above their village. But the mountain was dry. Long Hair fetched water through the heat of the summer and the cold days of winter, and she never complained.

One day, Long Hair took a walk up the mountain and found she was climbing higher than usual. When she stopped to rest, she found a strange, leafy plant that she had never seen before. Thinking that her pigs would enjoy it, she pulled the plant out of the ground to take it home. To her surprise, a huge, round radish came out in her hands, and out of the hole it had made in the ground rushed a stream of sparkling water.

"This is such good water," she thought as she drank her fill, and she sank back in contentment on the grass. Suddenly, a sharp wind arose, snatched the radish out of her hand, and dropped it back into its hole. The water stopped instantly. The wind went on blowing and buffeted Long Hair from place to place, until she took shelter behind some rocks, and found herself in the presence of an old man with golden hair.

"You have discovered my secret!" he shouted angrily. "You must never, ever, speak of it to anyone, or you will die. I am the Spirit of Lofty Mountain—this secret water is mine!" Before Long Hair could reply, she was tossed back to her own garden.

She remained silent that day as she went about her work. In the weeks that followed, her heart grew heavy, for she began to see how difficult life was for her people. She grew sadder and sadder as she watched the weary villagers, including the old and the weak and the very young, as they toiled home along the dry and stony road with their heavy loads of water from the faraway stream. Long Hair had never before noticed what a burden this was. But now her sorrow swelled and her hair began to turn grey. Then it grew white, until it was as white as freshly fallen snow. And still Long Hair worried, knowing that she could make it easier for the villagers to fetch water.

One morning, as she walked sadly along the road, Long Hair saw an old woman struggling with her water jars. The woman could hardly lift the jars, let alone carry them. All of a sudden she collapsed on the road and cut her head on a sharp stone. Her precious water spilled over the thirsty ground and was lost at once. As she helped the woman to her feet, Long Hair's heart flashed with anger and she decided to spurn the Mountain Spirit's warning. Calling all the people to follow her up the mountain, she announced, "There is plenty of water close by. It is ours, too—Lofty Mountain must share it with us."

Soon the villagers reached the spot high up, where the strange radish plant grew. Once again, Long Hair pulled at its big leaves and the radish came out of the earth, leaving the hole through which the stream flowed. Everyone was delighted and thanked Long Hair again and again. "We must chop the radish to pieces," she instructed them, "so that it can never again dam up our stream." When this was done, the cold water flowed faster and faster, and the people splashed and drank and rejoiced.

Suddenly, the wind began to gather on the mountain, and Long Hair remembered the words of the Mountain Spirit. As she did so, she was whisked away by the turbulent wind, which brought her again to the yellow-haired old man in his rock shelter. His face was even angrier than before and he shouted, "Evil girl! You have betrayed my secret and you must be punished. You will lie forever over the rocky side of my mountain where the stream rushes out of the shallow earth, and the freezing cold waters will race over you, pouring down through your long white hair. This is your punishment."

Long Hair shivered at the very thought, but she said bravely, "So be it. If that brings water to my people, I shall endure it. But please, O Spirit of Lofty Mountain, let me first go back to my mother to say goodbye and to find someone to take care of her when I am gone."

The Spirit groaned, for he was not used to saying yes to anyone. But in spite of himself, he was touched by the girl's request, so he said reluctantly, "You may go, but you must return before nightfall, or everyone will suffer."

The wind again howled, blowing Long Hair back to her own village, where the happy people had already begun to celebrate. Her heart grieved as she said goodbye to her pigs, and it nearly broke when she parted from her mother, knowing that she would never see her again, but not breathing a word of this for fear of upsetting her even more.

She went into the garden and stood weeping beneath her favorite tree, where she had so often rested. Suddenly, a man with green hair appeared out of the tree and spoke to her kindly. "Dear girl, wipe away your tears. I will help you, for you are generous and your heart is kind. I have carved a likeness of you in stone. It is a good likeness, but if we are to fool the Mountain Spirit into believing that it is really you, you must sacrifice your long white hair."

Without a moment's hesitation, Long Hair let the man cut off her hair and attach it to the head of the stone statue. Now Lofty Mountain would think the statue was Long Hair herself.

This time the wind blew more fiercely than ever, carrying Long Hair with the green man and the statue back up the mountain. Together they laid the statue face down, so that the long white hair hung over the precipice. The water then flowed through the air, forming a beautiful cascade of sparkling water over which rainbows played.

Now the wind took Long Hair up again and dropped her back beneath her favorite tree. The green-haired man was no longer there, but his voice spoke from the tree, saying, "Long Hair, you are kind and loving. Return to your mother for she needs you. Return to your friends and your village, where you will always be remembered for your kindness and courage. Live there in peace for as long as the waterfall tumbles down Lofty Mountain."

So Long Hair went back to her mother and they lived peacefully for many years. Soon her own head began to grow hair again, black and gleaming as it was before. And to this day the grateful villagers look up in thanks at

     Measuring Up® to the California Content Standards

1. In the first paragraph, what two significant details do you learn about the girl?

   _____

   _____

2. What role does the girl play in her community? What qualities does this show that she has?

   _____

   _____

3. Explain the village's problem. What has caused this problem?

   _____

   _____

4. What qualities does the Spirit of Lofty Mountain represent? Why do you think he has golden hair?

   _____

   _____

5. Why do you think that the girl's hair turns gray and then white as she realizes the hardship that the lack of water causes for her people?

   _____

   _____

6. Why does the girl tell the people to chop up the radish?

   _____

   _____

7. How does the girl react when the Spirit of the Mountain passes sentence on her? What does this tell you about her?

   _____

   _____

8. How does the man with green hair save the girl?

   _____

   _____

9. In what way does the girl's hair become the gift of water or sustenance for her people?

   _____

   _____

10. Why do you think that the girl's hair grows back at the end of this tale?

   _____

Assessment Practice

Directions Answer the questions based on the selection you just read.

1. This tale can be interpreted as an allegory because—

   A   the main character has unusually long hair.

   B   it contains several magical creatures.

   C   all the characters and events suggest the theme.

   D   the girl finds water for her village.

2. Which item below BEST explains why the girl can be interpreted as a savior figure?

   A   She is willing to sacrifice herself for the good of the community.

   B   Since her mother is ill, she takes care of her.

   C   At first, she doesn't tell anyone the Spirit of the Mountain's secret.

   D   She has long black hair that falls down to her feet.

3. The act of chopping up the radish represents—

   A   the letting lose of anger.

   B   the finality of her decision.

   C   the sharing of food in the community.

   D   the gratitude of the people.

4. Why is it appropriate that the man who saves Long Hair has green hair?

   A   This color represents envy.

   B   This color represents safety.

   C   This color represents generosity.

   D   This color represents life.

5. Why is it important that Long Hair has to sacrifice her hair to escape the wrath of the Spirit of the Mountain?

   A   It is all that she has.

   B   Hair is identified with water.

   C   Hair is identified with anger.

   D   It is her most important possession.

Reading Literature 9.3.7 Recognize and understand the significance of various literary devices, including figurative language, imagery, allegory, and symbolism, and explain their appeal.

Imagery is the use of words to create vivid mental images or pictures in the reader's head. Usually, these words appeal to one or more of the five sentences: sight, taste, sense, hearing, and touch.

> Words have **connotations** as well as **denotations**—their dictionary meanings. These connotations reinforce the image the writer wants to create. For example, one writer may choose the word *picky* to describe a person, while another calls this same person *discriminating*. *Picky* suggests that the person is difficult and finds problems where there aren't any. *Discriminating* suggests that the person makes fine, thoughtful distinctions. One word has negative connotations, the other, positive ones.

Imagery also establishes the **mood**, or feeling created by a work of literature. For example, images of daybreak and green pastures create a hopeful, tranquil mood, while images of thunderclouds overhead and barren trees create a hopeless, sorrowful mood.

Writers also choose words not for the meanings alone, but for the sounds of the words, which reinforce the meaning. The right sound in the right context may evoke an emotion in the reader and support the mood. If a poet has a choice of several words that are synonyms—if they all mean approximately the same thing—he or she may choose the shorter word rather than the longer one, or the word with harder consonant sounds over the word with softer consonant sounds, or the word with long vowel sounds over the one with short vowel sounds. The choice may be the opposite of any of these—because the sound may pluck a chord in the reader's heart.

This is true not just for single words, but for combinations of words. The flow of a line or sentence, the way the sounds in one word chime with the sounds in another word on the next line, the way repetition of a sound helps hammer home a theme—all these are arrows in the poet's quiver.

Many sound devices include **repetition**.

Rhyme	The repetition of vowel sounds at the ends of words.
Alliteration	The repetition of initial consonant sounds.
Rhythm	The pattern of stressed and unstressed syllables.

In addition to repeating sounds, an author may use repetition to reinforce an idea. By repeating key words and phrases, an author emphasizes them and tells the reader to pay attention to them.

Guided Reading Instruction

Directions Read the following poem. Use the questions in the margin to guide your reading. Then answer the questions that follow.

I Was Sleeping Where the Black Oaks Move
by Louise Erdrich

We watched from the house
as the river grew, helpless
and terrible in its unfamiliar body.
1 Wrestling everything into it,
the water wrapped around trees
until their life-hold was broken.
They went down, one by one,
and the river dragged off their covering.

2 Nests of the herons, roots washed to bones,
snags of soaked bark on the shoreline:
3 a whole forest pulled through the teeth
of the spillway. Trees surfacing
singly, where the rivers poured off
into arteries for fields below the reservation.

4 When at last it was over, the long removal,
they had all become the same dry wood.
We walked among them, the branches
whitening in the raw sun.

5 Above us drifted herons,
alone, hoarse-voiced, broken,
settling their beaks among the hollows.

6 Grandpa said, *These are the ghosts of the tree people,*
moving among us, unable to take their rest.

7 Sometimes now, we dream our way back to the heron dance.
Their long wings are bending the air
into circles through which they fall.
They rise again in shifting wheels.
How long must we live in the broken figures
their necks make, narrowing the sky.

Guided Questions

1 Find an example of alliteration in this line and the next.

2 What consonant sounds are repeated in this line and the next?

3 What feeling or mood is created here?

4 What sounds are used for alliteration in the next four lines? How does this sound relate to the central image of the poem?

5 To what two senses does the description of the herons most appeal?

6 What mood is created by Grandfather's words?

7 What is the dominant feeling conveyed in the final stanza? Cite two or three words or phrases that convey this feeling.

 Measuring Up® to the California Content Standards

1. What did the poet vividly describe in the first stanza?

_____

_____

2. Fill out the Sensory Detail Chart below with images from "I Was Sleeping Where the Black Oaks Move." You may not find a detail for every sense.

Sense	Image
Sight	
Taste	
Touch	
Hearing	
Smell	

Apply   **Directions** Read the story below. Then answer the questions that follow it.

The Writer
by Richard Wilbur

In her room at the prow of the house
Where light breaks, and the windows are tossed with linden,
My daughter is writing a story.

I pause in the stairwell, hearing
5   From her shut door a commotion of typewriter-keys
Like a chain hauled over a gunwale.

Young as she is, the stuff
Of her life is a great cargo, and some of it is heavy:
I wish her a lucky passage.

10 But now it is she who pauses,
    As if to reject my thought and its easy figure.
    A stillness greatens, in which

    The whole house seems to be thinking,
    And then she is at it again with a bunched clamor
15 Of strokes, and again is silent.

    I remember the dazed starling
    Which was trapped in that very room, two years ago;
    How we stole in, lifted a sash

    And retreated, not to affright it;
20 And how for a helpless hour, through the crack of the door,
    We watched the sleek, wild, dark

    And iridescent creature
    Batter against the brilliance, drop like a glove
    To the hard floor, or the desk-top,

25 And wait then, humped and bloody,
    For the wits to try again; and how our spirits
    Rose when, suddenly sure,

    It lifted off from a chair-back,
    Beating a smooth course for the right window
30 And clearing the sill of the world.

    It is always a matter, my darling,
    Of life or death, as I had forgotten. I wish
    What I wished you before, but harder.

1. In your own words, how does "a commotion of typewriter-keys" in line 5 sound? To what does the poet compare this sound?

   _____

   _____

2. Analyze the word-play in "I wish her a lucky passage." How is this word-play appropriate for the meaning of the poem?

   _____

   _____

3. The poet chose to make the bird in the poem a starling. What words in the poem alliterate with starling?

   _____

   _____

4. Reread lines 12–15. Analyze how the sounds of words in those lines reinforce the meaning and feeling of what occurs in those lines.

   _____

   _____

   _____

   _____

   _____

   _____

Assessment Practice

Directions Answer the questions based on the selection you just read.

1. **What does the poet suggest in line 9?**

    A   The cargo is also heavy.

    B   The daughter is planning a trip.

    C   Young people often face many problems.

    D   He is disappointed in his daughter.

2. **Line 26, "for the wits to try it again," is notable for—**

    A   departing from the rhyme scheme of the rest of the poem.

    B   alliteration of the hard *g* sound.

    C   personifying wit as a human trait.

    D   use of short *i* sounds.

3. **Which of the following phrases uses the sounds of words to reinforce the image of a bird colliding violently, noisily, into a piece of furniture?**

    A   "iridescent creature"

    B   "batter against the brilliance"

    C   "It lifted off from a chair-back"

    D   "clearing the sill of the world"

4. **Why does the poet refer to the girl as a starling?**

    A   to suggest failure to accomplish one's goals

    B   to suggest a dazed bird

    C   to suggest a precious cargo

    D   to suggest youth's repeated attempts to succeed

5. **Which image from the poem appeals MOST strongly to the sense of hearing?**

    A   My daughter is writing a story.

    B   Like a chain hauled over a gunwale.

    C   The whole house seems to be thinking

    D   We watched the sleek, wild, dark/And iridescent creature

Focus on California Content Standards

Lesson 20 — Interpret and Evaluate Ambiguity, Subtlety, Contradiction, Irony, and Incongruity

Reading Literature 9.3.8   Interpret and evaluate the impact of ambiguities, subtleties, contradictions, ironies, and incongruities in a text.

Ambiguity occurs when the writer leaves details or meanings unclear or uncertain. A text that is *ambiguous* has two or more possible meanings. Which meaning applies best to the text is left up to the reader to decide. Endings of stories are sometimes ambiguous. You, as the reader, are not quite sure what the final outcome is, but you have your ideas. For example, during a story the main character is faced with making a choice between love or money. At the end of the story, the writer tells you that the main character has made a choice but does not tell you what it is. Based on what you have read, you must form your own interpretation.

Ambiguity may be created by the use of subtleties, contradictions, and incongruities. **Subtleties** are fine distinctions between things, such as the distinction between *slighting* someone and *insulting* someone. **Contradictions** are seemingly opposing ideas or inconsistencies. For example, a character who praises democratic governments but vacations in countries with dictators would be contradictory. **Incongruities** are details that do not seem logical or that defy conventional reason. An example might be the following statement: "It was nearly midnight, and the sun was shining brightly."

Irony is another kind of discrepancy. It is the difference between what is expected and what is revealed. Three different types of irony are verbal irony, situational irony, and dramatic irony.

Verbal irony is the simplest kind to understand. It occurs when what someone says is the opposite of what that person means. For example, imagine you have been planning a hike in the park. You have been thinking about beautiful weather, the sun shining, and birds chirping in the trees. The day of the hike comes, and it's pouring rain. You turn to your friend and say, "Beautiful day, isn't it? Couldn't be better for a hike!" Of course, you mean just the opposite of what you say.

Situational irony occurs when what happens is just the opposite of what you expect to happen. For example, someone has an ugly old painting that he inherited from his aunt. He has to display it, because he wants to keep his aunt happy so that he will inherit her fortune. Upon her death, he gleefully burns the painting. But when the will is read, he finds that his aunt had no money to leave him. Her one valuable possession she had already given to him—a priceless masterpiece painted by Picasso.

Dramatic irony occurs when you, the reader or the viewer, knows something crucial that the main character in the story does not know. For example, imagine you are viewing a movie. A soldier longs to go home to his childhood sweetheart. This vision of the future keeps him going and gives him hope, even through the darkest hours of battle. You, the viewer, know something he does not know: His sweetheart has married his best friend. He has no one to go home to.

Guided Reading Instruction

Directions Read the following dramatic poem. Use the questions in the margin to guide your reading. Then answer the questions that follow.

One Perfect Rose
by Dorothy Parker

A single flow'r he sent me, since we met.
    All tenderly his messenger he chose:
Deep-hearted, pure, with scented dew still wet—
    One perfect rose.

I knew the language of the floweret;
    "My fragile leaves," it said, "his heart enclose."
Love long had taken for his amulet
    One perfect rose.

Why is it no one ever sent me yet
    One perfect limousine, do you suppose?
Ah no, it's always just my luck to get
    One perfect rose.

Guided Questions

1 Why did someone send this to the speaker?

2 Look at the language in this stanza. How is it suitable for a love poem?

3 How does the tone of voice change in these lines?

4 How is the way the words "One perfect rose" are used here different from in the first two stanzas?

1. In lines 1–4, how do you expect the speaker to feel about receiving the rose?

_____

_____

2. What does giving a rose usually represent?

_____

_____

3. What would the speaker rather receive than "one perfect rose"?

_____

_____

4. Explain why this poem is ironic.

_____

_____

Apply   **Directions** Read the passage below. Then answer the questions that follow it.

THE PRINCESS AND THE TIN BOX
by James Thurber

Once upon a time, in a far country, there lived a King whose daughter was the prettiest princess in the world. Her eyes were like cornflower, her hair was sweeter than the hyacinth, and her throat made the swan look dusty.

From the time she was a year old, the Princess had been showered with presents. Her nursery looked like Cartier's window. Her toys were all made of gold or platinum or diamonds or emeralds. She was not permitted to have wooden blocks or china dolls or rubber dogs or linen books, because such materials were considered cheap for the daughter of a king.

When she was seven, she was allowed to attend the wedding of her brother and throw real pearls at the bride instead of rice. Only the nightingale, with his lyre of gold, was permitted to sing for the Princess. The common blackbird, with his boxwood flute, was kept out of the palace grounds. She walked in silver-and-samite slippers to a sapphire-and-topaz bathroom and slept in an ivory bed inlaid with rubies.

On the day the Princess was eighteen, the King sent a royal ambassador to the courts of five neighboring kingdoms to announce that he would give his daughter's hand in marriage to the prince who brought her the gift she liked the most.

The first prince to arrive at the palace rode a swift white stallion and laid at the feet of the Princess an enormous apple made of solid gold, which he had taken from a dragon who had guarded it for a thousand years. It was placed on a long ebony table set up to hold the gifts of the Princess' suitors. The second prince, who came on a gray charger, brought her a nightingale made of a thousand diamonds, and it was placed beside the golden apple. The third prince, riding on a black horse, carried a great jewel box made of platinum and sapphires, and it was placed next to the diamond nightingale. The fourth prince, astride a fiery yellow horse, gave the Princess a gigantic heart made of rubies and pierced by an emerald arrow. It was placed next to the platinum-and-sapphire jewel box.

Now the fifth prince was the strongest and handsomest of all the five suitors, but he was the son of a poor king whose realm had been overrun by mice and locusts and wizards and mining engineers so that there was nothing much of value left in it. He came plodding up to the palace of the Princess on a plow horse, and he brought her a small tin box filled with mica and feldspar and hornblende which he had picked up on the way.

The other princes roared with disdainful laughter when they saw the tawdry gift the fifth prince had brought the Princess. But she examined it with great interest and squealed with delight, for all her life she had been glutted with precious stones and priceless metals, but she had never seen tin before or mica or feldspar or hornblende. The tin box was placed next to the ruby heart pierced with an emerald arrow.

"Now," the King said to his daughter, "you must select the gift you like best and marry the prince that brought it."

The Princess smiled and walked up to the table and picked up the present she liked the most. It was the platinum-and-sapphire jewel box, the gift of the third prince. "The way I figure it," she said, "is this. It is a very large and expensive box, and when I am married, I will meet many admirers who will give me precious gems with which to fill it to the top. Therefore, it is the most valuable of all the gifts my suitors have brought me, and I like it the best."

The Princess married the third prince that very day in the midst of great merriment and high revelry. More than a hundred thousand pearls were thrown at her and she loved it.

Moral: All those who thought that the Princess was going to select the tin box filled with worthless stones instead of one of the other gifts will kindly stay after class and write one hundred times on the blackboard, "I would rather have a hunk of aluminum silicate than a diamond necklace."

1. How does this tale start out like a traditional folktale?

_____

_____

2. What details in the second and third paragraphs suggest that this princess may be different from princesses in traditional tales?

_____

_____

3. What situation occurs in the fourth paragraph that is like what happens in traditional tales?

_____

_____

4. How is the gift of the fifth prince different from the gifts of the other princes? Based on your knowledge of traditional tales, how do you think the princess will react to this gift?

_____

_____

_____

5. Why does the princess choose the platinum and sapphire jewel box?

_____

_____

Assessment Practice

Directions Answer the questions based on the selection you just read.

1. **Which of the following details suggests that the princess in this tale may not behave as you expect princesses in fairy tales to behave?**

   A eyes like cornflower

   B hair sweeter than hyacinth

   C throat that made the swan look dusty

   D nursery that looked like Cartier's window

2. **Why does the reader expect the princess to fall for the fifth prince?**

   A He is strong and handsome.

   B He is the fifth suitor.

   C He is the son of a king.

   D He is riding on a plow horse.

3. **The moral of this story is unlike most morals in that it does NOT—**

   A tell what should be learned from this tale.

   B provide an uplifting message.

   C tell why the princess chose the right gift.

   D provide a memorable verse.

4. **What does the princess's choice of the gold box reveal about her?**

   A She is as greedy as she is practical.

   B She is sentimental and kind-hearted.

   C She is infatuated with the third prince.

   D She is a dutiful and loyal daughter.

5. **Why is this story ironic?**

   A It ends with a princess marrying a prince.

   B It doesn't end as the reader expects it to end.

   C It is filled with ambiguous details.

   D The ending is left open to the reader's interpretation.

Lesson 21 Understand Voice, Persona, and Narrator

Reading Literature 9.3.9 Explain how voice, persona, and the choice of narrator affect characterization and the tone, plot, and credibility of a text.

Every story has a teller, or narrator. The **narrator** describes events from a specific **point of view**. Some narrators know everything about all the characters in a story; other narrators have narrower viewpoints.

Sometimes, the person telling the story is one of the characters in the story—either the protagonist or a different character. The character tells the tale using first-person pronouns (*I, me, mine*) to describe his or her own actions. This technique is the **first person-point of view**. A **first-person narrator** knows only what he or she has experienced or learned about. Therefore, first person narrators may at times be unreliable or biased.

Usually, a writer gives this first person narrator a **persona**, or personality, which affects what he or she tells. In addition, the narrator speaks with a distinctive **voice**, that reveals this personality and the narrator's attitude toward other characters and events.

The two other major point of view techniques both use the third person, signaled by pronouns such as *he, she, him,* and *her*. A **third-person omniscient narrator** knows everything that goes on in the story, possibly including knowing every character's thoughts and feelings. A **third-person limited narrator** looks over the shoulder of one major character, presenting that character's traits in great detail, often including this character's thoughts, but *not* other characters' thoughts and feelings.

Guided Reading Instruction

Directions Read the following passage. Use the questions in the margin to guide your reading. Then answer the questions that follow.

Wallet
by Allen Woodman

1 Tired of losing his wallet to pickpockets, my father, at seventy, makes a phony one. **2** He stuffs the phony wallet with expired food coupons and losing Florida Lottery tickets and a fortune cookie fortune that reads, "Life is the same old story told over and over."

In a full-length mirror, he tries out the wallet in the back pocket of his pants. **3** It hangs out fat with desire. "All oyster," he says to me, "no pearl." We drive to the mall where he says he lost the last one. I am the wheelman, left behind in the car, while my father cases a department store.

4 He is an old man trying to act feeble and childlike, and he overdoes it like stage makeup on a community-theater actor. He has even bought a walking stick for special effect. Packages of stretch socks clumsily slip from his fingers. He bends over farther than he has bent in years to retrieve them, allowing the false billfold to rise like a dark wish and be grappled by the passing shadow of a hand.

Then the unexpected happens. The thief is chased by an attentive salesclerk. Others join in. The thief subdued, the clerk holds up the reclaimed item. "Your wallet, sir. Your wallet." As she begins opening it, searching for identification, my father runs toward an exit. The worthless articles float to the floor.

Now my father is in the car, shouting for me to drive away. There will be time enough for silence and rest. **5** We are both stupid with smiles and he is shouting. "Drive fast, drive fast."

Guided Questions

1 From what point of view is this story told?

2 Who is the narrator telling about?

3 What does the narrator mean when he says that the wallet "hangs out fat with desire"?

4 What is the narrator's attitude toward his father's escapade?

5 Why do they both smile?

---

1. Describe the persona of the narrator and the tone of voice he uses.

_____

_____

2. Because this story is told in the first person, you see the father through the son's eyes. What picture do you form of the father?

_____

_____

3. What do the father's and son's behavior at the end show about the relationship between these two characters?

_____

_____

4. If the father had told the story, what are at least two things he could have told you that his son cannot?

_____

_____

Apply **Directions** Read the passage below. Then answer the questions that follow it.

The Luckiest Time of All
from *The Lucky Stone*
by Lucille Clifton

Mrs. Elzie F. Pickens was rocking slowly on the porch one afternoon when her Great-granddaughter, Tee, brought her a big bunch of dogwood blooms, and that was the beginning of the story.

"Ahhh, now that dogwood reminds me of the day I met your Great-granddaddy, Mr. Pickens, Sweet Tee.

"It was just this time, spring of the year, and me and my best friend Ovella Wilson, who is now gone, was goin to join the Silas Greene. Usta be a kinda show went all through the South called it the Silas Greene show. Somethin like the circus. Me and Ovella wanted to join that thing and see the world. Nothin wrong at home or nothin, we just wanted to travel and see new things and have high times. Didn't say nothin to nobody but one another. Just up and decided to do it.

"Well, this day we plaited our hair and put a dress and some things in a crokasack and started out to the show. Spring day like this.

"We got there after a good little walk and it was the world, Baby, such music and wonders as we never had seen! They had everything there, or seemed like it.

"Me and Ovella thought we'd walk around for a while and see the show before goin to the office to sign up and join.

"While we was viewin it all we come up on this dancin dog. Cutest one thing in the world next to you, Sweet Tee, dippin and movin and head bowin to that music. Had a little ruffly skirt on itself and up on two back legs twistin and movin to the music. Dancin dancin dancin till people started throwin pennies out of they pockets.

"Me and Ovella was caught up too and laughin so. She took a penny out of her pocket ad threw it to the ground where that dog was dancin, and I took two pennies and threw 'em both.

"The music was faster and faster and that dog was turnin and turnin. Ovella reached in her sack and threw out a little pin she had won from never being late at Sunday school. And me, laughin and all excited, reached in my bag and threw out my lucky stone!

"Well, I knew right off what I had done. Soon as it left my hand it seemed like I reached back out for it to take it back. But the stone was gone from my hand and Lord, it hit that dancin dog right in his nose.

"Well, he lit out after me, poor thing. He lit out after me and I flew! Round and round the Silas Greene we run, through every place me and Ovella had walked before, but now that dancin dog was a runnin dog and all the people was laughin at the new show, which was us!

"I felt myself slowin down after a while and I thought I would turn around a little bit to see how much gain that cute little dog was makin on me. When I did I got such a surprise! Right behind me was the dancin dog and right behind him was the finest fast runnin hero in the bottoms of Virginia.

"And that was Mr. Pickens when he was still a boy! He had a length of twine in his hand and he was twirlin it around in the air just like the cowboy at the Silas Greene and grinnin fit to bust.

"While I was watchin how the sun shined on him and made him look like an angel come to help a poor sinner girl, why, he twirled that twine one extra fancy twirl and looped it right around one hind leg of the dancin dog and brought him low.

"I stopped then and walked slow and shy to where he had picked up that poor dog to see if he was hurt, cradlin him and talkin to him soft and sweet. That showed me how kind and gentle he was, and when we walked back to the dancin dog's place in the show he let the dog loose and helped me to find my stone. I told him how shiny black it was and how it had the letter A scratched on one side. We searched and searched and at last he spied it!

"Ovella and me lost heart for shows then and we walked on home. And a good little way, the one who was gonna be your Great-granddaddy was walkin on behind. Seeing us safe. Us walkin kind of slow. Him seein us safe. Yes." Mrs. Pickins' voice trailed off softly and Tee noticed she had a smile on her face.

"Grandmama, that stone almost got you bit by a dog that time. It wasn't so lucky that time, was it?"

Tee's Great-grandmother shook her head and laughed out loud.

"That was the luckiest time of all, Tee Baby. It got me acquainted with Mr. Amos Pickens, and if that ain't luck, what could it be! Yes, it was luckier for me than for anybody, I think. Least mostly I think it.

Tee laughed with her Great-grandmother though she didn't exactly know why.

"I hope I have that kind of good luck stone one day," she said.

"Maybe you will someday," her Great-grandmother said.

And they rocked a little longer and smiled together.

1. Because Mrs. Elzie F. Pickens tells her own story, you learn a lot about her thoughts and feelings. Why did she and her friend Ovella want to join the Silas Greene? What does this tell you about her?

_____

_____

2. What is Mrs. Pickens reaction to the little dog? What does her comment suggest about her feelings for her great-granddaughter?

_____

_____

3. Why does Mrs. Pickens throw her lucky stone at the dog?

_____

_____

4. Why does Mrs. Pickens consider this stone so lucky?

_____

_____

5. Imagine you are Mr. Pickens. Tell about meeting Elzie from your point of view.

_____

_____

_____

_____

_____

_____

_____

_____

_____

Assessment Practice

Directions Answer the questions based on the selection you just read.

1. **What statement below BEST describes the narrator's tone?**

   A cold and objective

   B sly and deceptive

   C warm and nostalgic

   D bitter and unkind

2. **Which statement below BEST shows that Elzie wanted Mr. Pickens to catch up with her?**

   A "I told him how shiny black it was and how it had the letter A scratched on one side."

   B "Seein us safe. Us walkin kind of slow. Him seein us safe."

   C "Ovella and me lost heart for shows then and we walked on home."

   D "And a good little way, the one who was gonna be your Great-granddaddy was walkin on behind."

3. **In this story, Mrs. Pickens tells all of the following EXCEPT—**

   A how she feels about the dog.

   B why she wants to join the show.

   C how she feels about Mr. Pickens.

   D how Mr. Pickins feels about her.

4. **Why does Elzie like Mr. Pickens right away?**

   A He is kind and gentle.

   B He is frightened of dogs.

   C He is extremely brave.

   D He is an experienced cowboy.

5. **Which item BEST describes the persona of Mrs. Elzie F. Pickens?**

   A a happy, loving woman with a positive attitude toward life

   B an awkward woman who is uncomfortable with people

   C a happy woman with nothing left but her memories

   D a flippant and saucy woman with an attitude

Reading Literature 9.3.10 Identify and describe the function of dialogue, scene designs, soliloquies, asides, and character foils in dramatic literature.

Dramatic literature is meant to be performed. Actors tell the story through **dialogue**, or what they say to one another. Their words reveal the plot and what the characters are like.

Sometimes, instead of talking to other characters, a character turns and speaks directly to the audience. This is called an **aside**. Sometimes a character has a long speech in which he speaks to himself. This speech, called a **soliloquy**, is like an inner conversation that you in the audience can overhear. Like any inner conversation, it reveals a lot about the speaker.

As you read in Chapter 14, the main character, or protagonist, seeks to solve a problem or settle a conflict during the course of the play. The character who tries to prevent the protagonist from resolving the problem is called the antagonist. How the protagonist resolves the conflict leads to the resolution. Sometimes, a play also contains a character known as the **character foil**. This character has traits that are just the opposite of the protagonist's. In fact, by illustrating what the protagonist is NOT like, the character foil helps the audience understand what the protagonist IS like.

Because the audience learns so much through dialogue and what the characters do on the stage, how the actors say their lines and how and where they move is very important. Playwrights include **stage directions** in their scripts telling actors exactly what to do and how to do it. They also tell actors how to say their lines.

Stage design refers to the way the setting for the play looks on stage. The stage design establishes where and when the events are taking place. Included in the stage design are the lighting effects and the actual sets as well as the props (properties) used by the actors, such as furniture, umbrellas, books—everything you see on stage.

Guided Reading Instruction

Directions Read the following passage. Use the questions in the margin to guide your reading. Then answer the questions that follow.

from **What I Did Last Summer**
by A.R. Gurney, Jr.

> The scene from this play is set in Canada in 1945. Charlie Higgins, a fourteen-year-old boy, wants to date Bonny, a fourteen-year-old girl working as a life guard.

Guided Questions

1 BONNY: (*Bonny spreads the towel, as if she were on a beach. She speaks quietly to the audience.*) Sometimes I think this play is secretly about me. That's what I secretly think. Because, for me, this is a crucial summer. All sorts of important things are beginning to happen. My father's letting me skipper the boat occasionally. And my mother says I can smoke, as long as it's in front of her. And I've got a paid baby-sitting job three times a week. (*She calls out.*) It's not cold, Susie. Just go in slowly. Bit by bit. And it'll be fine. (*To audience.*) And tonight, one of the most crucial things of all might happen. Tonight we might be riding this roller coaster. It's called The Cyclone, and on a calm night you can hear it roar, even though the amusement park is over five miles away! Oh it's the scariest thing! It's built right out over the lake, all rickety and shaky, and they say when you climb to the top, you can see all the way to town. And when you start down, it's so basically terrifying that women have thrown their babies over the side! It costs five tickets per person to ride, and there's a big sign right at the gate saying you have to be at least sixteen before you can ride it. But Ted knows the Canadian boys who take tickets, and right now he's seeing if they can sneak us on. (*Calls out.*) Nobody goes out beyond the sandbar, please! Stay in the shallow water where I can see you. (*Ted comes on eagerly, from U.L.*)

TED: Everything's copasetic.

BONNY: They'll let us on.

TED: No problem.

BONNY: Oh I'm shaking like a leaf. Did you tell Charlie?

TED: How could I tell Charle? He's over at the Pig Woman's again.

BONNY: We'll have to wait and see if he can come too.

TED: Why Charlie?

1 The stage directions tell you that Bonny is going to speak in an aside to the audience. What is she supposed to be doing while she is talking about herself?

BONNY: Because last summer we all promised to ride it together.

TED: They won't let him on. He's too young.

BONNY: He's my age.

TED: That's different. I told them you were my girl.

2 BONNY: Your girl!

TED: So they'd let you through.

BONNY: You mean you didn't mention Charlie?

TED: I said I was bringing my girl.

BONNY: Oh. (*She calls out.*) Stay together, everybody! Everybody stay close together! (*Pause.*)

3 TED: So what do you say?

BONNY: How would we get there?

TED: How do you think? By car.

BONNY: With you driving? Or your father?

TED: I got my license, remember?

BONNY: My mother doesn't want me to go out alone at night in cars with older boys. She was even mad I took you sailing with me.

TED: That wasn't a car. And it wasn't at night.

BONNY: Well I don't know. She thinks you're too old for me.

TED: She didn't think that last summer.

2 How do you think Bonny says this line? Why?

3 If you were a director, how would you tell the actor playing Ted to say this line?

4 **BONNY:** Well maybe you weren't last summer. (*Calling out.*) Yes I saw Susie. I saw you do that somersault! It was very good, Susie.

TED: Don't tell her then.

BONNY: Don't tell her?

TED: Just meet me out by the main road.

BONNY: Without Charlie?

TED: Look, Charlie's going his way, why can't we go ours? Come on. I'll fix it so we ride in the front. And I'll take you to the Frozen Custard place afterwards. And introduce you to my whole gang from high school.

5 **BONNY:** Gosh. . . .

TED: (*Touching her arm.*) Sure. It'll be like a date. A real date.

BONNY: You're distracting me, Ted. I'm supposed to be watching these . . . (*She looks out at the lake.*) . . . kids. (*She jumps to her feet.*) Uh-oh.

TED: What?

BONNY: How many heads do you see out there?

TED: (*Counting quickly.*) One . . . two . . . three . . . four . . .

BONNY: There's supposed to be five!

TED: (*Pointing.*) And five, over there!

6 **BONNY:** Thank God! (*Calling out angrily.*) Susie, when you decide to swim underwater, would you tell people, please?

TED: Close call, huh?

BONNY: That wouldn't have happened if I had used the buddy system.

4 What effect is created by Bonny's constantly turning away to call to the children?

5 At this point, do you think that Bonny is ready to say yes or no? Why?

6 How do you think Ted feels about these constant interruptions?

TED: I hate the buddy system.

BONNY: Well at least it's safe. (*Clapping her hands.*) Everyone out of the water, please. I'm instigating a new rule! (*She starts OFF U.R.*)

TED: What about our date?

BONNY: Tell you what: I'll ask my father.

TED: He'll say no.

1. What impression do you form of Bonny through the aside?

   _____

   _____

2. In this play, both Ted and Charlie have been paying attention to Bonny. Based on what you know of her personality, why do you think she might ultimately favor Ted?

   _____

   _____

3. How does Tim try to make Charlie seem less attractive in Bonny's eyes?

   _____

   _____

4. Bonny sets up a buddy system for the children she is watching. In what way has she been using Charlie as her own buddy system?

   _____

   _____

Apply   **Directions** Read the passage below. Then answer the questions that follow it.

FROM A YOUNG LADY OF PROPERTY
by Horton Foote

In this scene from a play set in 1925, Wilma, a young woman of fifteen, has lost her mother, and her father is planning to remarry. She feels an emptiness and tries to decide what she wants her future to be.

WILMA: Heh, Arabella. Come sit and swing.

ARABELLA: All right. Your letter came.

WILMA: Whoopee. Where is it?

ARABELLA: Here. (*She gives it to her. Wilma tears it open. She reads.*)

WILMA: (*Reading.*) Dear Miss Thompson: Mr. Delafonte will be glad to see you any time next week about your contemplated screen test. We suggest you call the office when you arrive in the city and we will set an exact time. Yours truly, Adele Murray. Well . . . Did you get yours?

ARABELLA: Yes.

WILMA: What did it say?

ARABELLA: The same.

WILMA: Exactly the same?

ARABELLA: Yes.

WILMA: Well, let's pack our bags. Hollywood, here we come.

ARABELLA: Wilma . . .

WILMA: Yes?

ARABELLA: I have to tell you something . . . Well . . . I . . .

WILMA: What is it?

ARABELLA: Well . . . promise you won't hate me, or stop being my friend. I never had a friend, Wilma, until you began being nice to me, and I couldn't stand it if you weren't my friend any longer . . .

WILMA: Oh, my cow. Stop talking like that. I'll never stop being your friend. What do you want to tell me?

ARABELLA: Well . . . I don't want to go to see Mr. Delafonte, Wilma . . .

WILMA: You don't?

ARABELLA: No. I don't want to be a movie star. I don't want to leave Harrison or my mother or father . . . I just want to stay here the rest of my life and get married and settle down and have children.

WILMA: Arabella . . .

ARABELLA: I just pretended like I wanted to go to Hollywood because I knew you wanted me to, and I wanted you to like me . . .

WILMA: Oh, Arabella . . .

ARABELLA: Don't hate me, Wilma. You see, I'd be afraid . . . . I'd die if I had to go to see Mr. Delafonte. Why, I even get faint when I have to recite before the class. I'm not like you. You're not scared of anything.

WILMA: Why do you say that?

ARABELLA: Because you're not. I know.

WILMA: Getting lost in a city. Being bitten by dogs. Old lady Leighton taking my daddy away . . . (*A pause.*)

ARABELLA: Will you still be my friend?

WILMA: Sure. I'll always be your friend.

ARABELLA: I'm glad. Oh, I almost forgot. Your Aunt Gert said for you to come home.

WILMA: I'll go in a little. I love to swing in my front yard. Aunt Gert has a swing in her front yard, but it's not the same. Mama and I used to come out here and swing together. Some nights when Daddy was out, I used to wake up and hear her out here swinging away. Sometimes she'd let me come and sit beside her. We'd swing until three or four in the morning. (*A pause. She looks into the yard.*) The pear tree looks sickly, doesn't it? The fig trees are doing nicely though. I was out in back and the weeds are near knee high, but the fig trees just seem to thrive in the weeds. The freeze must have killed off the banana trees . . . (*A pause. Wilma stops swinging—she walks around the yard.*) Maybe I won't leave either. Maybe I won't go to Hollywood after all.

ARABELLA: You won't?

WILMA: No. Maybe I shouldn't. That just comes to me now. You know sometimes my old house looks so lonesome it tears at my heart. I used to think it looks lonesome just whenever it had no tenants, but now it comes to me it has looked lonesome ever since Mama died and we moved away, and it will look lonesome until some of us move back here. Of course, Mama can't, and Daddy won't. So it's up to me.

ARABELLA: Are you gonna live here all by yourself?

WILMA: No. I talk big about living here by myself, but I'm too much of a coward to do that. But maybe I'll finish school and live with Aunt Gert and keep on renting the house until I meet some nice boy with good habits and steady ways, and marry him. Then we'll move here and have children and I bet this old house won't be lonely any more. I'll get Mama's old croquet set and put it out under the pecan trees and play croquet with my children, or sit in this yard and swing and wave as people to they pass by.

ARABELLA: Oh, I wish you would. Mama says that's a normal life for a girl, marrying and having children. She says being an actress is all right, but the other's better.

WILMA: Maybe I've come to agree with your mama. Maybe I was going to Hollywood out of pure lonesomeness. I felt so alone with Mrs. Leighton getting my daddy and my mama having left the world. Daddy could have taken away my lonesomeness, but he didn't want to or couldn't. Aunt Gert says nobody is lonesome with a house full of children, so maybe that's what I just ought to stay here and have . . .

ARABELLA: Have you decided on a husband yet?

WILMA: No.

ARABELLA: Mama says that's the bad feature of being a girl, you have to wait for the boy to ask you and just pray that the one you want wants you. Tommy Murray is nice, isn't he?

WILMA: I think so.

ARABELLA: Jay Godfrey told me once he wanted to ask you for a date, but he didn't dare because he was afraid you'd turn him down.

WILMA: Why did he think that?

ARABELLA: He said the way you talked he didn't think you would go out with anything less than a movie star.

WILMA: Maybe you'd tell him different . . .

ARABELLA: All right. I think Jay Godfrey is very nice. Don't you?

WILMA: Yes, I think he's very nice and Tommy is nice . . .

ARABELLA: Maybe we could double-date sometimes.

WILMA: That might be fun.

ARABELLA: Oh, Wilma. Don't go to Hollywood. Stay here in Harrison and let's be friends forever. . . .

WILMA: All right. I will.

ARABELLA: You will?

WILMA: Sure, why not? I'll stay here. I'll stay and marry and live in my house.

ARABELLA: Oh, Wilma. I'm so glad. I'm so very glad.

1. At the beginning of this scene, what is Wilma's reaction to receiving the letter? How is Arabella's reaction just the opposite?

_____

_____

2. Why hadn't Arabella told Wilma that she didn't really want to go to Hollywood? What does this tell you about her?

_____

_____

3. When Wilma talks about her house being lonesome, what is she really talking about?

_____

_____

4. Why does Arabella think she should get married? Why does Wilma think that she should get married, too?

_____

_____

5. Look at Wilma's last line. If you were directing an actor to say it, what would you tell her?

_____

_____

Assessment Practice

Directions Answer the questions based on the selection you just read.

1. **According to Arabella, how is she different from Wilma?**

   A   She gets scared by life.

   B   She is brave and outgoing.

   C   She wants to be a movie star.

   D   She listens to her mother.

2. **Which line of dialogue BEST shows that Wilma is introspective and self-aware?**

   A   Well, let's pack our bags. Hollywood, here we come.

   B   I'll never stop being your friend.

   C   I talk big about living here by myself, but I'm too much of a coward to do that.

   D   You know sometimes my old house looks so lonesome it tears at my heart.

3. **Read this stage direction from the selection.**

   (*A pause. Wilma stops swinging—she walks around the yard.*)

   What does the stage direction indicate?

   A   Wilma is thinking of selling the house.

   B   Wilma is about to change her mind.

   C   Wilma will go to Hollywood.

   D   Wilma is angry at her father.

4. **Why do the stage directions say to pause after Wilma tells Arabella the things she is afraid of?**

   A   This indicates that she is not really afraid of anything.

   B   This indicates that she has been lying or avoiding the truth

   C   This indicates that she has run out of ideas.

   D   This indicates that she is thinking about what she has just said.

5. **Which item below best describes Wilma?**

   A   determined

   B   weak-willed

   C   insensitive

   D   content

Focus on California Content Standards

Lesson 23 Use Different Approaches to Analyze Literature

Reading Literature 8.3.7 Analyze a work of literature, showing how it reflects the heritage, traditions, attitudes, and beliefs of its author. (Biographical approach)
Reading Literature 9.3.11 Evaluate the aesthetic qualities of style, including the impact of diction and figurative language, on tone, mood, and theme, using the terminology of literary criticism. (Aesthetic approach)
Reading Literature 9.3.12 Evaluate the way in which a work of literature is related to the themes and issues of its historical period. (Historical approach)

There are three approaches you can take to analyzing literature. You can look at how the work is connected to the author's life. You can examine the aesthetic qualities, or you can consider how it is related to its historical period.

When you take the **biographical approach**, you look at how the author's life, background, attitudes, and beliefs affect the work. For example, if you are reading a story about a dramatic rescue during the Vietnam War and you know the writer served in Vietnam during this war, you might assume that the story is influenced by his first-hand experiences and his attitudes.

When you take the **aesthetic approach**, you concentrate on the author's style, or way of writing. You look at how the author's diction, or choice of language, affects the tone, mood, or theme of the text. For example, you might look at how the author's choice of language creates a feeling of sadness and regret. Elements that help create the author's special style include

- **parallelism**—the expression of similar ideas in the same grammatical form

- **repetition**—the repeating of a key word or element for effect

- **evocative words**—the use of words that stir strong feelings or emotions

- **figurative language**—the use of devices such as simile, metaphor, and personification

- **sound devices**—the use of devices such as rhythm, rhyme, alliteration, and assonance to create a musical quality

When you take the **historical approach**, you consider the historical context of the work. You think about the time period and the issues that concerned people and see how they affect the plot, the characters, and the theme. For example, if you read a story set during the Civil War, you would think about what was happening at this time and how this historical context relates to the text.

Guided Reading Instruction

Directions Read the following passage. Use the questions in the margin to guide your reading. Then answer the questions that follow.

from **The Bonesetter's Daughter**
by Amy Tan

1   I was raised with the Liu clan in the rocky Western Hills south of Peking. The oldest recorded name of our village was Immortal Heart. Precious Auntie taught me how to write this down on my chalkboard. *Watch now, Doggie,* she ordered, and drew the character for "heart": *See this curving stroke? That's the bottom of the heart, where blood gathers and flows. And the dots, those are the two veins and the artery that carry the blood in and out.* As I traced over the character, she asked: *Whose dead heart gave shape to this word? How did it begin, Doggie? Did it belong to a woman? Was it drawn in sadness?*

I once saw the heart of a fresh-killed pig. It was red and glistening. And I had already seen plenty of chicken hearts in a bowl, waiting to be cooked. They looked like tiny lips and were the same color as Precious Auntie's scars. But what did a woman heart look like? "Why do we have to know whose heart it was?" I asked as I wrote the character.

2   And Precious Auntie flapped her hands fast: *A person should consider how things begin. A particular beginning results in a particular end.*

I remember her often talking about this, how things begin. Since then I have wondered about the beginning and end of many things. Like Immortal Heart village. And the people who lived there, myself included. By the time I was born, Immortal Heart was no longer lucky. The village lay between hills in a valley that dropped into a deep limestone ravine. **3** The ravine was shaped like the curved chamber of a heart, and the heart's artery and veins were the three streams that once fed and drained the ravine. But they had gone dry. **4** So had the divine springs. Nothing was left of the waterways but cracked gullies and the stench of a fart.

Yet the village began as a sacred place. According to legend, a visiting emperor himself had planted a pine tree in the middle of the valley. The tree was to honor his dead mother, and his respect for his mother was so great he vowed that the tree would live forever. When Precious Auntie first saw the tree, it was already more than three thousand years old.

Rich and poor alike made a pilgrimage to Immortal Heart. They hoped that the tree's vital energy would rub off on them. **5** They stroked the trunk, patted the leaves, then prayed for baby sons or big fortunes, a cure for dying, an end to curses. Before leaving, they chipped off some bark, snapped off some twigs. They took them away as souvenirs. Precious Auntie said this was what killed the tree, too much admiration. When the tree died, the souvenirs lost their strength. And because the dead tree was no longer immortal, it was no longer famous, nor was our village. That tree was not even ancient, people said afterward, maybe only two or three hundred years old. As for the story about the emperor

Guided Questions

1 Circle the name of the village. How can a village be like a heart?

2 Put Precious Auntie's response in your own words.

3 What figure of speech does the narrator use to describe the ravine? What figure of speech does she use to describe the streams?

4 Circle the word *divine*. Then, circle the word in the next paragraph that carries the same connotations.

5 What style elements does the narrator use in this paragraph to describe people's treatment of the tree?

honoring his mother? That was a fake feudal legend to make us think the corrupt were sincere. Those complaints came out the same year that the old Ching Dynasty fell down and the new Republic sprang up.

The nickname of our village is easy for me to remember: Forty-six Kilometers from Reed Moat Bridge. Reed Moat Bridge is the same as Marco Polo Bridge, what people now call the turnoff point to and from Peking. GaoLing's probably forgotten the old name, but I have not. During my girlhood, the directions to get to Immortal Heart went like this: "First find the Reed Moat Bridge, then walk backward forty-six kilometers."

6 That joke made it sound as if we lived in a pitiful little hamlet of twenty or thirty people. Not so. When I was growing up, nearly two thousand people lived there. It was crowded, packed from one edge of the valley to the other. We had a brick maker, a sack weaver, and a dye mill. We had twenty-four market days, six temple fairs, and a primary school that GaoLing and I went to when we were not helping our family at home. We had all kinds of peddlers who went from house to house, selling fresh bean curd and steamed buns, twisted dough and colorful candies. And we had lots of people to buy those goods. A few coppers, that was all you needed to make your stomach as happy as a rich man's.

The Liu clan had lived in Immortal Heart for six centuries. For that amount of time, the sons had been inkstick makers who sold their goods to travelers. They had lived in the same courtyard house that had added rooms, and later wings, when one mother four hundred years ago gave birth to eight sons, one a year. The family home grew from a simple three-pillar house to a compound with wings stretching five pillars each. In later generations, the number of sons was less, and the extra rooms became run-down and were rented to squabbling tenants. Whether those people laughed at coarse jokes or screamed in pain, it did not matter, the sounds were the same, ugly to hear.

7 All in all, our family was successful but not so much that we caused great envy. We ate meat or bean curd at almost every meal. We had new padded jackets every winter, no holes. We had money to give for the temple, the opera, the fair. But the men of our family also had ambitions. They were always looking for more. They said that in Peking, more people wrote important documents. Those important documents required more good ink. Peking was where more of the big money was. Around 1920, Father, my uncles, and their sons went there to sell the ink. From then on, that was where they lived most of the time, in the backroom of a shop in the old Pottery-Glazing District.

In our family, the women made the ink. We stayed home. We all worked—me, GaoLing, my aunts and girl cousins, everybody. Even the babies and Great-Granny had a job of picking out stones from the dried millet we boiled for breakfast. We gathered each day in the ink-making studio. According to Great-Granny, the studio began as a grain shed that sat along the front wall of the courtyard house. Over the years, one generation of sons added brick walls and a tile roof. Another strengthened the beams and lengthened it by two pillars. The next tiled the floors and dug pits for storing the ingredients. Then other descendants made a cellar for keeping the inksticks away from the heat and cold. "And now look," Great-Granny often bragged. "Our studio is an ink palace."

6 What effect is created by the parallel structure in this paragraph?

7 Circle the word *more* each time the author uses it in this paragraph. What is she trying to emphasize by repeating this word?

Because our ink was the best quality, we had to keep the tables and the floors clean year-round. With the dusty yellow winds from the Gobi, this was not easy to do. The window openings had to be covered with both glass and thick paper. In the summer, we hung netting over the doorways to keep out the insects. In the winter, it was sheep hides to keep out the snow.

8   Summer was the worst season for ink-making. Heat upon heat. The fumes burned our eyes and nostrils and lungs. From watching Precious Auntie tie her scarf over her marred face, we got the idea of putting a wet cloth over our mouths. I can still smell the ingredients of our ink. There were several kinds of fragrant soot: pine, cassia, camphor, and the wood of the chopped-down Immortal Tree. Father hauled home several big logs of it after lightning cracked the dead tree right down the middle, exposing its heart, which was nearly hollow because of beetles eating it inside out. There was also a glue of sticky paste mixed with many oils—serpentine, camphor, turpentine, and tung wood. **9**   Then we added a sweet poisonous flower that helped resist insects and rats. That was how special our ink was, all those lasting smells.

8 Circle the word in this paragraph that ties it back to the opening of this passage.

9 What effect is created by the image "sweet poisonous flower"?

Directions Part of the power of this passage comes from the contrast between words and images of life and death. Fill out the chart below. Include at least five words or images in each column.

Life	Death
	dead heart
	fresh-killed pig
	cracked gullies
	chipped off bark
	screamed in pain
	poisonous flowers

Apply **Directions** Read the passage below. Then answer the questions that follow it.

from MATCHIMANITO
by Louise Erdrich

We started dying before the snow, and, like the snow, we continued to fall. We were surprised that so many of us were left to die. For those who survived the spotted sickness from the south and our long flight west to Dakota land, where we signed the treaty, and then a wind from the east, bringing exile in a storm of government papers, what descended from the north in 1914 seemed terrible, and unjust.

By then we thought disaster must surely have spent its force, that disease must have claimed all of the Anishinabe that the earth could hold and bury.

But along with the first bitter punishments of early winter a new sickness swept down. The consumption, it was called by young Father Damien, who came in that year to replace the priest who had succumbed to the same devastation as his flock. This disease was different from the pox and fever, for it came on slowly. The outcome, however, was just as certain. Whole families of Anishinabe lay ill and helpless in its breath. On the reservation, where we were forced close together, the clans dwindled. Our tribe unraveled like a coarse rope, frayed at either end as the old and new among us were taken. My own family was wiped out one by one. I was the only Nanapush who lived. And after, although I had seen no more than fifty winters, I was considered an old man.

I guided the last buffalo hunt. I saw the last bear shot. I trapped the last beaver with a pelt of more than two years' growth. I spoke aloud the words of the government treaty and refused to sign the settlement papers that would take away our woods and lake. I axed the last birch that was older than I, and saved the last of the Pillager family.

Fleur.

We found her on a cold afternoon in late winter, out in her family's cabin near Matchimanito Lake, where my companion, Edgar Pukwan, of the tribal police, was afraid to go. The water there was surrounded by the highest oaks, by woods inhabited by ghosts and roamed by Pillagers, who knew the secret ways to cure or kill, until their art deserted them. Dragging our sled into the clearing, we saw two things: the smokeless tin chimney spout jutting from the roof, and the empty hole in the door where the string was drawn inside. Pukwan did not want to enter, fearing that the unburied Pillager spirits might seize him by the throat and turn him windigo. So I was the one who broke the thin-scraped hide that made a window. I was the one who lowered himself into the stinking silence, onto the floor. I was also the one to find the old man and woman, the little brother and two sisters, stone cold and wrapped in gray horse blankets, their faces turned to the west.

Afraid as I was, stilled by their quiet forms, I touched each bundle in the gloom of the cabin, and wished each spirit a good journey on the three-day road, the old-time road, so well trampled by our people this deadly season. Then something in the corner knocked. I flung the door wide. It was the eldest daughter, Fleur, so feverish that she'd thrown off her covers. She huddled against the cold wood range, staring and shaking. She was wild as a filthy wolf, a big bony girl whose sudden bursts of strength and snarling cries terrified the listening Pukwan. I was the one who struggled to lash her to the sacks of supplies and to the boards of the sled. I wrapped blankets over her and tied them down as well.

 Measuring Up® to the California Content Standards

Pukwan kept us back, convinced that he should carry out the agency's instructions to the letter: he carefully nailed up the official quarantine sign, and then, without removing the bodies, he tried to burn down the house. But though he threw kerosene repeatedly against the logs and even started a blaze with birch bark and chips of wood, the flames narrowed and shrank, went out in puffs of smoke. Pukwan cursed and looked desperate, caught between his official duties and his fear of Pillagers. The fear won out, He finally dropped the tinders and helped me drag Fleur along the trail.

And so we left five dead at Machimanito, frozen behind their cabin door.

1. What vast tragedy, taking place all across North America, provides the overall historical context of the passage?

_____

_____

2. What specific aspect of that larger context does the passage focus on?

_____

_____

3. How might the narrator's life be different if his historical context were one century earlier? Suggest at least two possible differences.

_____

_____

_____

4. How might the narrator's life be different if his historical context were one century later? Speculate on at least two possible differences.

_____

_____

_____

5. In your opinion, what is the author's view of her story's historical context? Supply evidence from the text.

_____

_____

_____

_____

Assessment Practice

Directions Answer the questions based on the selection you just read.

1. **What is the main purpose of the first paragraph?**

   A to show the hardships the Native Americans faced

   B to show the effects of the spotted sickness

   C to show that the flight to the Dakota lands was long

   D to show that the government was unfair

2. **What diseases that were common at the time does the narrator refer to as spotted sickness and consumption?**

   A smallpox and tuberculosis

   B anthrax and influenza

   C polio and multiple sclerosis

   D cancer and hypertension

3. **Father Damien is mentioned early in the story because—**

   A members of a tribe often called their tribal leaders "Father."

   B doctors were sent by the government to the reservation.

   C the Catholic Church sent priests to convert the Indians.

   D Damien was a name popular with Indians at the time.

4. **Which item below best helps the reader understand the historical context of this story?**

   A Buffalo were plentiful at the time of this story.

   B The government sometimes took Indian land.

   C It was easy for Native Americans to live off the land.

   D Reservations were in the woods.

5. **That story reveals that—**

   A Native Americans did not like to go near the dead.

   B Native Americans could not have their own police.

   C Native Americans favored the cures of the government doctors.

   D Native American homes did not have windows.

6. **To what does the phrase "the three-day road, the old-time road, so well trampled by our people this deadly season" refer?**

   A the trek from Georgia to Dakota

   B the train trip from the reservation to Washington, D.C.

   C the road to the afterlife

   D the warpath against the settlers

The following story involves a generational disagreement about the value of manual labor. Read the story and answer questions 1–10.

The Shepherd's Daughter
by William Saroyan

It is the opinion of my grandmother, God bless her, that all men should labor, and at the table, a moment ago, she said to me: You must learn to do some good work, the making of some item useful to man, something out of clay, or out of wood, or metal, or cloth. It is not proper for a young man to be ignorant of an honorable craft. Is there anything you can make? Can you make a simple table, a chair, a plain dish, a rug, a coffee pot? Is there anything you can do?

And my grandmother looked at me with anger.

I know, she said, you are supposed to be a writer, and I suppose you are. You certainly smoke enough cigarettes to be anything, and the whole house is full of the smoke, but you must learn to make solid things, things that can be used, that can be seen and touched.

There was a king of the Persians, said my grandmother, and he had a son, and this son fell in love with a shepherd's daughter. He went to his father and he said, My Lord, I love a shepherd's daughter, and I would have her for my wife. And the king said, I am king and you are my son, and when I die you shall be king, how can it be that you would marry the daughter of a shepherd? And the son said, My Lord, I do not know but I know that I love this girl and would have her for my queen.

The king saw that his son's love for the girl was from God, and he said, I will send a message to her. And he called a messenger to him and he said, Go to the shepherd's daughter and say that my son loves her and would have her for his wife. And the messenger went to the girl and he said, The king's son loves you and would have you for his wife. And the girl said, What labor does he do? And the messenger said, Why, he is the son of the king; he does no labor. And the girl said, He must learn to do some labor. And the messenger returned to the king and spoke the words of the shepherd's daughter.

The king said to his son, The shepherd's daughter wishes you to learn some craft. Would you still have her for your wife? And the son said, Yes, I will learn to weave straw rugs. And the boy was taught to weave rugs of straw, in patterns and in colors and with ornamental designs, and at the end of three days he was making very fine straw rugs, and the messenger returned to the shepherd's daughter, and he said, These rugs of straw are the work of the king's son.

And the girl went with the messenger to the king's palace, and she became the wife of the king's son.

One day, said my grandmother, the king's son was walking through the streets of Baghdad, and he came upon an eating place which was so clean and cool that he entered it and sat at a table.

This place, said my grandmother, was a place of thieves and murderers, and they took the king's son and placed him in a large dungeon where many great men of the city were being held, and the thieves and murderers were killing the fattest of the men and feeding them to the leanest of them, and making sport of it. The king's son was the leanest of the men, and it was not known that he was the son of the king of the Persians, so his life was spared, and he said to the thieves and murderers, I am a weaver of straw rugs and these rugs have great value. And they brought him straw and asked him to weave and in three days he weaved three rugs, and he said, Carry these to the palace of the king of the Persians, and for each rug he will give you a hundred gold pieces of money. And the rugs were carried to the palace of the king, and when the king saw the rugs he saw that they were the work of his son and he took the rugs to the shepherd's daughter and he said, "These rugs were brought to the palace and they are the work of my son who is lost." And the shepherd's daughter took each rug and looked at it closely and in the design of each rug she saw in the written language of the Persians a message from

her husband, and she related this message to the king.

And the king, said my grandmother, sent many soldiers to the place of the thieves and murderers, and the soldiers rescued all the captives and killed all the thieves and murderers, and the king's son was returned safely to the palace of his father, and to the company of his wife, the little shepherd's daughter. And when the boy went into the palace and saw again his wife, he humbled himself before her and he embraced her feet, and he said, My love, it is because of you that I am alive, and the king was greatly pleased with the shepherd's daughter.

Now, said my grandmother, do you see why every man should learn an honorable craft?

I see very clearly, I said, and as soon as I earn enough money to buy a saw and a hammer and a piece of lumber I shall do my best to make a simple chair or a shelf for books.

1. **How does the reader know that this is a short story?**

   A   It is set in two different time periods.

   B   It contains made up characters and events.

   C   It tells about a shepherd's daughter and a prince.

   D   It is about a grandmother and her grandson.

2. **When the grandmother says to the narrator, "Is there anything you can do," she is showing that she—**

   A   doesn't consider writing real work.

   B   wants her grandson to do whatever makes him happy.

   C   supports her grandson's desire to be a writer.

   D   thinks that her grandson has a talent for carpentry.

3. **Which of the following pairs of characters do not come into conflict with each other in this story?**

   A   the narrator and his grandmother

   B   the narrator and the prince

   C   the prince and the king

   D   the prince and the shepherd's daughter

4. **What conflict does the grandmother try to resolve by telling her story?**

   A   the conflict over whether the prince should marry a shepherd's daughter

   B   the conflict over whether the prince should learn to weave straw rugs

   C   the conflict over whether her grandson should be a writer or learn a trade

   D   the conflict over who is smarter, she or her grandson

5. What is the main reason why the prince is able to successfully resolve the conflict with the thieves and murderers?

   A   He has married the shepherd's daughter.

   B   He has learned a craft.

   C   He has less meat on his bones than some of the other prisoners.

   D   He is the son of the king.

6. Why does the author have the narrator say that he will make a chair and a shelf for books at the end of the story?

   A   to show that the narrator now agrees with his grandmother

   B   to show that the narrator needs to earn money

   C   to show that the narrator's goals haven't really changed at all

   D   to show that the narrator has won the conflict

7. Which statement BEST describes what happens in this story?

   A   A grandmother tries to teach her grandson about the value of labor.

   B   A grandson learns from his grandmother how to weave rugs.

   C   A prince marries the daughter of a shepherd.

   D   A grandmother teaches her grandson the value of marrying well.

8. This story is a good example of which of the following literary devices?

   A   foreshadowing

   B   flashback

   C   story within a story

   D   use of generalization

 9. Read this sentence from the story.

> Now, said my grandmother, do you see why every man should learn an honorable trade?

Based on this statement, why is the ending of the story ironic?

   A   The grandmother's story reinforced the man's commitment to writing.

   B   The man learned to use a saw and a hammer.

   C   The man knows that the prince was not really honorable.

   D   The grandmother turns out to be a good writer.

10. Which word BEST describes the narrator's tone in this story?

   A   bitter

   B   sentimental

   C   reflective

   D   amused

Read the selection below. Then answer questions 1–10.

Talent
by Annie Dillard

There is no such thing as talent. If there are any inborn, God-given gifts, they are in the precocious fields of music, mathematics, and chess; if you have such a gift, you know it by now. All the rest of us, in all the other fields, are not talented. We all start out dull and weary and uninspired. Apart from a few like Mozart, there never have been any great and accomplished little children in the world. Genius is the product of education.

Perhaps it's a cruel thing to insist that there is no such thing as talent. We all want to believe—at least I do—that being selfless was "easy" for Albert Schweitzer, that Faulkner's novels just popped into his head, that Rembrandt painted because he "had to." We want to believe all these nonsensical things in order to get ourselves off the hook. For if these people had no talent, then might the rest of us have painting or writing or great thinking as an option? We, who have no talent? I think the answer is yes, absolutely.

So I maintain that the people who have made something of their lives—the Pasteurs and Cézannes and Melvilles—were neither more talented nor more disciplined nor more energetic nor more driven than the rest of us. They were simply better educated. Some of them did it the hard way, studying all the difficult works of their fields at home on their own. Others studied in school. But they all studied. You won't find a writer who hasn't studied the details of the works of other writers—although occasionally you find an American writer like Hemingway or Whitman who deliberately pretended to be spontaneous and unstudied, probably in order to mislead the competition. And occasionally you find a writer like Thoreau, a very well educated Harvard man whose reading was in the Greek classics and in whose work most people overlook the evidences of scholarship and effort simply because they don't want to see them.

It's hard work, doing something with your life. The very thought of hard work makes me queasy. I'd rather die in peace. Here we are, all equal and alike and none of us much to write home about—and some people choose to make themselves into physicists or thinkers or major-league pitchers, knowing perfectly well that it will be nothing but hard work. But I want to tell you that it's not as bad as it sounds. Doing something does not require discipline; it creates its own discipline.

People often ask me if I discipline myself to write, if I work a certain number of hours a day on a schedule. They ask this question with envy in their voices and awe on their faces and a sense of alienation all over them, as if they were addressing an armored tank or a talking giraffe or Niagara Falls. We all want to believe that other people are natural wonders; it gets us off the hook.

Now, it happens that when I wrote my first book of prose, I worked an hour or two a day for a while, and then in the last two months, I got excited and worked very hard, for many hours a day. People can lift cars when they want to. People can recite the Koran, too, and run in marathons. These things aren't ways of life; they are merely possibilities for everyone on certain occasions of life. You don't lift cars around the clock or write books every year. But when you do, it's not so hard. It's not superhuman. It's very human. You do it for love. You do it for love and respect for your own life; you do it for love and respect for the world; and you do it for love and respect for the task itself.

       Measuring Up® to the California Content Standards

If I had a little baby, it would be hard for me to rise up and feed that little baby in the middle of the night. It would be hard; but it certainly wouldn't be a discipline. It wouldn't be a regimen I imposed on myself out of masochism, nor would it be the flowering of some extraordinary internal impulse. I would do it, grumbling, for love and because it has to be done.

Of course it has to be done. And something has to be done with your life too: something specific, something human. But don't wait around to be hit by love. Don't wait for anything. Learn something first. Then while you are getting to know it, you will get to love it, and that love will direct you in what to do. So many times when I was in college I used to say of a course like Seventeenth Century Poetry or European History, "I didn't like it at first, but now I like it." All of life is like that—a sort of dreary course which gradually gets interesting if you work at it.

I used to live in perpetual dread that I would one day read all the books that I would ever be interested in and have nothing more to read. I always figured that when that time came I would force myself to learn wildflowers, just to keep awake. I dreaded it, because I was not very interested in wildflowers but thought I should be. But things kept cropping up and one book has led to another and I haven't had to learn wildflowers yet. I don't think there's much danger of coming to the end of the line. The line is endless. I urge you to get in it, to get in line. It's a long line—but it's the only show in town.

1. **Read this sentence from the article.**

> I used to live in perpetual dread that I would one day read all the books that I would ever be interested in and have nothing more to read.

What does the word *perpetual* mean in this sentence?

A   terrible

B   hopeless

C   continuing

D   determined

2. **What words from the first paragraph does the author use to suggest that we all start off in the same boat?**

A   *music, mathematics,* and *chess*

B   *talent, inborn,* and *gifts*

C   *dull, weary,* and *uninspired*

D   *great, accomplished,* and *genius*

3. **How does the author link the idea that writing is hard work with the way she writes?**

A   She repeats the word *discipline.*

B   She discusses her writing style.

C   She uses metaphors.

D   She suggests that the discipline is hard work.

4. **Which of the following sentences from the article is an example of parallelism?**

A   Apart from a few like Mozart, there never have been any great and accomplished little children in the word.

B   I would do it, grumbling, for love and because it has to be done.

C   Now, it happens that when I wrote my first book of prose, I worked an hour or two a day for a while, and then in the last two months, I got excited and worked very hard, for many hours a day.

D   They ask this question with envy in their voices and awe on their faces and a sense of alienation all over them, as if they were addressing an armored tank or a talking giraffe or Niagara Falls.

5. **In the first two paragraphs, why does the author repeat the word *talent* or a form of the word?**

A   to make the point that there is no such thing as talent

B   to emphasize how extraordinary talented people are

C   to show that not everyone is talented

D   to encourage people to think about whether they are talented

6. **Which question could MOST effectively be developed into a research paper?**

A   Am I talented as I think?

B   Who were Rembrandt and Faulkner?

C   Why is Whitman considered a great American writer?

D   How would you describe Hemingway's life and work?

     Measuring Up® to the California Content Standards

7. **Which sentence below BEST supports the idea that people want to believe that those who do great work are extraordinary or essentially different from the rest of us?**

A If I had a little baby, it would be hard for me to rise up and feed that little baby in the middle of the night.

B People often ask me if I discipline myself to write, if I work a certain number of hours a day on a schedule.

C They ask this question with envy in their voices and awe on their faces and a sense of alienation all over them, as if they were addressing an armored tank or a talking giraffe or Niagara Falls.

D Apart from a few like Mozart, there never have been any great and accomplished little children in the world.

8. **What does the phrase *none of us much to write home about* mean in the following sentence?**

> Here we are, all equal and alike and none of us much to write home about—and some people choose to make themselves into physicists or thinkers or major-league pitchers, knowing perfectly well that it will be nothing but hard work.

A None of us has interesting stories to tell.

B None of us is particularly special.

C All of us can become good writers.

D Writing takes skill and practice.

9. **Read this sentence from the article.**

> So I maintain that the people who have made something of their lives—the Pasteurs and Cézannes and Melvilles—were neither more talented nor more disciplined nor more energetic nor more driven than the rest of us.

What is the meaning of the word *energetic*?

A lacking energy

B requiring a lot of energy

C full of energy

D giving energy to others

 10. **Which statement below BEST expresses the theme of this article?**

A Achieving something in your life comes from hard work and education.

B Only a few people are able to achieve great things in life.

C Whenever you fail, you should pick yourself up and try again.

D Some people achieve great things early in their lives.

Chapter 4 Writing Strategies

In Chapter 4, you will study and practice how to:

- establish a controlling impression of coherent thesis;
- develop a main idea and supporting details;
- synthesize and evaluate information from multiple sources;
- revise for logic, coherence, and appropriateness.

Chapter 5 Writing Conventions

In Chapter 5, you sill study and practice how to:

- use clauses, phrases, and the mechanics of punctuation;
- construct sentences;
- conform to proper English usage.

Chapter 6 Writing Applications

In Chapter 6, you will study and practice how to write:

- a biographical narrative;
- a response to literature;
- an expository composition;
- a persuasive composition;
- a business letter.

Lesson 24   Establish a Controlling Impression or Coherent Thesis

Focus on California Content Standards

Writing Strategies 9.1.1   Establish a controlling impression or coherent thesis that conveys a clear and distinctive perspective on the subject and maintain a consistent tone and focus throughout the piece of writing.

A piece of writing should be **unified**. This means that it holds together seamlessly. How does a writer make sure that every idea and detail fit together?

The writer establishes one **controlling impression** on the topic. This is the writer's point of view about the topic. The writer also provides a **coherent thesis**, the clearly expressed main idea about the topic the writer develops in his or her writing. Usually, the thesis is expressed directly in a **thesis statement**. Sometimes, however, an author's thesis is implied so strongly in the ideas and details of the text that it does not have to be directly stated. The thesis statement helps convey the **tone** of the work—the writer's attitude toward the subject. For example, if the author is writing about how hydroelectric dams damage the environment, his tone regarding dams will be mostly negative.

In well–organized writing, all ideas and details support the thesis statement. The writer organizes the work so that ideas and details flow from one another and from the thesis. When this is done successfully, the work has coherence and a logical progression of ideas. **Coherence** means that the work has a structure that holds the ideas together; everything makes sense. **Logical progression** means that the ideas flow smoothly and sensibly from one to the next.

Depending on the purpose, the writer might choose one of the following organizational structures for a piece of writing:

Compare and Contrast—to show how things are alike and different

Cause and Effect—to show reasons and results, such as in discussing the results of a historical event or in explaining scientific facts or theories

Chronological Order—to show the sequence in which events happen, such as a story from real life or the steps of a process

Order of Importance—to present ideas and information starting with the most important to the least important point, or from least to most important point, especially when you are presenting a persuasive argument or explaining why something happened

Spatial Order—to describe location, such as when you are writing about the arrangement of furniture in a room

Guided Reading Instruction

Directions Read the following passage. Use the questions in the margin to guide your reading. Then answer the questions that follow.

What Happened to the Anasazi?
by Luz Cepeda

1 Why did the Anasazi build their dwellings high up on dangerous cliffs? And why, less than a century later, did the Anasazi leave those dwellings? These questions represent a mystery that archeologists have not yet solved.

2 For centuries, in the Four Corners area where Utah, Colorado, Arizona, and New Mexico meet, Anasazi people built large apartment communities in sandstone canyons and on buttes and mesas. Their adobe buildings were as much as five stories high and sometimes contained 800 rooms. Four hundred miles of roads linked the 30,000 people who lived in the many villages of this culture.

Suddenly, during the 1200s, the Anasazi changed their style of dwelling, as if in response to some crisis. They began building their amazing apartment complexes on the sides of cliffs instead of on valley floors. Why did people choose to live in homes where even a short walk to get water could mean a fall of hundreds of feet?

Just as mysteriously, by the end of the 1200s, the population deserted the cliffs and migrated southeast to the Rio Grande area of New Mexico, where their descendents, the Pueblo peoples, still live today. **3** The reason, according to some scientists, may have been a severe drought, which we know occurred from 1276 to 1299. However, the Anasazi had been through equally bad droughts before without abandoning their homeland. **4** Some people think that the cliff dwellings were built in fear of invaders from the north, and were abandoned when the invaders defeated the Anasazi. However, archaeologists have found no solid evidence that such an invasion took place. A recent theory says that war among the Anasazi themselves caused the turmoil. **5** Will we ever know the true answer? Maybe when I become an archaeologist I will find it!

Guided Questions

1 State the thesis of this essay in your own words.

2 Underline details that give a vivid impression of Anasazi culture.

3 What two extraordinary changes occurred in Anasazi culture in the 1200s?

4 Circle three terms in this paragraph that indicate chronological order.

5 Briefly state three theories of why the Anasazi left their cliff dwellings.

1. Most of the essay is presented in chronological order. What parts are not in chronological order?

_____

_____

2. Why did the author depart from chronological order at those points?

_____

_____

3. What form of organization is used in this essay besides chronological order? Why is this combination appropriate to the topic?

_____

_____

4. What would you like to know about the topic that the essay does not tell you?

_____

_____

Apply   **Directions** Read the prompt below. Then answer the questions that follow it.

Write an essay discussing the plusses and minuses of moving to a new home.

1. Brainstorm some good and bad effects that might be caused by moving.

_____

_____

_____

_____

_____

_____

2. What organizational pattern will you choose and why? You may combine patterns if you wish.

_____

_____

_____

3. Write a thesis statement for your essay.

_____

_____

4. Write the first draft of your essay on a separate piece of paper. Arrange your ideas and details according to your organizational plan.

_____

_____

Assessment Practice

Directions Read the passage that follows. Then answer questions 1–5.

T'ai Chi, the "Supreme Ultimate"
by Robert Ling

[1] Have you ever seen a group of people in a park performing a series of gentle exercise movements that looked like martial arts in slow motion? [2] If so, you have seen t'ai chi, a Chinese form of exercise that has become widely popular in the United States. [3] The words "t'ai chi" mean "supreme ultimate" in Chinese, and many people who practice it believe that t'ai chi is indeed the best kind of healthful exercise there is. [4] It helps you develop balance, flexibility, and coordination. [5] It gives you confidence and a general feeling of well-being. [6] It can be used for self-defense if its slow, gentle moves are sped up.

[7] T'ai chi arose hundreds of years ago—no one knows exactly when or how. It developed out of older martial arts, such as kung-fu. [8] Its movements are graceful and have beautiful names such as "White Crane Spreads Wings" and "Move Hands Like Clouds." [9] However, each of those lovely, delicate moves has a specific purpose related to self-defense, perhaps as a strike or a block or as a way of turning aside an opponent's attack. [10] The motto of t'ai chi is "four ounces of effort defeats a thousand pounds of force." [11] Can four ounces really defeat a thousand pounds?

[12] Several different styles of t'ai chi are practiced, including the Yang style, which is the most popular, and the Cheng style, which is older and more traditional. [13] T'ai chi is great for older people, since it is a gentle sport, but young adults and teens also enjoy practicing it. [14] If you start now, then by the time you're older, you may be a t'ai chi master!

1. **The coherent impression left by this essay is that—**

   A   t'ai chi is mainly an exercise for old people.

   B   t'ai chi developed from kung-fu but is not really effective for self–defense.

   C   "real" t'ai chi is only practiced in China.

   D   t'ai chi is a gentle, healthy exercise that can also be used for self-defense.

2. **Which sentence in the essay should be deleted because it adds no information and does not lead anywhere?**

   A   Sentence 1

   B   Sentence 7

   C   Sentence 11

   D   Sentence 14

3. **Which type of structure does the author use to organize the essay as a whole?**

   A   order of importance

   B   spatial order

   C   cause and effect

   D   chronological order

4. **What aspects of its topic does the essay focus on?**

   A   the author's personal experiences doing t'ai chi

   B   basic information about what t'ai chi is

   C   legends of famous t'ai chi masters

   D   instructions on how to do t'ai chi

5. **Which detail uses comparison and contrast?**

   A   T'ai chi moves have beautiful, delicate names, but they can be used for self-defense.

   B   T'ai chi means "supreme ultimate."

   C   You can start practicing t'ai chi when you are young.

   D   T'ai chi helps with balance, flexibility, coordination, confidence, and general well-being.

Lesson 25 — Develop Main Idea and Supporting Details

Writing Strategies 9.1.4 Develop the main ideas within the body of the composition through supporting evidence (e.g., scenarios, commonly held beliefs, hypotheses, definitions).

The **topic** is what a piece of writing is about—its subject. For example, your topic might be home aquariums. The **main idea** is the most important idea the writer expresses about the topic. Your main idea in a paper about aquariums might be that freshwater aquariums are easier to maintain than saltwater aquariums. Sometimes, the writer states the main idea in a **topic sentence**. When a topic sentence controls the entire article, it is called the **thesis statement**.

A **main idea** needs to be developed and backed up by **supporting details**. These may include:

- facts—informational statements that can be proved

- examples—specific instances or cases that support the point

- quotations—the exact words of people related to the topic

- opinions from authorities—judgments made by people who know the subject and are knowledgeable about the topic

- scenarios—outline or models of possible sequences of events

- hypotheses—possible explanations or assumptions

- definitions—statements expressing the meanings of concepts or things

Guided Reading Instruction

Directions Read the following portion of the first draft of a student essay. Use the questions in the margin to guide your reading. Then answer the questions that follow.

JFK
by Rena Jankowski

1 Was John F. Kennedy a wise president and a great man? The tragedy is that we will never know, for the young 35th president of the United States never got the chance to serve a complete term or live a full life. Because he was killed by a bullet on November 22, 1963, historians—and ordinary citizens—can only guess what Kennedy might have become if he had been granted a longer life span.

2 However, if we look at what Kennedy did manage to do in his brief 46 years, we can get a glimpse of a complex, charming person who was capable of many things. Although born to wealth, his childhood was far from easy, for he was sickly and often hospitalized. In spite of this, he wrote a published book, *Why England Slept*, when he was only a college student, and then went on to serve heroically in World War II. As skipper of patrol boat PT-109, he saved the life of a wounded crew member after the boat was torpedoed. Kennedy swam for a long distance, towing the man. As a result, Kennedy injured his back and would suffer pain for much of the rest of his life. **3**

As a political figure, Kennedy was known for his personal style. Handsome and intelligent, he delighted in making witty responses to reporters at press conferences. **4** His personal popularity helped him when he announced ambitious programs, such as the goal of sending astronauts to the moon by the end of the 1960s. Many people at the time doubted it could be done, but Kennedy had the personal magnetism to convince the nation to try—and it worked. **5**

If Kennedy were still alive today, he would be an old man. What achievements would he look back on with pride? Sadly, we will never know them all.

Guided Questions

1 What is the thesis statement of this essay?

2 What is the topic of this paragraph?

3 What kinds of supporting details are presented in this paragraph?

4 If the writer had included one or two witty things that Kennedy said, using Kennedy's exact words, what kind of supporting detail would that be?

5 What information could you add to this paragraph to develop it more fully?

 Measuring Up® to the California Content Standards

1. How might opinions from authorities strengthen this essay?

   _____

   _____

   _____

2. In what specific places in the essay would you insert opinions from authorities?

   _____

   _____

   _____

3. The concluding paragraph of this essay restates the main idea of the first paragraph. How does the writer keep the conclusion from seeming too repetitious?

   _____

   _____

   _____

4. What are the strengths and weaknesses of the topic of this essay, as a student essay?

   _____

   _____

   _____

Apply   **Directions** Read the prompt below. Then answer the questions that follow it.

> Write an essay analyzing the qualities that make a good leader.

1. Main Idea or Thesis for Essay

    _____

    _____

2. What qualities did each of the people you listed have?

    _____

    _____

3. Now brainstorm ideas for your essay by jotting down words and phrases that come to mind when you think about good leaders.

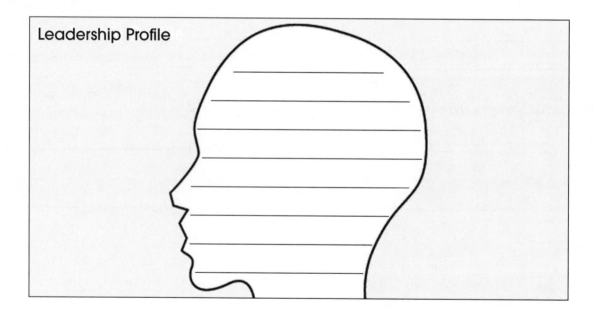

4. Read over your answers to items 1–3 above. What is the most important idea about leadership that you would like to express? Write it as a thesis statement.

    _____

    _____

Measuring Up® to the California Content Standards

Assessment Practice **Directions** Read the passage that follows. Then answer questions 1–5.

Unintended Inventions
by Urica Simpson

[1] If you'd like to create a great invention, try making some mistakes. [2] That's one lesson that can be learned from the history of inventions. [3] Many of the things we take for granted today were invented by accident, by people who were looking for other results entirely.

[4] For example, take eleven-year-old Frank Epperson. [5] One cold day early in the twentieth century, Frank was on his back porch, mixing soda powder and water with a stick. [6] He forgot to bring his mixture in at bedtime, so the soda water froze overnight with the mixing stick stuck inside. [7] A frozen beverage on a stick-what might that be? [8] Frank didn't do anything about it at the time, but years later, as an adult, he remembered his invention and called it the Popsicle.

[9] If you want to eat a Popsicle, one place not to put it is a microwave oven. [10] But did you know that the idea for the microwave oven came to its inventor by chance? [11] Scientist Percy Spencer was in his laboratory one day when he realized that the chocolate bar in this pocket had suddenly melted. [12] It had happened when he walked past a machine that sent out microwaves for radar. [13] The ordinary person might not think that radar and microwave ovens have anything in common, but Percy Spencer found meaning in that chance event.

[14] Lots of other things, from Post-It notes to the World Wide Web, have been invented by people who didn't realize at first what they had stumbled upon. [15] So is making mistakes enough to make you a great inventor? [16] No, the key is to understand your mistakes when they happen. [17] Keep your mind open to unforeseen results and unexpected opportunities. [18] Even if you don't invent a wonderful appliance, you'll probably become a more interesting person.

1. **Which is the thesis statement of the essay?**

   A Sentence 2

   B Sentence 3

   C Sentence 14

   D Sentence 18

2. **Which of the following passages from the essay does not cite an example?**

   A " If you'd like to create a great invention, try making some mistakes."

   B " Scientist Percy Spencer was in his laboratory one day when he realized that the chocolate bar in this pocket had suddenly melted."

   C " For example, take eleven-year-old Frank Epperson."

   D " Lots of other things, from Post-It notes to the World Wide Web, have been invented by people who didn't realize at first what they had stumbled upon."

3. **According to the essay, which of the following is the best way of becoming an inventor?**

   A Take out an application for a patent.

   B Search the Internet for solutions to your problem.

   C Look for unexpected opportunities in your mistakes.

   D Get a job with a company of inventors.

4. **Which of the following sentences states a fact, not an opinion?**

   A Sentence 4

   B Sentence 7

   C Sentence 14

   D Sentence 17

5. **Which of the following ideas is supported by details or evidence in the essay?**

   A Great inventions come from careful planning and execution.

   B It's more important to be an interesting person than to invent something.

   C Ordinary people are not capable of the type of thinking needed to invent.

   D It's acceptable to make mistakes if you learn from them.

Writing Strategies 9.1.5 Synthesize information from multiple sources and identify complexities and discrepancies in the information and the different perspectives found in each medium (e.g., almanacs, microfiche, news sources, in-depth field studies, speeches, journals, technical documents).

When you write a research paper, you use information from multiple sources. Once you have gathered your sources, you evaluate how useful each one will be.

- Decide how complete and accurate the information in a source is. What are the author's qualifications? Does the author show a bias? How up to date is the information? What other information do you need to gather?

- Determine the relevance of each source to your topic and your particular purpose. For example, letters from soldiers during the Civil War would be a good source of first-hand information about the war. An article in a medical journal would be a good source of in-depth information about a disease and its effects.

- Look for discrepancies, or disagreements, among your sources. For example, two biographers writing about the same person might give different dates of major events in the person's life. Be sure to check another source to verify the information.

- Decide whether any of the information in one of your sources needs to be clarified. For example, an author might assume the reader understands technical terms that the general reader does not know. Look for another source to clarify the information.

The two main places to do informational research are the library and the Internet. Most libraries now offer access to the Internet, so they are a two-in-one source.

Most libraries have a circulation section and a reference section. Materials may be borrowed from the circulation section, but not from the reference section. Research for school papers will usually take you to both areas. Library materials include:

- **Trade books:** books written by individuals on specific topics, such as biographies, autobiographies, personal recollections, and collections of letters.

- **Reference books:** dictionaries, encyclopedias, thesauruses, almanacs, field studies, directories, yearbooks, bibliographies, indexes, biographical indexes, etc., in specialized fields as well as in general; including continually updated reference series such as the *Readers' Guide to Periodical Literature*, the *New York Times Index, Facts on File*, and *Contemporary Authors*. Good reference books are often the best place to start your research and obtain basic information.

- **Microfilm and microfiche:** camera-film records of documents, such as old newspapers, which can be viewed on projectors at the library, and sometimes printed out.

- **Electronic media:** videotapes, audiotapes, CDs, CD-ROMs, audiobooks, etc.

- **Periodicals:** magazines and journals.

- **The Vertical File:** a file of pamphlets, circulars, clippings, and miscellaneous printed information on varied topics arranged alphabetically in a file cabinet.

The **Internet** is a worldwide linkage of electronic information networks. To find information on the Internet (or Net), you use a **search engine**, an online service that quickly scours the entire Net to find references to your topic. You provide key words that you think will bring up the most useful Web sites. One of the most popular search engines is Google™. Sometimes the search engine will provide hundreds of sites related to your key words. Often it is not useful to go beyond the first page of related sites.

Guided Reading Instruction

Directions Read the following passage of the first draft of a student essay. Use the questions in the margin to guide your reading.

Becoming Mark Twain
by Ronald Yuan

Novelist, humorist, newspaperman, public speaker, book publisher, failed prospector, would-be inventor, and former cub pilot on a Mississippi riverboat, Mark Twain is one of the larger-than-life real heroes who popped up in the American West in the 1800s. He was born in 1835 in Missouri under the name of Samuel Langhorne Clemens. **1** Growing up in the river port of Hannibal, he witnessed the evils of slavery, which he later wrote about in his great novel, *The Adventures of Huckleberry Finn* (1884). **2** At the same time, he thrilled to the sight of riverboats plying north and south with their paddle wheels churning the water; and his apprenticeship with a printer marked his first acquaintance with the business of writing.

As a young man, Clemens tried many different occupations and failed at most of them. Early during the Civil War, he headed west to Nevada with his brother and tried to strike it rich in the silver boom that was then going on. However, claim jumpers stole his only claim. "Broke and discouraged," according to William Weber Johnson **3** in *The Forty-Niners*, Clemens became a reporter for the *Nevada Territorial Enterprise* and the Virginia City *Examiner*. **4** He took the pen name Mark Twain, a two-word phrase, which is riverboat jargon for water two fathoms, or twelve feet, deep.

As luck would have it, Twain was forced to flee Nevada and ended up in San Francisco. There, his writing skill flowered as he worked alongside such notable California writers as Bret Harte and Ambrose Bierce **5** for such periodicals as the San Francisco *Call*. Twain became a popular humorist, and in 1865, he won national fame with the publication of his comic short story, "The Celebrated Jumping Frog of Calaveras County." **6**

Guided Questions

1 What sources might the writer have used to get information about Twain's boyhood?

2 What sources would give the publication date of *The Adventures of Huckleberry Finn*?

3 Who is William Weber Johnson?

4 Where might you find the texts of newspaper articles that Mark Twain wrote as a young reporter?

5 Where could you find out more about Bret Harte and Ambrose Bierce?

6 If you wanted to read "The Celebrated Jumping Frog of Calaveras County," how would you go about looking for it?

Directions Suppose you were a television producer. You are planning a miniseries on the life and times of Mark Twain. It will be about not only Twain himself, and his work, but the culture of the United States from 1835 until 1910. The miniseries will include America's literature, art, and music during the period and the people who created it. List ten possible sources of information for your miniseries, and for each source, state what kind of information you would expect to find in it.

Type of Source	Possible Information

Apply   **Directions** Read the prompt below. As part of your research for the essay, list five specific questions you would like answered. For each question, jot down one or two possible sources of information.

> Write an essay describing the changes that have occurred in your school since it first opened.

Question	Possible Source
1.	
2.	
3.	
4.	
5.	

Assessment Practice   **Directions** Read the portion of the student essay below. Then answer the questions that follow it.

Jupiter, the Mysterious Giant
by Anthony Singleton

[1] Imagine a spinning ball of gas weighing more than 300 times as much as the Earth, and more than 11 times as wide as our planet. [2] This ball has an atmosphere of poisonous methane and ammonia, with clouds moving swiftly across its surface and storms as large as small planets. [3] It has 61 natural moons, some of them planet size in themselves, and some merely the size of asteroids.

[4] We are talking about Jupiter, of course, the largest planet in our solar system, named fittingly enough for the king of the ancient Roman gods. [5] Science fiction has often portrayed what a manned trip to Jupiter might be like, but you can forget it as far as real-life astronautic trips there are concerned. [6] Jupiter lacks a solid surface to land on, and its gravity is so powerful that humans would not be able to survive it. All we can do is send probes with cameras and other sensing equipment to study what Jupiter is like—and that is doing a lot. [7] Since the Voyager and Galileo probes beginning in

1979, we have learned a great deal about what Jupiter is made of, and about such questions as how many moons the big planet has.

[8] These probes have allowed us to ask new questions, too. [9] For example, can Jupiter's second moon, Europa, contain life? [10] Its icy surface is webbed with cracks. [11] Many scientists believe that beneath the ice there is a watery ocean. [12] What's in the ocean? [13] Maybe someday one of our probes will find out.

1. **What would be the BEST source for basic factual information about Jupiter?**

    A   a speech by a NASA official about increasing funds for the latest Jupiter probe

    B   a magazine article on why space exploration is important

    C   a science fiction novel about astronauts going to Jupiter

    D   a general encyclopedia such as World Book or the Encyclopedia Britannica

2. **Keeping in mind that the writer's assignment was to write a research article on the planet Jupiter, where did the writer MOST LIKELY get the information in Sentence 4 that the planet Jupiter was named after a Roman god?**

    A   a book of Roman mythology

    B   a history of how things got their names

    C   an astronomy book about the solar system

    D   an up-to-date world atlas

3. **What is the MOST LIKELY reason that four different encyclopedias and textbooks, all of high quality, give four different figures for the number of Jupiter's moons: 14, 16, 39, and 61?**

    A   They were published in different years, and many new moons of Jupiter have been discovered recently.

    B   The definition of moon differs from author to author.

    C   The number 61 is a wild mistake; the others are reasonable guesses.

    D   Three of the four sources were translated from non-English languages.

4. **Which of the following would NOT be a good source for up-to-date information on the latest probes of the solar system?**

    A   the science section of a daily newspaper such as the *New York Times*

    B   a visual atlas of the solar system published this year.

    C   a book of the writings of the first astronauts who landed on the moon

    D   a lecture on space probes at a city planetarium

5. **If you want to keep informed about whether scientists find evidence of life on Europa over the next few years, what is your BEST strategy?**

    A   Read every issue of a respected science magazine, such as *New Scientist*.

    B   Start your own Internet Web site and ask everyone who visits it to give you the latest information about Europa.

    C   Telephone or e-mail a professional astronomer and ask if he or he believes that Europa will turn out to have life.

    D   Keep your home telescope trained on Europa and look at it every clear night.

Writing Strategies 9.1.2 Use precise language, action verbs, sensory details, appropriate modifiers, and the active rather than the passive voice.

Writing Strategies 9.1.9 Revise writing to improve the logic and coherence of the organization and controlling perspective, the precision of word choice, and the tone by taking into consideration the audience, purpose, and formality of the context.

The first rough piece of writing you do for any given project is called a **draft**. A first draft is always imperfect; it can always be improved. To improve your composition, you may **revise** it. You change words, add words, delete words, turn sentences around, combine sentences, place things in different orders, and sometimes rethink large portions of your text. There is no set number of drafts that it takes to complete a polished piece of writing. A writer revises until the composition is coherent and effective. Revisions can be made on paper, on a computer screen, or both.

Revising is a two-step process:

- **Evaluating** or judging your composition's content, organization, style, and appropriateness to purpose, audience, and occasion.

- **Making changes** based on your evaluation.

Organization

Does the text's organization match my purpose?

Are the ideas connected logically and in a way that is easy to follow?

Do the ideas hold together?

Should sentences be rearranged to make them flow more smoothly?

Content

Are the ideas well developed?

Have I supported my ideas?

Is more information, or more detailed support, needed?

Is there unnecessary material that should be edited out?

Style

Is the paper well written?

Is my voice original and individual or full of clichés?

Are the words and phrases exact or precise?

Have I used vivid verbs and appropriate modifiers?

Are the sentences varied?

Are most of the sentences in the active rather than the passive voice?

Appropriateness

Does the content match the audience and the purpose of the occasion?

Does the form I chose for my paper match the audience, purpose, and occasion?

Does my voice, style, and tone match the audience, purpose, and occasion?

Guided Reading Instruction

Directions Read the following passage. Use the questions in the margin to guide your reading. Then answer the questions that follow.

How to Make an Omelette
by Guy Collins

To make a great omelette, the first thing you need to do is buy an omelette pan. (Or have an adult buy it. An adult should supervise this whole process, of course.) This is a small metal pan with rounded sides and a wood handle—rounded sides so you can stir the eggs as they cook, and wood handle so **1** ~~so not to have burned one's hand~~ you don't burn your hand. After "seasoning" the pan with oil according to the directions on the tag, never use it for anything but omelettes, and clean it only with water or, better still, salt and a paper towel—never soap.

1 Why did the author change the wording of this clause?

First prepare and cut up your filling ingredients—cheese, ham, green peppers, or whatever. Then, break **2** ~~the~~ two eggs into a bowl and beat them with a tablespoon of milk. Heat the pan at high heat, add butter, and wait until the sizzling stops and the butter foam has mostly disappeared. Then, dump the beaten eggs into the pan. Let them set for about five seconds. **3** ~~It doesn't have to be exactly five seconds—it can be six or eight or ten.~~ Then, start moving the pan back and forth over the burner so that the eggs don't stick. At the same time **4** with your fork stir the eggs in the pan so that the cooked parts lift up from the surface and the wet, raw parts get cooked. ~~With your fork.~~ Pushing with one hand on the handle and stirring with the fork in ~~the other hand~~, you're giving **5** ~~it~~ all the egg mixture a chance to get quickly cooked but not overcooked. **6** ¶ After about a minute, you should have a lumpy, fully cooked, but still moist heap of eggs in the pan. Turn off the heat and immediately pour the filling over the eggs. Then, with the fork, fold the egg in half over itself. **7** ~~Then eat!~~ Slide the omelette onto your plate, season with salt and pepper, and eat!

2 Why did the author replace "the" with "two?"

3 Why was this sentence deleted?

4 Why was the position of "with your fork" changed?

5 Why was "it" changed to "all the egg mixture?"

6 Why did the author decide to begin a new paragraph here?

7 Why were the instructions to the reader to begin eating moved?

1. Use the following evaluation guide to critique the essay, "How to Make an Omelette." Use the questions on page 184 to guide you.

Evaluation Form	
Area	**Comments**
Content	
Organization	
Style	
Appropriateness	

2. What did you learn from evaluating this essay that can help you with your own writing?

_____

_____

_____

_____

Apply   **Directions** Read the prompt below. Then follow the instructions after it.

> Write an essay that describes something you know how to do well. It may be a "how-to" essay but it does not have to be.

1. On the lines below, brainstorm ideas about your topic.

_____

_____

_____

_____

_____

_____

_____

_____

_____

_____

_____

2. Choose a purpose and audience for your response to the prompt.

_____

3. Make an informal outline briefly stating the main idea of each paragraph in your essay. You may have more than three paragraphs if necessary.

Paragraph 1: _____

Paragraph 2: _____

Paragraph 3: _____

4. Write your first draft.

Measuring Up® to the California Content Standards

5. Exchange your paper with a partner. Use the evaluation guide to help you offer suggestions on improving one another's work.

Evaluation Form	
Area	**Comments**
Content	
Organization	
Style	
Appropriateness	

Assessment Practice

Directions Read the beginning of the student essay below. Then answer the questions that follow it.

Finding the Lost Coast
by Kyoko L. Kishi

[1] One Friday morning last August, we were all sitting at breakfast when Dad said suddenly, "Let's get out of town this weekend!" [2] So we did! [3] We drove way north to Cape Mendocino in Humboldt County. [4] There, the visitor will find long, empty beaches with ropes of dark green kelp lying on the wet gray sand. [5] In the background, steep, foggy mountains keep the beaches sheltered from development. [6] As soon as I saw it, I knew it was a place I'd want to live.

[7] I'll never forget the moment when we got to the beach and looked back and saw a black horse standing on a green slope with fog swirling round him. [8] Looking like the whole Lost Coast was his kingdom. [9] I stood still and looked at it for a long time. [10] We parked in the parking lot of a county park and then walked to the beach. [11] Then my parents called me and I forced myself to say goodbye to "my" horse and rejoin our little expedition. [12] It was worth it, because of all the unforgettable stuff we saw. [13] There were sea urchins living in little pools at the base of gnarled rock stacks, drifting in and out with the splashes of waves. [14] Then there was the driftwood: big pieces of smooth gray wood molded by the waves, with furrows and holes that made them look like abstract sculptures. [15] Dad wanted to take one of them home as a living-room bench, but it was said by Mom that we should leave nature the way it is. [16] We strolled on the beach for hours, and then drove to Ferndale, where we had dinner and stayed at a lovely inn.

 Measuring Up® to the California Content Standards

1. **Why is the underlined part of sentence 4 inappropriate in this context?**

   A   The word *visitor* is too vague.

   B   The tone is too formal for this narrator and her purpose.

   C   The visitor will not actually find those things at Cape Mendocino.

   D   The vocabulary is too informal and conversational for this context.

2. **Which is the BEST revision of sentence 8?**

   A   Looking like the whole lost coast was his Kingdom.

   B   Looked like the whole Lost Coast was his kingdom.

   C   He looked like the whole Lost Coast was his kingdom.

   D   Looking, it seemed to me, like the whole Lost Coast was his kingdom.

3. **What is the problem in the order of sentences in the second paragraph?**

   A   Sentence 10 should be at the beginning of the paragraph.

   B   Sentences 8 and 9 should be reversed in order.

   C   Sentence 12 should be deleted, because it has no purpose.

   D   Sentences 14 and 15 should be reversed in order.

4. **The underlined word *stuff*, in sentence 12, should be replaced with the word or words—**

   A   plants.

   B   tourist attractions.

   C   sights.

   D   junk.

5. **How should the underlined part of sentence 15 be rewritten?**

   A   but then Mom is saying we should leave nature the way it is.

   B   but it was said by Mom that we should leave nature.

   C   but it was soon claimed by Mom that we should scorn nature to itself.

   D   but Mom said that we should leave nature the way it is.

Flo wrote the following rough draft of a report for social studies. It may contain errors. Read the report and answer questions 1 through 5.

(1) It was the weather. (2) Our beautiful, predictably warm and sunny Southern California climate was the main reason the movie industry came to Hollywood.

(3) In the year 1907, Hollywood was a quiet, lovely suburb of Los Angeles, known for hillside mansions and a hundred-plus-room hotel. (4) Back east, in New York and New Jersey and Chicago, people were first beginning to make motion pictures, but the residents of Southern California knew little about it until Colonel William Selig, head of the Selig Polyscope Company of Chicago, began shooting a film of *The Count of Monte Cristo*. (5) Bad weather in the Windy City shut the production down, and a better climate in which to make movies outdoors was sought by Selig. (6) Finally he went all the way west to the beach at Santa Monica.

(7) Delighted by the possibility of making movies all year long in a warm, attractive landscape, Selig soon opened a Los Angeles studio. (8) Several other eastern studios too. (9) The first one to set up shop in Hollywood was the Nestor Film Company, formerly of Bayonne, New Jersey. (10) The first film made in Hollywood was *The Law of the Range*.

(11) By the 1910s, this part of the state was home to many of the pioneers who first figured out the complicated task of how to make a movie. (12) DeMille's business partner kept horses in the barn, and when the horses were watered, DeMille had to pick up his feet or get sloshed. (13) For example, Cecil B. DeMille and his company rented part of a barn on Vine Street to make their first feature, *The Squaw Man*. (14) That was Hollywood in the old days: casual, rough, but already swelling with the studios, sets, and theaters that would mark it as one of the most important towns in the world.

  Measuring Up® to the California Content Standards

1. **What would be the BEST source for further details about the making of the first Hollywood movies?**

   A   a biographical dictionary

   B   a magazine article on the subject

   C   an encyclopedia

   D   letters written by a Hollywood resident of the time

2. **In sentence 5, "a better climate in which to make movies outdoors was sought by Selig" should BEST be rewritten as—**

   A   a warmer climate in which to make movies outdoors was sought by Selig.

   B   better weather Selig sought for making movies outdoors.

   C   a better climate in which to make movies outdoors was promised by Selig.

   D   Selig sought a better climate in which to make movies outdoors.

3. **Which would be the most coherent reordering of sentences in the last paragraph of the essay?**

   A   Delete Sentence 14 from the essay.

   B   Reverse the order of sentences 12 and 13.

   C   Place sentence 14 at the beginning of the paragraph.

   D   Switch the positions of sentences 11 and 13.

4. **In sentence 8, the word *too* would BEST be replaced by—**

   A   followed suit.

   B   as well.

   C   also.

   D   ensued additionally in the aftermath.

5. **Which detail directly supports the idea that Southern California's climate caused moviemakers to move here?**

   A   Hollywood in 1907 was a peaceful, lovely suburb.

   B   Cecil B. DeMille's first California production company was housed in a barn.

   C   Colonel Selig left Chicago because of bad weather there.

   D   The first movie company in Hollywood was the Nestor Film Company.

Writing Conventions 9.1.1 Identify and correctly use clauses (e.g., main and subordinate), phrases (e.g., gerund, infinitive, and participial), and mechanics of punctuation (e.g., semicolons, colon, ellipses, hyphens).

Use clauses and phrases to make your writing clear, descriptive, and varied. Punctuate all sentences correctly, especially when you use semicolons, colons, ellipses, and hyphens.

A **clause** is a group of words that has a verb and a subject. An **independent** or **main** clause expresses a complete thought. It can stand by itself as a sentence, or it can be linked to another clause. A **dependent** or **subordinate** clause does not express a complete idea, so it must be linked to an independent clause.

Before matches made it easy to start a fire, people had to keep a fire going all the time.
      [dependent clause]   **[independent clause]**

A **phrase** is a group of words without a subject and a verb used as a single part of speech.

- A **gerund** is a verb that acts as a noun. Gerunds always end in -ing. A **gerund phrase** includes a gerund and any modifiers (describing words) and may include a gerund object as well.

  Eating healthily was the subject of the pamphlet.
  The firefighters ran into the station without *removing their muddy boots.*

- A **participle** is a verb that acts as an adjective. It usually ends in *-ing*, *-ed*, or *-en*. A **participial phrase** contains a participle and its modifiers.

  The tree was *thoroughly burned* and could not be saved.
  Throughout the San Diego area, the *constantly burning* brush was dangerous.
  That drug is a *proven* remedy for first-degree burns.

- An **infinitive** is a verb that usually comes after the word *to* and functions as a noun, an adjective, or an adverb. An **infinitive phrase** contains an infinitive and its object and modifiers.

  His only desire was *to serve dutifully.*
  To fight forest fires takes courage and endurance.

Use punctuation marks to help you clarify the meaning of sentences with clauses and phrases.

- Use a **semicolon** between independent clauses not linked with a coordinating conjunction (*and, nor, but, for, or, so,* or *yet*).

  Fire is our good friend; fire is our deadly foe.

- Use a **colon** between independent clauses when the second clause explains the first. The second clause begins with a capital letter.

  Fire is vital in our lives: It heats our homes, lights our cities, and cooks our food.

- Use **ellipses**, three spaced dots, to show that something has been omitted.

  The firefighter said, "It's really dangerous . . . but we have the blaze under control."

- Use a **hyphen** in some compound adjectives, numbers, and prefixes.

  The *well-organized* squad of *twenty-four* firefighters are *pro-American*.

Guided Reading Instruction

Directions Read the student essay below. Use the questions in the margin to guide your reading.

Firefighters Fight More Than Fire
by Courtney Kassinger

1 When a traffic accident traps passengers in a car, Firefighters are there to

help. **2** Firefighters wait^ing for the emergency calls It is often harrowing but

important **3** **4** Because approximately seventy-five percent of the calls that

come into fire departments are medical emergencies. **5** Firefighters help^ing people

injured in a bridge collapse, a mine accident, and a hiking accident These are

common occurrences. **6** Firefighters use special equipment such as the jaws of

life. to pry They work by prying apart the metal doors and roof of a mangled car.

7 "It's all in a day's work. ○○○ Many firefighters are Emergency Medical

Technicians: We are trained to give medical care until a person can get to the

hospital. Some EMTs receive advanced training as well. We're always happy to

help," says firefighter Ruth Greenspan.

Guided Questions

1 Why did the writer combine the first two clauses? *To join*

2 How did the writer improve the next two sentences?

3 Why did the writer add this sentence to the previous one?

4 Why did the writer insert a hyphen between the words *seventy* and *five*?

5 How did the writer combine these two sentences? *He turned it into a gerund.*

6 Why did the writer combine these sentences?

7 Do you think that eliminating the words in the quote improves it? Why or why not?

Apply   **Directions** Edit the first draft of the essay below. Look for opportunities to combine sentences using phrases and clauses. Correct any errors.

Forest Fires
by José Alvarez

Fire spotters in lookout towers watch for smoke. They are the first line of defense in a forest fire. Fighting a fire involves applying chemicals. Fire fighters also use on-site efforts. Often by parachuting right into the fire. Fire retardant chemicals are dropped on fires from airplanes to slow down and cool the flames. The chemicals are nicknamed "sky jello" because of their color and texture. Firefighters are battling a fire deep in the forest. They have to know their way around. GPSs (global positioning systems) help forest rangers. The forest rangers provide up to the minute maps for the firefighters. Forest fires are dangerous. Yet planned and controlled fires also remove extra fuel. Firefighters help prevent and control forest fires. They help preserve the forests for today and tomorrow.

Assessment Practice

For questions 1 through 5, choose the answer that is the most effective substitute for each sentence or underlined part of the sentence. If no substitution is necessary, choose "Leave as is."

1. **We picked up the injured bird. We could see that it had a broken wing.**

    A   We picked up the injured bird, we could see that it had a broken wing.

    B   We picked up the injured bird; and its broken wing.

    C   Picking up the injured bird, we could see that it had a broken wing.

    D   Leave as is.

2. **Running out of gas on the highway can be an upsetting experience.**

    A   Having run out of gas on the highway

    B   Running out of gas on the highway,

    C   Running out of gas on the highway:

    D   Leave as is.

3. **We have a fixed policy. We will not be undersold.**

    A   We have a fixed policy, and we will not be undersold.

    B   We have a fixed policy. . . . We will not be undersold.

    C   We have a fixed policy; and we will not be undersold.

    D   Leave as is.

4. **The quick witted explorer Hernando Cortés had his sailors cultivate the cocoa bean; as a result, Western European nations soon discovered and enjoyed the treat.**

    A   The quick witted explorer Hernando Cortés had his sailors cultivate the cocoa bean, as a result, Western European nations soon discovered and enjoyed the treat.

    B   The quick-witted explorer Hernando Cortés had his sailors cultivate the cocoa bean; as a result, Western European nations soon discovered and enjoyed the treat.

    C   The quick witted explorer Hernando Cortés had his sailors cultivate the cocoa bean: and as a result, Western European nations soon discovered and enjoyed the treat.

    D   Leave as is.

5. **We were outside in the garden. The cat knocked over the vase in the living room.**

    A   We were outside in the garden, the cat knocked over the vase in the living room.

    B   Being outside in the garden, the cat knocking over the vase in the living room.

    C   While we were outside in the garden, the cat knocked over the vase in the living room.

    D   Leave as is.

Writing Conventions 9.1.2 Understand sentence construction (e.g., parallel structure, subordination, proper placement of modifiers) and proper English usage (e.g., consistency of verb tenses).

The following points will help you write logical and effective sentences.

- **Parallel Structure** Put ideas of the same rank into the same grammatical structure.

  NOT   *Mailing* a letter early is better than to *run* the risk of its arriving late.

  BUT   *Mailing* a letter early is better than *running* the risk of its arriving late.

- **Subordination** Place less important ideas in the subordinate clause.

  NOT   He wore a big hat to the game. The TV camera focused on him.

  BUT   Because he wore a big hat to the game, the TV camera focused on him.

- **Proper Placement of Modifiers** To avoid confusion, place a modifier as close as possible to the word it describes.

  NOT   George caught sight of the train passing *through the kitchen door*.

  BUT   *Through the kitchen door* George caught sight of the train passing.

- **Consistency of Tenses** Keep the verbs in your sentence in the same tense unless you are dealing with events that happen at different times.

  NOT   He *rushed* into the house and *closes* the door in my face.

  BUT   He *rushed* into the house and *closed* the door in my face

Guided Reading Instruction

Directions Read the first part of the student essay below. Use the questions in the margin to guide your reading.

The World of Water
Hi-jing Yu

1 When you last went to the beach, you ~~see~~ *saw* that the ocean is always moving. **2** Because the tide rises and falls every day, the pull of gravity comes from the sun and moon. **3** Currents help the water carry heat to cold places, move plants and animals along, and ~~are propelling~~ *propel* boats from port to port.

4 The Gulf Stream is one of the world's strongest currents and it ~~kept~~ *keeps* a lot of people warm. **5** It almost starts south of Florida and travels all the way to Europe. **6** When they flow toward the north and carry warmth from the equator to cooler areas, the currents come to the Gulf of Mexico. **7** We came upon the Pacific Ocean rounding the corner. **8** It was so beautiful, peaceful, and ~~calmed us~~ *calm*.

1 Why did the writer make this change?

2 Why did the writer switch the order of clauses?

3 Why did the writer change *are propelling* to *propel*?

4 What error did the writer correct in this sentence?

5 What problem did the writer fix here?

6 How did the writer improve this sentence?

7 What is the purpose of this change?

8 What problem did this change correct?

Apply   **Directions** Continue reading this student essay and help Hi-Jing edit it. Look for problems in parallel structure, subordinate ideas, placement of modifiers, and consistency of tenses. Write your corrections on the text.

Gifts from the Sea
Hi-jing Yu

Oceans give us many gifts, including salt, food, and powering from water. Today, salt farms in China still produce salt that was being used mainly for seasoning food. People in shallow water build low walls from earth. The water evaporates. The salt crystals are left. Fishing boats use huge nets to catch herring, tuna, and mackerel, while big fish such as swordfish and tuna were caught with a harpoon. Seaweed is used to make toothpaste, ice cream, and for painting. From the water around Japan, the Japanese use the seaweed that grows there. Coal and oil take a long time to replace. Water power is important because it does not use up resources such as these.

Assessment Practice

For questions 1 through 5, choose the answer that is the most effective substitute for each sentence or underlined part of the sentence. If no substitution is necessary, choose "Leave as is."

1. **Washing dishes, doing the laundry, and to take out the trash are household chores that some people get done on weekends.**

   A Washing dishes, doing the laundry, and taking out the trash

   B Washing dishes, doing the laundry, and having taken out the trash

   C Washing dishes, to do the laundry, and to take out the trash

   D Leave as is.

2. **Joe found a letter in the mailbox that didn't belong to him.**

   A Joe finds a letter in the mailbox that didn't belong to him.

   B In the mailbox that didn't belong to him Joe found a letter.

   C Joe found a letter that didn't belong to him in the mailbox.

   D Leave as is.

3. **In a modern car factory, sheets of metal and assorted parts go in one end; cars came out the other end.**

   A parts go in one end; cars come out the other end.

   B parts go in one end; cars had been coming out the other end.

   C parts going in one end; cars came out the other end.

   D Leave as is.

4. **Whether people visit California for pleasure or work, they admire the beautiful scenery.**

   A Whether they admire the beautiful scenery, people visit California for pleasure or work.

   B Whether people visit California, they admire the beautiful scenery for pleasure or work.

   C Whether people visit California for pleasure or work, they admired the beautiful scenery.

   D Leave as is.

5. **Damon heard the huge flock of migrating birds in his tent that he had pitched near the lake.**

   A In his tent that he had pitched near the lake, Damon heard the huge flock of migrating birds.

   B Damon heard in his tent that he had pitched near the lake the huge flock of migrating birds.

   C The huge flock of migrating birds was heard by Damon in his tent that he had pitched near the lake.

   D Leave as is.

Writing Conventions 9.1.3 Demonstrate an understanding of proper English usage and control of grammar, paragraph and sentence structure, diction, and syntax.

Keep the following guidelines in mind when you revise and proofread your work.

Usage

- Have you followed the rules of standard English usage?

- Did you check to make sure the words you used mean what you think they mean?

- Have you checked for commonly mistaken words such as *beside* and *besides*?

Structure

- Are your paragraphs well organized?

- Did you use simple, compound, and complex sentences to create a varied style?

- Have you used clauses in the right places?

- Did you put matching ideas in parallel structure?

- Are all modifiers placed as closely as possible to the words they modify?

- Did you use all verb tenses consistently?

Diction

- Did you use specific words that fit your topic?

- Did you use colorful words to help readers form vivid images?

Grammar

- Do your subjects and verbs agree?

- Have you checked for agreement of pronouns and antecedents?

- Is every sentence complete, without sentence fragments and run-ons?

- Have you correctly used verb tenses?

Mechanics

- Have you spelled all words correctly?

- Have you punctuated each sentence correctly?

- Have you capitalized proper nouns and the first words in sentences?

Guided Reading Instruction

Directions Read the following passage. Use the questions in the margin to guide your reading. Then answer the questions that follow.

My Hero
Tuyet Tran

1 I admire my grandfather because he was patient and ~~always~~ working hard ^hard ^. **2** In vietnam in the old days, people did not have many of the modern conveniences that we take for granted today, such as electricity, indoor plumbing, or cars. **3** The lack of technology and his poverty made life difficult ^but^ My grandfather persevered. **4** My grandfather had a lot of ~~patients~~ ^patience^. **5** First thing every morning, he lit the fire in the stove ^and placed a simple tripod made of steel called a "Cieng" above the coals.^ **6** Sometimes it ~~takes~~ ^took^ him thirty minutes or even more to get the fire started because the wood, grass, or rice stalks ~~are~~ ^were^ damp. **7** He slowly and carefully tended the fire, ^so that^ we could have our bowl of hot rice when we got up in the morning.

8 My grandfather never seemed to sit still ; from dawn to dark, he worked without a break. **9** In the old days, houses in Vietnam ~~was~~ ^were^ made of big stalks of bamboo that often needed to be repaired. **10** My grandfather replaced ^broken stalks of^ bamboo, took care of his ^five^ grandchildren, and even cooked food for other families ^while his daughter worked,^. **11** Because we had no water indoors, |from wood and banana leaves| my grandfather built a small bathroom outside. **12** I admire my grandfather, ~~alot~~ ^a lot^ because he kept me warm, fed me, and kept me safe and comfortable. **13** he is my hero ~~for his courage and kind heart and he has helped me in many wonderful ways.~~

1 What problem did the writer find and correct in this sentence?

2 Why did the writer make this change?

3 Why did the writer combine these two sentences?

4 Why did the writer change *patients* to *patience*?

5 Why did the writer add this phrase?

6 Why did the writer make this change?

7 What error did the writer correct here?

8 Why did the writer add a colon here?

9 Why did the writer change *was* to *were*?

10 Why did the writer add these words?

11 Why did the writer switch the order of the clauses?

12 Why did the writer change *alot* to *a lot*?

13 Why did the writer make these two changes?

Apply   **Directions** Help Jean-Baptiste correct the first draft of his essay below. Use editing and proofreading symbols to mark your corrections.

Where Did All the Dinos Go?
Jean-Baptiste Vera

Dinosaurs nearly roamed the earth for 150 million years then they suddenly died out but no one knows exactly why. Dinosaur bones have been found in so many different parts of the world. scientists have had a hard time coming up with a single explanation for there sudden disappearance.

There are a lot of theories however and some of them are wild. Some observers, for example, have suggested that the dinosaurs could have died because of sickness. That seems unlikely. They were dispersed all over the world. There is also a theory that dinosaurs dissappeared because of overcrowding. One of several well-regarded theories concern food sources. According to these scientists, the dinosaurs ate too many bad things. They did not have a well-developed sense of taste. The dinosaurs did not realize that they are eating something that would harm them.

These theories remain just that—theories. However, research is continuing and maybe some day we had the answer to this fasinating mystery.

Assessment Practice

For questions 1 through 5, choose the answer that is the most effective substitute for each sentence or underlined part of the sentence. If no substitution is necessary, choose "Leave as is."

[1] In 1950, 400 American sportswriters and broadcasters selected Jim Thorpe as the greatest all around athlete and football player of the first half of the 20th century. [2] A sac and fox indian, Thorpe was born in Oklahoma in 1888. [3] Although he was a very good high school athlete. He stunned the entire world with his brilliant performance at the 1912 Olympic Games in Stockholm. [4] There, he won gold medals in both the pentathlon and the decathlon; to date, no other athlete has ever duplicated his amazing achievement. [5] A year later, the International Olympic Committee learned that Thorpe had accepted money in 1911 to play baseball so they took away Thorpe's amateur status, stripped him of his medals, and were erasing his achievements from the record books.

1. **In 1950, 400 American sportswriters and broadcasters selected <u>Jim Thorpe as the greatest all around athlete and football player of the first half of the 20th century.</u>**

   A   Jim Thorpe as the greatest all around athlete and football player of the first half of the 20th century.

   B   Jim Thorpe; as the greatest all around athlete and football player of the first half of the 20th-century.

   C   Jim Thorpe as the greatest all-around athlete and football player of the first half of the 20th century.

   D   Leave as is.

2. **<u>A sac and fox indian,</u> Thorpe was born in Oklahoma in 1888.**

   A   A Sac and Fox indian, Oklahoma in 1888.

   B   A Sac and Fox Indian,

   C   A sac and fox Indian

   D   Leave as is.

3. **<u>Although he was a very good high school athlete.</u> He stunned the entire world with his brilliant performance at the 1912 Olympic Games in Stockholm.**

   A   He was a very good high school athlete,

   B   Although he was a very good high school athlete,

   C   Although he was a very good high school athlete:

   D   Leave as is.

4. **There, he won gold medals in both the pentathlon and the decathlon; to date, no other athlete has ever duplicated his amazing achievement.**

   A   There, he won gold medals in both the Pentathlon and the Decathlon; to date, no other athlete has ever duplicated his amazing achievement.

   B   There, he won gold medals in both the pentathlon and the decathlon, to date, no other athlete has ever duplicated his amazing achievement.

   C   There he won gold metals in both the pentathlon and the decathlon; to date, no other athlete has ever duplicated his amazing achievement.

   D   Leave as is.

5. **A year later, the International Olympic Committee learned that Thorpe had accepted money in 1911 to play baseball so they took away Thorpe's amateur status, stripped him of his medals, and were erasing his achievements from the record books.**

   A   A year later, the International Olympic Committee learned that Thorpe had accepted money in 1911 to play baseball, they took away Thorpe's amateur status, stripped him of his medals, and were erasing his achievements from the record books.

   B   A year later, the International Olympic Committee learned that Thorpe had accepted money in 1911 to play baseball, so they took away Thorpe's amateur status, stripping him of his medals, and were erasing his achievements from the record books.

   C   A year later, the International Olympic Committee learned that Thorpe had accepted money in 1911 to play baseball, so they took away Thorpe's amateur status, stripped him of his medals, and erased his achievements from the record books.

   D   Leave as is.

The following is a rough draft of an article a student wrote for the school newspaper about finding scholarship money for college. It may contain errors in grammar, punctuation, sentence structure, and organization. Some of the questions may refer to underlined or numbered sentences or phrases within the text. Read the article and then answer questions 1–10.

Paying for College

[1] According to some sources, $250 million in scholarship funds nearly goes unclaimed every year. [2] Other people, in contrast, argue that it is very hard for students and <u>their parents</u> to find these financial aid sources on their own. [3] College financial aid officers claim that the money would all be used if applicants looked more thoroughly for funds. [4] Consequently, a new industry is developing helping people looking for college scholarships. [5] This industry <u>used</u> computerized databases to locate as many as a hundred possible sources of financial aid for each applicant. [6] Most of the private funding <u>come</u> from traditional sources. [7] These sources include religious organizations, veterans groups, labor unions, and businesses. [8] There are also sources targeted for specific applicants. [9] For instance, there are scholarships for people who are twins, are children of New England fisherman, <u>or who have been writing with their left hands</u>. [10] Financial aid experts emphasize the main goal in the quest for scholarships. [11] You must find the aid package that best suits your needs. [12] "There's plenty of scholarship money available, they claim."

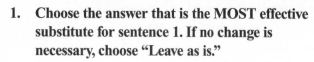

1. Choose the answer that is the MOST effective substitute for sentence 1. If no change is necessary, choose "Leave as is."

   A   According to some sources, $250 million in scholarship funds goes unclaimed nearly every year.

   B   According to nearly some sources, $250 million in scholarship funds goes unclaimed every year.

   C   According to some sources, nearly $250 million in scholarship funds goes unclaimed every year.

   D   Leave as is.

2. Choose the answer that is the MOST effective substitute for the underlined part of sentence 2. If no change is necessary, choose "Leave as is."

   A   there parents.

   B   they're parents.

   C   their parent's

   D   Leave as is.

3. How can you improve the organization of this paragraph?

   A   Switch sentences 2 and 3.

   B   Switch sentences 3 and 4.

   C   Delete sentence 4.

   D   Leave as is.

4. What is the BEST way to write sentence 4?

   A   Consequently, a new industry is developing that helped people looking for college scholarships.

   B   Consequently, a new industry is developing to help people looking for college scholarships.

   C   A new industry is consequently developing that is helping people looking for college scholarships.

   D   For people looking for college scholarships, a new industry is developing to help them.

5. Choose the answer that is the MOST effective substitution for the underlined portion of sentence 5. If no change is necessary, choose "Leave as is."

   A   will be using

   B   had used

   C   uses

   D   Leave as is.

6. Choose the answer that is the MOST effective substitution for the underlined portion of sentence 6. If no change is necessary, choose "Leave as is."

   A   comes

   B   came

   C   derive

   D   Leave as is.

7. What is the most effective way to combine sentences 7 and 8?

   A   These sources include religious organizations, veterans groups, labor unions, and businesses there are also sources targeted for specific applicants.

   B   These sources include religious organizations, veterans groups, labor unions, and businesses, there are also sources targeted for specific applicants.

   C   There are also sources targeted for specific applicants; these sources include religious organizations, veterans groups, labor unions, and businesses.

   D   These sources include religious organizations, veterans groups, labor unions, and businesses; there are also sources targeted for specific applicants.

8. Choose the answer that is the MOST effective substitute for the underlined portion of sentence 9. If no change is necessary, choose "Leave as is."

A   or have written with their left hands.

B   or are writing with their left hands.

C   or are left-handed.

D   Leave as is.

9. What is the most effective way to combine sentences 10 and 11?

A   Financial aid experts emphasize the main goal in the quest for scholarships you must find the aid package that best suits your needs.

B   Financial aid experts emphasize the main goal in the quest for scholarships, you must find the aid package that best suits your needs.

C   Financial aid experts emphasize the main goal in the quest for scholarships: You must find the aid package that best suits your needs.

D   Financial aid experts emphasize the main goal in the quest for scholarships: you must find the aid package that best suits your needs.

10. What is the BEST way to write sentence 12?

A   "There's plenty of scholarship money available," they claim.

B   "There's plenty of scholarship money available", they claim.

C   They claim that there's plenty of scholarship money available.

D   Leave as is.

Focus on California Content Standards

Write biographical narratives. 9.2.1
a. Relate a sequence of events and communicate the significance of the events to the audience.
b. Locate scenes and incidents in specific places.
c. Describe with concrete sensory details the sights, sounds, and smells of a scene and the specific actions, movements, gestures, and feelings of the characters; use interior monologue to depict the characters' feelings.
d. Pace the presentation of actions to accommodate changes in time and mood.
e. Make effective use of descriptions of appearance, images, shifting perspectives, and sensory details.

A **biographical narrative** tells a story about a real person. The subject may be a historical figure or a person you know from everyday life. For example, a biographical narrative may tell about Dr. Jonas Salk, who discovered the polio vaccine, or it may tell about your own family doctor, who let you listen through her stethoscope. When you write a biographical narrative, keep the following points in mind.

- **Tell the story in chronological order.** Narrate the events in sequence, beginning with what happened first and ending with what happened last. Remember that exceptions are possible, however: You may use flashback to sketch in the background of the past, and foreshadowing to hint at the future.

- **Include interesting details.** Details help get your reader interested and also help show the reader why the events are significant to you.

- **Describe where the events take place.** Show how the subject of your biographical narrative was affected or shaped by the setting of his or her life. Describe any changes in setting.

- **Use specific details and sensory language.** Describe specific sights, sounds, and smells to help your reader see, hear, and feel the events.

- **Show what the person you have chosen for your narrative is thinking.** Use interior monologue and body language to help the reader understand your subject's thoughts, feelings, and motivations.

- **Pace your writing.** Exciting, suspenseful events should seem to move quickly, while sad or somber events should progress at a slower pace. You might devote more words to events that took a long time and fewer words to events that took a short period of time. On the other hand, you might decide to speed up a time-consuming event by narrating it in few words. Use your judgment, your sense of a good story, to maintain a pace that creates the desired mood.

Guided Reading Instruction

Directions Read the following biographical narrative. Use the questions in the margin to guide your reading.

Tio Leon's Wagon
by Nicholas Gutierrez

1 I wish I had been alive to see Tio Leon when he first began setting up his lunch wagon on the corner across the street from the construction site. **2** That was back in the early 1950s, when eighteen-year-old Tio Leon had decided all on his own to leave the fishing village in Jalisco and try the United States. **3** He didn't tell anybody his decision because he knew they might be able to talk him out of it. Only he kissed his Mama the night before and made her promise not to tell, and it must have been a terribly hard promise for her to keep. **4**

As soon as he got to San Diego he began looking for work, of course, but the construction sites turned him down because he was too skinny. "I can do anything!" he tried to tell them, in his limited English, but they just said, "Get out of here, kid," and sent him away. He ended up delivering groceries for a store, but he kept thinking, "I want more out of life than this." He was already thinking of us—his family, his descendants.

As he traveled around the oceanside neighborhood, delivering groceries on a rusty old foot-brake bike with a basket between its handlebars, he noticed the way the workmen would sit eating their lunches out of paper sacks. **5** It made him think, "What if they had a nice hot lunch they could buy right at the site?" **6**

In a nearby junk heap he found a kid's red metal wagon. He bought a tiny stove, the kind you take on a camping trip, with one burner. He loaded up with supplies: tortillas from the tortilleria down the street, and picadillo that he made himself at home, a shredded head of lettuce, sliced tomatoes, and limes and onions. The next morning, he wheeled his wagon to the construction site and sold out his first load of picadillo tacos.

Day after day he returned, and the construction workers lined up hungrily at the little red wagon. With his earnings he soon bought a used lunch van and set it up in the vacant lot across the street. The workers liked sitting on rocks in the lot, in the warm noonday sun, and watching the seagulls squawk overhead, flying above the marina. **7** Now Tio Leon had four burners and a grill, and could add new items: carnitas and chicken and posole and tortas. He began buying fresh fish fillets at the market before sunrise, and marinating it all morning in a chipotle sauce and grilling it for fish tacos.

8 As Tio Leon prospered, he paid for his younger brother, my grandfather Abuelo Paulo, to join him. Within two years they weren't a lunch wagon anymore, they were the owners of a restaurant, and they married the two nice young women they hired to help them. Today, I wait tables at the restaurant to save money for college—and I always recommend Tio Leon's Original Fish Tacos. **9**

Guided Questions

1 Who is the narrator of this biographical narrative? What is his relation to the subject?

2 Where and when do the events of this biographical narrative occur?

3 How does the narrative depart from strict chronological order?

4 How many different characters' perspectives have been shown so far in the narrative?

5 What details in the second and third paragraphs help make the characters and events more vivid?

6 Why does the writer tell what Tio Leon asked himself?

7 Circle the sensory words and phrases in this passage the writer included to help you visualize the setting.

8 What change occurs in the pace of the narrative in the last paragraph? Why?

9 How does the writer convey the significance the subject has for him?

Assessment Practice

✎ REMINDER

- ✎ Write your response to the prompt on the next page.

- ✎ Place a title on your response if you like.

- ✎ Try to sound out words you do not know how to spell. You may not use a dictionary.

- ✎ Write legibly. You may print or use cursive.

- ✎ Be neat.

Writing Task:

A person can affect the history of an entire family or community with a seemingly small action. Think of someone who has done this. It can be a person from history or someone you know from life.

Write a biographical narrative about the action this person took that affected others. Tell the event mainly in chronological order. Include sensory details, a clearly described setting, and interior monologue.

Checklist for Your Writing

Use the checklist below to help you do your best work.
Be sure to:
- ❏ read the description of the writing task carefully;
- ❏ clearly tell the sequence of events;
- ❏ indicate the importance or significance of the events;
- ❏ describe the setting;
- ❏ use sensory details;
- ❏ include interior monologue;
- ❏ pace the events.

Write responses to literature. 9.2.2
a. Demonstrate a comprehensive grasp of the significant ideas of literary works.
b. Support important ideas and viewpoints through accurate and detailed references to the text or to other works.
c. Demonstrate awareness of the author's use of stylistic devices and an appreciation of the effects created.
d. Identify and assess the impact of perceived ambiguities, nuances, and complexities within the text.

In a **literary response**, you show your understanding of a literary work that you have read. Keep the following points in mind when you write a literary response.

- **Present a thesis statement that shows that you have grasped the meaning of the literary work.** A thesis statement establishes the focus of your essay.

- **In each paragraph in the body of your essay, include a main idea statement that supports your thesis.** This statement usually appears at the beginning of the paragraph, but it may appear at the end or in the middle.

- **Use details from the selection to support your ideas.** Details are a form of evidence for your argument. Be sure you use your details accurately. If you use quotations, be sure to quote the literary work accurately.

- **Discuss the author's use of stylistic devices.** Go beyond merely identifying stylistic devices. Discuss the effect these devices have on the work. For example, if the author uses lots of short declarative sentences, how does this stylistic choice affect the work?

- **Discuss the effect of any ambiguities in the text.** For example, is a certain character both good and evil? Does the author both approve and disapprove of the character? Explain how the ambiguities, and their possible interpretations, affect the impact of the work.

- **End with a strong concluding statement.**

Guided Reading Instruction

Directions Read the following literary response. Use the questions in the margin to guide your reading.

Behind the Minister's Black Veil
by Francine Choi

1   Nathaniel Hawthorne's short story "The Minister's Black Veil" is subtitled "A Parable," and indeed it is a story that contains powerful moral lessons, using its characters as symbolic figures even though they are also realistic people from a quiet little New England village. The fact that Hawthorne combines the realistic and symbolic levels so effectively makes this story effectively chilling and thought-provoking.

2   This combined effect is visible from the story's opening paragraph. It is a totally ordinary Sunday morning in Milford. Families, bachelors, and maidens are walking to church, drawn by the cheerful tolling of the bell. But what has happened? The minister, Mr. Hooper, is wearing a black veil over his face. What detail could be both flimsier and more ominous in this context? Rumors fly. Has good Mr. Hooper gone mad? How little it takes to upset the equilibrium of a tidy little town!

    Only one person has the courage to ask Hooper directly for the reason why he wears the veil: his fiancée, Elizabeth. Hooper tells her—and the reader—that he is not doing penance for any specific sin, but for human sin in general—the sins we all bear. Elizabeth can't take it. She begs him to show her his face, but he won't, and she leaves. And Hooper, obeying his personal vow, spends the rest of his life lonely, an object of dread and curiosity behind his crepe mask.

3 Is Hawthorne saying that people can't take the truth? Is he saying that even our loved ones can only accompany us so far in our private journeys? Either interpretation adds to the reader's feeling that the author, by covering his protagonist's face, is uncovering deep and painful realities. **4**

    On his deathbed, Hooper finally delivers his ultimate insight into the causes and effects of his wearing the veil. It has been a sign of mourning for a world in which everyone hides sins and everyone lives falsely: "I look round me, and, lo!, on every visage a Black Veil!" he cries with his last breath. **5** It is as if Hawthorne himself is crying it out to us, his readers. Everyone lives falsely, and he who points it out is shunned. It is a disturbing lesson from a sunny little American town. **6**

Guided Questions

1 In your own words, express the thesis of the first paragraph.

2 What sensory details from the story does writer Francine Choi include to strengthen her response?

3 Francine shows how plot and character support Hawthorne's ideas in the story. What specific aspect of plot and character does she describe, and what impacts do they have on the story?

4 What ambiguities, or different possible interpretations, does Francine Choi discuss? What impact do these ambiguities seem to have on Hawthorne's story?

5 Why did the writer choose to quote Hooper's last line of dialogue?

6 What is the conclusion of the literary response, and how does it refer back to the opening thesis?

Assessment Practice

Directions Read the selection below. Then write a response to the prompt that follows it.

Mike and the Grass
by Erma Bombeck

When Mike was three he wanted a sandbox and his father said, "There goes the yard. We'll have kids over here day and night and they'll throw sand into the flower beds and cats will make a mess in it and it'll kill the grass for sure." And Mike's mother said, "It'll come back."

When Mike was five, he wanted a jungle gym set with swings that would take his breath away and bars to take him to the summit and his father said, "Good grief. I've seen those things in backyards and do you know what they look like? Mud holes in a pasture. Kids digging their gym shoes in the ground. It'll kill the grass." And Mike's mother said, "It'll come back."

Between breaths, when Daddy was blowing up the plastic swimming pool, he warned, "You know what they're going to do to this place? They're going to condemn it and use it for a missile site. I hope you know what you're doing. They'll track water everywhere and you'll have a million water fights and you won't be able to take out the garbage without stepping in mud up to your neck and when we take this down, we'll have the only brown lawn on the block."

"It'll come back," smiled Mike's mother.
When Mike was twelve, he volunteered his yard for a campout. As they hoisted the tents and drove in the spikes, his father stood at the window and observed, "Why don't I just put the grass seed out in cereal bowls for the birds and save myself the trouble of spreading it around? You know for a fact that those tents and all those big feet are going to trample down every single blade of grass, don't you? Don't bother to answer," he said. "I know what you're going to say. 'It'll come back.'"

The basketball hoop on the side of the garage attracted more crowds than the Winter Olympics. And a small patch of lawn that started out with a barren spot the size of a garbage-can lid soon grew to encompass the entire side yard. Just when it looked like the new seed might take root, the winter came and the sled runners beat it into ridges and Mike's father shook his head and said, "I never asked for much in this life... "only a patch of grass."

And his wife smiled and said, "It'll come back."

The lawn this fall was beautiful. It was green and alive and rolled out like a sponge carpet along the drive where gym shoes had trod... "along the garage where bicycles used to fall . . . and around the flower beds where little boys used to dig with iced teaspoons.

But Mike's father never saw it. He anxiously looked beyond the yard and asked with a catch in his voice, "He will come back, won't he?"

✎ **REMINDER**

✎ Write your response to the prompt on the next page.

✎ Place a title on your response if you like.

✎ Try to sound out words you do not know how to spell.
You may not use a dictionary.

✎ Write legibly. You may print or use cursive.

✎ Be neat.

Writing Task:

In "Mike and the Grass," Mike's dad repeatedly complains that Mike will ruin the lawn by playing on it in various ways. His wife smilingly assures him that the grass will come back. At the end, Mike's dad has a thick, green lawn, but he no longer notices or cares.

Why doesn't Mike's Dad care about the lawn anymore? What does his final question, "He will come back, won't he?" mean, and how would you answer that question? Write an essay explaining these aspects of the story's meaning. Use details and examples from the story to support your ideas.

Checklist for Your Writing
Use the checklist below to help you do your best work.
Be sure to:
❏   read the description of the writing task carefully;
❏   provide a strong introduction, body, and conclusion;
❏   use specific details to support your response;
❏   demonstrate that you have understood the selection and the author's intent;
❏   write in an interesting style;
❏   correct any mistakes in grammar, usage, and mechanics.

Measuring Up® to the California Content Standards

Write expository compositions, including analytical essays and research reports. 9.2.3
a. Marshal evidence in support of a thesis and related claims, including information on all relevant perspectives.
b. Convey information and ideas from primary and secondary sources accurately and coherently.
c. Make distinctions between the relative value and significance of specific data, facts, and ideas.
d. Include visual aids by employing appropriate technology to organize and record information on charts, maps, and graphs.
e. Anticipate and address readers' potential misunderstandings, biases, and expectations.
f. Use technical terms and notations accurately.

An **expository composition** provides information and ideas about a topic. It might be about anything from how birds fly to how and why Silicon Valley grew. Some expository compositions are completely objective, while others may contain the author's subjective interpretation of the topic. Keep the following points in mind in your expository writing:

- **Present a thesis statement that clearly and interestingly expresses your controlling idea.** The introductory paragraph is the place to put this statement.

- **Develop the body of the composition by including ideas that back up the thesis.** In general, give each idea a paragraph of its own.

- **Provide details that support each idea.** Examples, facts, statistics, and expert opinions are among the kinds of supporting details.

- **You may include information to back up your ideas from primary or secondary sources.** A primary source consists of first-hand information. A secondary source provides information that has already been researched by another writer.

- **Discuss the relative value of the ideas and details you include.** By doing this, you show that you have thought about the information.

- **Be clear and well organized.** Choose an organizational pattern that suits your content and language that suits your audience and purpose.

- **End with a strong conclusion.** This may summarize your main points, restate your main idea, and leave your audience with something to think about.

Guided Reading Instruction

Directions Read the expository composition below. Use the questions in the margin to guide your reading.

Rome, My Favorite Empire
by Thomas O'Connor

Guided Questions

1 What makes an empire great? It may have something to do with how vast the empire was and how long it lasted. By those criteria, ancient Egypt and China may have been the greatest empires in human history. However, I think that ancient Rome was the equal of these in importance, even though it may not have lasted as long. The empire based in the city of Rome lasted for about 500 years, compared to the 3,000 that Egypt remained an empire. In addition, Rome was a mighty republic for almost 500 years before it became an empire. During those centuries, Rome prepared the way for the modern Western world that we now live in—and that is why I admire the Romans and look to them for inspiration.

1 State the writer's thesis in your own words.

2 I believe that the whole world today can learn from the Roman skill at governing. Rome conquered many nations, but once they were conquered, their people were treated fairly and given opportunities to succeed. At its height, the empire was at peace: The period from approximately 100 to 200, the Pax Romana, or "Roman peace," was one of the few times in all history that the entire Western world was without war. Roman law is still the basis of much European law today. Roman roads provided links for communication and trade across an entire continent. Roman armies were well-organized and superbly trained. Roman architecture was both beautiful and useful—not only buildings, but aqueducts and reservoirs for water supply.

2 How does the writer back up his thesis?

The above accomplishments were material things, but even more than that, I admire the spirit of the ancient Romans. **3** During the republic and the early empire, Roman patricians (the aristocrats) used their high position not for personal gain but for the good of the nation. They led honest, sober lives of integrity. An example was Cincinnatus, who was made dictator of Rome during a crisis, but who, after winning a war against neighboring tribes, returned to his farm to live in peace. The rich and powerful in today's world could learn from that example—and in fact, George Washington and some other early American leaders consciously modeled themselves on Cincinnatus. (And the city of Cincinnati, Ohio, honors his name still.) **4**

3 What idea does the writer develop in this paragraph?

5 The Romans were only human, and in its later years, the empire became corrupt. That was one reason why it fell. But that in a way is yet another lesson people today can learn from Rome—an ancient empire that can convey wisdom to the present.

4 What is the purpose of including the example of Cincinnatus?

5 How does the writer's conclusion tie the essay together?

Assessment Practice

✎ Write your response to the prompt on the next page.

✎ Place a title on your response if you like.

✎ Try to sound out words you do not know how to spell. You may not use a dictionary.

✎ Write legibly. You may print or use cursive.

✎ Be neat.

Writing Task:

In what ways do you think people two thousand years from now will admire and learn from the United States of today?

Write an expository essay in which you express your ideas on this topic of future history. Be sure to support your response with specific details, such as examples, facts, and statistics.

Checklist for Your Writing

Use the checklist below to help you do your best work.

Be sure to:

❑ read the description of the writing task carefully;

❑ support your ideas with specific details and examples;

❑ provide a strong introduction, body, and conclusion;

❑ use specific details to support your response;

❑ vary your sentences;

❑ correct any mistakes in grammar, usage, and mechanics.

Write persuasive compositions. 9.2.4
a. Structure ideas and arguments in a sustained and logical fashion.
b. Use specific rhetorical devices to support assertions (e.g., appeal to logic through reasoning; appeal to emotion or ethical belief; relate a personal anecdote, case study, or analogy).
c. Clarify and defend positions with precise and relevant evidence, including facts, expert opinions, quotations, and expressions of commonly accepted beliefs and logical reasoning.
d. Address readers' concerns, counterclaims, biases, and expectations.
e. Use technical terms and notations accurately.

In a **persuasive composition** a writer tries to persuade readers to do something or to believe something. Types of persuasive essays include newspaper editorials and election flyers. Keep the following points in mind when writing a persuasive essay:

• **Present a strong thesis statement that states your opinion or assertion.** Your assertion is the idea that you want readers to agree with or the action that you want them to take.

• **Make logical, emotional, or ethical appeals to persuade your readers.** You might appeal to logic by using clear reasoning and providing facts and other evidence. You might appeal to emotion by using loaded words—words with strong positive or negative connotations. You might appeal to the readers' ethical concerns by discussing values you and your audience share.

• **Support your opinion or assertion.** You might include case studies, examples, personal anecdotes, and analogies to support your thesis.

• **Address your audience's concerns.** Understand the possible objections, biases, and expectations your readers may have, and try to answer them.

Guided Reading Instruction

Directions Read the following passage. Use the questions in the margin to guide your reading.

Needed: Speed Bumps on Market Avenue
by Noreen Hughes

1   Have you ever tried to walk across Market Avenue on a busy afternoon, say about five o'clock? I did just the other day, and it was not a pleasant experience. As you know, Market Avenue is five lanes across—two in each direction plus a turn lane in the center—and typically the traffic in the inner lanes goes zipping by while the cars in the outer lanes go at a crawling pace in search of the few available parking spaces. The "Walk" sign stays on for such a short time a slow walker can easily get caught in the middle of the street while trying to cross, especially the many older pedestrians on Market carrying shopping bags from store to store. Even leaving aside the pedestrian issues, there are numerous accidents on Market when cars with impatient drivers try to pass each other or turn in front of each other. One driver is trying to get through the shopping district as fast as possible, and the other is slowing down to read a "Sale" sign. The result: Wham! Bang! Crunch!

My solution? It's simply this: Install speed bumps on Market Avenue in the shopping district. That would slow all cars down to 25 miles per hour or less and greatly reduce collisions. **2**   Many of the drivers shopping on that street want to go slowly anyway; it's only the non-shoppers, the drivers just "passing through," who would be slightly inconvenienced. But is it really an inconvenience to go a little more slowly? **3**   Not if it means avoiding a possible accident. After all, which gets you to your destination faster: "crawling" at a mere 20 mph, or zooming through at 35 but crashing and having to wait for the police and the tow truck (and possibly having to go to the hospital)? **4**

Speed bumps have been used successfully for years in many cities, including our own. **5**   Several residential neighborhoods, including mine, have speed bumps to slow down traffic in areas where children play. Why can't the same solution be used in a commercial area, not because of children playing but because of cars smacking destructively into one another and pedestrians frightened to cross? **6**

Police Chief Robertson said in the *Daily American* just the other day, "We have to clear an average of two 'fender benders' each day from Market Avenue, and that in itself ties up traffic for long periods." **7**   I suggest that that is too many accidents! If you agree with me and with Chief Robertson—if you want to keep our streets safe for walking and shopping and for responsible, law-abiding drivers—let's all begin to raise this issue at neighborhood council meetings and in the pages of the *American*. If speed bumps can save even one life, or prevent one serious injury, it will be worth it for our whole community. **8**

1 What strategy does writer Noreen Hughes use in her first paragraph?

2 What is Noreen's basic assertion?

3 What possible objection on the part of readers does Noreen address?

4 How does Noreen address this objection?

5 What logical appeal does Noreen use here?

6 What technique does Noreen use in the phrases *children playing, cars smacking destructively into one another,* and *pedestrians frightened to cross?*

7 What is the purpose of including a quotation from the police chief?

8 What techniques does Noreen use to conclude her persuasive argument?

Assessment Practice

✎ **REMINDER**

✎ **Write your response to the prompt on the next page.**

✎ **Place a title on your response if you like.**

✎ **Try to sound out words you do not know how to spell. You may not use a dictionary.**

✎ **Write legibly. You may print or use cursive.**

✎ **Be neat.**

Writing Task:

Should traffic laws, such as speed limits, be enforced more strictly, or are they already enforced strictly enough?

Write a persuasive composition in which you try to convince the readers to agree with your opinion. Use specific reasons and examples.

Checklist for Your Writing

Use the checklist below to help you do your best work.
Be sure to:
❑ read the description of the writing task carefully;
❑ provide a persuasive argument;
❑ provide specific reasons and examples to support your argument;
❑ provide a strong introduction, body, and conclusion;
❑ vary your sentences;
❑ correct any mistakes in grammar, usage, and mechanics.

Measuring Up® to the California Content Standards

Write business letters. 9.2.5
a. Provide clear and purposeful information and address the intended audience appropriately.
b. Use appropriate vocabulary, tone, and style to take into account the nature of the relationship with, and the knowledge and interests of, the recipients.
c. Highlight central ideas or images.
d. Follow a conventional style with page formats, fonts, and spacing that contribute to the documents' readability.

A **business letter** is a formal correspondence about a business-related matter. For example, you might write a business letter to apply for a job, to complain about poor service in a store, or to request information for a report. Keep these points in mind when writing a business letter.

- **Choose either a block form or a modified block form.** In block form, all six parts of the letter align at the left-hand margin. Modified block form is more common: The heading, the closing, and the signature are placed on the right side of the page.

- **Address your audience appropriately.** Your tone should be formal and respectful and your language should follow the conventions of standard English usage.

- **At the opening of your letter, clearly state your reason for writing.** Remember that business people are busy, so get to the point right away.

- **In the body of your letter, state your major points.** Provide any necessary information the reader will need.

- **Close the letter formally.** Use a phrase such as "Sincerely yours" or "Yours truly."

Guided Reading Instruction

Directions Read the following business letter. Use the questions in the margin to guide your reading.

777 East Sunrise Drive
Los Angeles, California 90000
December 1, 2003 **1**

Ms. Shelley Gold
Colossal Talent Associates, Inc.
1 Colossal Drive
Beverly Hills, California 90052

Dear Ms. Gold:

2 I am a ninth grader at Excelsior High School here in Los Angeles, and I hope to enter the motion picture business someday as an agent or producer. Next summer, I will be sixteen, old enough to hold a job. I was wondering if you anticipate having the need for a summer intern at Colossal.

3 Although I am young, I feel I am fully qualified to begin learning the movie business from those like yourself who are best qualified to teach it. I also feel that I have aptitudes that would make me a useful addition to the staff at your agency. I have been writing and directing movies, using the family video recorder, for several years, and recently, my fifteen-minute short, "La Vida y El Muerte," won Honorable Mention in the "Tomorrow's Stars" competition held by *NewCal* Magazine. I enclose a copy of *NewCal's* review, which calls "La Vida y El Muerte" "an intriguing youthful vision of the vast scope of existence." I would be glad to send you a copy of the videotape upon request.

4 My outside interests have not led me to neglect my primary responsibilities, however. I am a hard worker who maintains an A- average in school. I am president and founder of the Future Filmmakers Club, and received the Perfect Attendance Award from the principal last year. (I am on the way to another such award this year.) To learn more about my school work and my personality, please feel free to contact Jason Johnson, Principal, Excelsior High School, 1286 Blank Expressway SE, Los Angeles, CA 90000, or Julieta Villa at the same school address. Ms. Villa is faculty advisor to the Future Filmmakers Club.

5 I look forward to hearing from you about the possibility of working for Colossal. If you would like me to visit your office for an interview, I am available any weekday after 3:30 P.M. My phone number is 555-0110. Thank you for your time and consideration.

Sincerely yours,

Eduardo Gutierrez, Jr.

Eduardo Gutierrez, Jr.

Guided Questions

1 What does the placement of the header tell you about the form of this letter?

2 What is the purpose of this letter?

3 What information does the writer include in this paragraph that would help him achieve his purpose?

4 How would the information in this paragraph help the writer achieve his purpose?

5 What is the purpose of the last paragraph?

Assessment Practice

✎ Write your response to the prompt on the next page.

✎ Follow business letter format.

✎ Try to sound out words you do not know how to spell. You may not use a dictionary.

✎ Write legibly. You may print or use cursive.

✎ Be neat.

Writing Task:

You bought a great-looking new pair of shoes, but two days afterward they began hurting your feet and causing blisters. The shoe store has refused to refund your money, because you have worn the shoes and because you threw out the receipt. Now, you decide to mail the shoes directly to the shoe company in the hope that they will be nicer.

Write a letter accompanying the returned shoes to Whose Shoes? Inc., 1888 Fidelman Street, Bronx, New York 10400. Explain the nature of your problem and what you want done. Use proper business letter format.

Checklist for Your Writing

Use the checklist below to help you do your best work.
Be sure to:

❑ read the description of the writing task carefully;

❑ use proper business letter format;

❑ explain the complaint and tell what you want done;

❑ correct any mistakes in grammar, usage, and mechanics.

Read the selection below. Then write a response to the prompt that follows it.

The Day Grandfather Tickled a Tiger
A True Story by Ruskin Bond

Timothy, our tiger cub, was found by my grandfather on a hunting expedition in the Terai jungles near Dehra, in northern India. Because Grandfather lived in Dehra and knew the jungles well, he was persuaded to accompany the hunting party.

Grandfather, strolling down a forest path some distance from the main party, discovered a little abandoned tiger about eighteen inches long, hidden among the roots of a banyan tree. After the expedition ended, Grandfather took the tiger home to Dehra, where Grandmother gave him the name Timothy.

Timothy's favorite place in the house was the living room. He would snuggle down comfortably on the sofa, reclining there with serene dignity and snarling only when anyone tried to take his place. One of his chief amusements was to stalk whoever was playing with him, and so, when I went to live with my grandparents, I became one of the tiger's pets. With a crafty look in his eyes, and his body in a deep crouch, he would creep closer and closer to me, suddenly making a dash for my feet. Then, rolling on his back and kicking with delight, he would pretend to bite my ankles.

By this time he was the size of a full-grown golden retriever, and when I took him for walks in Dehra, people on the road would give us a wide berth. At night he slept in the quarters of our cook, Mahmoud. "One of these days," Grandmother declared, "we are going to find Timothy sitting on Mahmoud's bed and no sign of Mahmoud!"

When Timothy was about six months old, his stalking became more serious, and he had to be chained up more frequently. Even the household started to mistrust him and, when he began to trail Mahmoud around the house with what looked like villainous intent, Grandfather decided it was time to transfer Timothy to a zoo.

The nearest zoo was at Lucknow, some two hundred miles away. Grandfather reserved a first-class compartment on the train for himself and Timothy and set forth. The Lucknow zoo authorities were only too pleased to receive a well-fed and fairly civilized tiger.

Grandfather had no opportunity to see how Timothy was getting on in his new home until about six months later, when he and Grandmother visited relatives in Lucknow. Grandfather went to the zoo and directly to Timothy's cage. The tiger was there, crouched in a corner, full-grown, his magnificent striped coat gleaming with health.

"Hello, Timothy," Grandfather said.

Climbing the railing, he put his arms through the bars of the cage. Timothy approached and allowed Grandfather to put both arms about his head. Grandfather stroked the tiger's forehead and tickled his ears. Each time Timothy growled, Grandfather gave him a smack across the mouth, which had been his way of keeping the tiger quiet when he lived with us.

Timothy licked Grandfather's hands. Then he showed nervousness, springing away when a leopard in the next cage snarled at him, but Grandfather shooed the leopard off, and Timothy returned to licking his hands. Every now and then the leopard would rush at the bars, and Timothy would again slink back to a neutral corner.

A number of people had gathered to watch the reunion, when a keeper pushed his way through the crowd and asked Grandfather what he was doing. "I'm talking to Timothy," said Grandfather. "Weren't you here when I gave him to the zoo six months ago?"

"I haven't been here very long," said the surprised keeper. "Please continue your conversation. I have never been able to touch that tiger myself. I find him very bad-tempered."

Grandfather had been stroking and slapping Timothy for about five minutes when he noticed another keeper observing him with some alarm. Grandfather recognized him as the keeper who had been there when he had delivered Timothy to the zoo. "You remember me," said Grandfather. "Why don't you transfer Timothy to a different cage, away from this stupid leopard?"

"But—sir," stammered the keeper. "It is not your tiger."

"I realize that he is no longer mine," said Grandfather testily. "But at least take my suggestion."

"I remember your tiger very well," said the keeper. "He died two months ago."

"Died!" exclaimed Grandfather.

"Yes, sir, of pneumonia. This tiger was trapped in the hills only last month, and he is very dangerous!"

The tiger was still licking Grandfather's arms and apparently enjoying it more all the time. Grandfather withdrew his hands from the cage in a motion that seemed to take an age. With his face near the tiger's he mumbled, "Good night, Timothy." Then, giving the keeper a scornful look, Grandfather walked briskly out of the zoo.

✎ **REMINDER**

✎   Write your response to the prompt on the next page.

✎   Place a title on your response if you like.

✎   Try to sound out words you do not know how to spell.
You may not use a dictionary.

✎   Write legibly. You may print or use cursive.

Writing Task 1:

In "The Day Grandfather Tickled a Tiger," the narrator recalls how his grandfather raised a tiger cub found abandoned in the forest. When the tiger grows up, it has to be transferred to a zoo. When Grandfather visits the zoo to see his tiger friend, something unexpected happens.

Write a literary response in which you analyze the meaning of the unexpected outcome of Grandfather's visit. Use details and examples from the story to support your ideas.

Checklist for Your Writing

Use the checklist below to help you do your best work.
Be sure to:
❑   read the description of the writing task carefully;
❑   provide a strong introduction, body, and conclusion;
❑   use specific details to support your response;
❑   demonstrate that you have understood the selection and the author's intent;
❑   write in an interesting style and vary your sentences;
❑   correct any mistakes in grammar, usage, and mechanics.

✎ REMINDER

✎ **Write your response to the prompt on the next page.**

✎ **Place a title on your response if you like.**

✎ **Try to sound out words you do not know how to spell. You may not use a dictionary.**

✎ **Write legibly. You may print or use cursive.**

✎ **Be neat.**

Writing Task 2:

Most people want success in life. But what does success mean? Is it the same for everyone, or is it different for each individual?

Write an essay explaining what success means to you. Share your reasons for identifying each quality. Give reasons for your ideas, and support your ideas with details and examples.

Checklist for Your Writing

Use the checklist below to help you do your best work.
Be sure to:

❏ read the description of the writing task carefully;
❏ support your ideas with specific details and examples;
❏ provide a strong introduction, body, and conclusion;
❏ select words that are suitable for your audience and purpose;
❏ vary your sentences;
❏ correct any mistakes in grammar, usage, and mechanics.

Comic Books Made Simple
by Daryl Edelman

[1] In general, comic books are made by team effort in an assembly-line process. [2] The editor shepherds the comic book. [3] It passes from writer to penciler, letterer, inker, and finally, colorist.

[4] The writer and editor begin the process by brainstorming ideas for a story. [5] They decide on a plot. [6] Once that is agreed upon, the ball is in the writer's court.

[7] The writer then writes a script, a page-by-page, panel-by-panel description of what the penciler is to draw. [8] Panels are boxed frames, which the penciler lays out on the blank page. [9] If the writer calls for a four-panel page, there will be four boxes with a drawing in each on the page. [10] The writer tells the setting, characters, action, captions, and sound effects in each panel. [11] He or she also writes the dialogue, which goes in word balloons. [12] Word balloons are round shapes with a tail pointing to the character who is speaking. [13] Additionally, the writer can call for a thought balloon in which a character's thoughts are lettered. [14] These are like word balloons except that they have scalloped edges like a cloud.

[15] The penciler draws on 11" by 17" bristol board, a heavy, absorbent paper. [16] After drawing everything the writer has called for, the penciler sends the penciled pages and the writer's script to the letterer. [17] The word balloons, thought balloons, captions, and sound effects have already been laid out by the penciler showing where they are to be placed. [18] The letterer uses ink to write in everything. [19] After the letterer is done, he or she sends the lettered, penciled page on to the inker.

[20] Inkers draw in ink over the pencil drawing. [21] They do not simply trace <u>but they are adding texture, weight, and shadow.</u> [22] Sometimes there are two inkers, first one to ink in the human figures, then one to ink in the background, such as buildings, trees, and machinery. [23] After the pages have been penciled, lettered, and inked, they are copied onto 8 1/2" by 11" inch paper and sent to the colorist.

[24] The colorist uses condensed watercolor ink to color in the black and white art. [25] He or she uses detailed references to make sure that each person, place, and thing is colored correctly. [26] Then the colorist writes codes, notes to the factory that tell what percentage of blue, yellow, red are to be mixed to make each color, in the margins of the page. [27] All the colors in a comic book are made by mixing blue, red, and yellow!

[28] The editor, who oversees the entire process, then gives the lettered and inked bristol board and the color guide to the production department. [29] Color film is made and the film is sent to the printing press. [30] The comic is printed on pulp paper, collated, and stapled, then shipped to a newsstand or comic book store near you.

1. Which of the following sentences, if inserted before sentence 1, would make the MOST effective opening sentence?

A A team effort involves a lot of people working well together to meet a common goal.

B The history of comic books is a long and complex one, which includes many interesting stories.

C Even if you have read many comic books in your life, you may never have given a thought to how they are made.

D Comic books are a specialized art form, so making a comic book involves the work of many artists.

2. What is the MOST effective way to combine sentences 2 and 3?

> The editor shepherds the comic book. It passes from writer to penciler, letterer, inker, and finally, colorist.

A The editor shepherds the comic book, because it passes from writer to penciler, letterer, inker, and finally, colorist.

B Since the editor shepherds the comic book, it passes from writer to penciler, letterer, inker, and finally, colorist.

C When the editor shepherds the comic book, it passes from writer to penciler, letterer, inker, and finally, colorist.

D The editor shepherds the comic book as it passes from writer to penciler, letterer, inker, and finally, colorist.

3. Which of the following ideas is supported by details or evidence in the essay?

A The penciler plays an important role in coming up with ideas for stories.

B The colorist does not actually color in the drawing.

C The main job of telling the story falls on the writer.

D The job of the penciler is to tell the writer what to do.

4. Which of the following would be the BEST source for further information about how comic books are created today?

A a biography of Walt Disney

B an encyclopedia article about computer animation in movies

C an instruction manual for comic book writers and designers

D a history of the early days of comic books

5. What is the MOST effective way to revise sentences 5 and 6?

> They decide on a plot. Once that is agreed upon, the ball is in the writer's court.

A Once they agree on the plot, the ball is in the writer's court.

B They decide on a plot, and after they agree on that, the ball is in the writer's court.

C Before they decide on a plot, the ball is in the writer's court.

D The ball is in the writer's court for the writer and editor to decide on a plot.

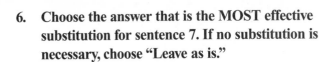

6. **Choose the answer that is the MOST effective substitution for sentence 7. If no substitution is necessary, choose "Leave as is."**

> The writer then writes a script, a page-by-page, panel-by-panel description of what the penciler is to draw.

A The writer then writes a script, this is a page-by-page, panel-by-panel description of what the penciler is to draw.

B The writer then writes a page-by-page script, whereas he gave a panel-by-panel description to the penciler.

C Then the writer writes a script for the penciler, having included a page-by-page, panel-by-panel description.

D Leave as is.

7. **Choose the answer that is the MOST effective substitution for sentences 10 and 11. If no substitution is necessary, choose "Leave as is."**

> The writer tells the setting, characters, action, captions, and sound effects in each panel. He or she also writes the dialogue, which goes in word balloons. Word balloons are round shapes with a tail pointing to the character who is speaking.

A In each panel, the writer tells the setting, characters, action, captions, and sound effects and writes the dialogue in word balloons— round shapes with a tail pointing to the character who is speaking.

B The writer tells in each panel the setting, characters, action, captions, and sound effects, and he or she also writes the dialogue, which goes in word balloons, which are round shapes with a tail pointing to the character who is speaking.

C The writer tells the setting, characters, action, captions, and sound effects and writes the dialogue in each panel in word balloons that are round shapes with a tail pointing to the character who is speaking.

D Leave as is.

8. **Choose the answer that is the MOST effective substitution for sentence 17. If no substitution is necessary, choose "Leave as is."**

> The word balloons, thought balloons, captions, and sound effects have already been laid out by the penciler showing where they are to be placed.

  A The penciler shows the placement of the word balloons, thought balloons, captions, and sound effects.

  B The penciler has already laid out where the word balloons, thought balloons, captions, and sound effects are to be placed.

  C Having already laid out the word balloons, thought balloons, captions, and sound effects, the penciler shows where they are to be placed.

  D Leave as is.

9. **Choose the answer that is the MOST effective substitution for the underlined part of sentence 21. If no substitution is necessary, choose "Leave as is."**

> They do not simply trace <u>but they are adding texture, weight, and shadow.</u>

  A but they are adding texture, as well as they create weight and shadow

  B but they have added texture, weight, and shadow

  C but they add texture, weight, and shadow

  D Leave as is.

10. **Choose the answer that is the MOST effective substitution for sentence 26. If no substitution is necessary, choose "Leave as is."**

> Then the colorist writes codes, notes to the factory that tell what percentage of blue, yellow, red are to be mixed to make each color, in the margins of the page.

  A Then the colorist writes codes, or notes to the factory, that tell what percentage of blue, yellow, and red are to be mixed in the margins of the page.

  B Then in the margins of the page the colorist writes codes, notes to the factory that tell what percentage of blue, yellow, and red are to be mixed to make each color.

  C Then the colorist writes codes, notes to the factory that tell what percentage of blue, yellow, red should have been mixed to make each color in the margins of the page.

  D Leave as is.

Read the selection below. Then construct a response to the writing prompt that follows it.

Zoo
by Edward D. Hoch

The children were always good during the month of August, especially when it began to get near the twenty-third. It was on this day that the great silver spaceship carrying Professor Hugo's Interplanetary Zoo settled down for its annual six-hour visit to the Chicago area.

Before daybreak the crowds would form, long lines of children and adults both, each one clutching his or her dollar, and waiting with wonderment to see what race of strange creatures the Professor had brought this year.

In the past they had sometimes been treated to three-legged creatures from Venus, or tall, thin men from Mars, or even snakelike horrors from somewhere more distant. This year, as the great round ship settled slowly to earth in the huge tri-city parking area just outside of Chicago, they watched with awe as the sides slowly slid up to reveal the familiar barred cages. In them were some wild breed of nightmare—small, horse-like animals that moved with quick, jerking motions and constantly chattered in a high-pitched tongue. The citizens of Earth clustered around as Professor Hugo's crew quickly collected the waiting dollars, and soon the good Professor himself made an appearance, wearing his many-colored rainbow cape and top hat. "Peoples of Earth," he called into his microphone.

The crowd's noise died down and he continued. "Peoples of Earth, this year you see a real treat for your single dollar—the little-known horse-spider people of Kaan—brought to you across a million miles of space at great expense. Gather around, see them, study them, listen to them, tell your friends about them. But hurry! My ship can remain here only six hours!"

And the crowds slowly filed by, at once horrified and fascinated by these strange creatures that looked like horses but ran up the walls of their cages like spiders. "This is certainly worth a dollar," one man remarked, hurrying away. "I'm going home to get the wife."

All day long it went like that, until ten thousand people had filed by the barred cages set into the side of the spaceship. Then, as the six-hour limit ran out, Professor Hugo once more took the microphone in hand. "We must go now, but we will return next year on this date. And if you enjoyed our zoo this year, telephone your friends in other cities about it. We will land in New York tomorrow, and next week on to London, Paris, Rome, Hong Kong, and Tokyo. Then on to other worlds!"

He waved farewell to them, and as the ship rose from the ground, the Earth peoples agreed that this had been the very best Zoo yet. . . .

Some two months and three planets later, the silver ship of Professor Hugo settled at last onto familiar jagged rocks of Kaan, and the odd horse-spider creatures filed quickly out of their

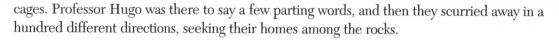
cages. Professor Hugo was there to say a few parting words, and then they scurried away in a hundred different directions, seeking their homes among the rocks.

In one house, the she-creature was happy to see the return of her mate and offspring. She babbled a greeting in the strange tongue and hurried to embrace them. "It was a long time you were gone. Was it good?"

And the he-creature nodded. "The little one enjoyed it especially. We visited eight worlds and saw many things."

The little one ran up the wall of the cave. "On the place called Earth it was the best. The creatures there wear garments over their skins, and they walk on two legs."

"But isn't it dangerous?" asked the she-creature.

"No," her mate answered, "There are bars to protect us from them. We remain right in the ship. Next time you must come with us. It is well worth the nineteen commocs it costs."

And the little one nodded. "It was the very best Zoo ever. . . ."

REMINDER

 Write your response to the prompt on the next page.

 Place a title on your response if you like.

 Try to sound out words you do not know how to spell. You may not use a dictionary.

 Write legibly. You may print or use cursive.

Writing Task 1:

The short story "Zoo" gains its power by playing with the reader's expectation by shifting points of view. What happens in the first part of the story turns out to be very different from what happens in the second part.

Write a literary response in which you analyze the use of points of view in this story. Compare and contrast the perspectives of the characters and your own perspective as reader, too. Use details from the story and your own ideas to support your answer.

Checklist for Your Writing

Use the checklist below to help you do your best work.
Be sure to:
- ❏ read the description of the writing task carefully;
- ❏ provide a strong introduction, body, and conclusion;
- ❏ use specific details to support your response;
- ❏ demonstrate that you understand the short story and its meaning;
- ❏ write in an interesting style and vary your writing;
- ❏ correct any mistakes in grammar, usage, and mechanics.

Students' responses will vary. Use the CAHSEE Scoring Rubric: Response to Writing Prompt to evaluate them.

English Language Arts, Early Preparation   Copying is illegal.   Measuring Up® to the California Content Standards

 **REMINDER**

 Write your response to the prompt on the next page.

Place a title on your response if you like.

Try to sound out words you do not know how to spell. You may not use a dictionary.

Write legibly. You may print or use cursive.

Writing Task 2:

Do fences make good neighbors, or would people be better off without any fences between them? In this crowded world, do we need to establish boundaries to get along? People have pondered these questions for ages.

Write an essay telling whether you think people need fences to get along. Use specific details, examples, and reasons to persuade your readers.

Checklist for Your Writing

Use the checklist below to help you do your best work.
Be sure to:
- ❑ read the description of the writing task carefully;
- ❑ provide a strong introduction, body, and conclusion;
- ❑ use specific details to support your response;
- ❑ write in an interesting style and vary your writing;
- ❑ correct any mistakes in grammar, usage, and mechanics.

Read the short story below. Then answer questions 1–10.

To Catch the Wind
A Tale from the Marshall Islands
Retold by Joyce Sidman

Timur and his brothers lived far out in the middle of the ocean on Ailinglapalap Atoll, a tiny ring of islands. All day, trade winds bent the coconut palms, and all night, stars glittered like foam on the crest of a wave.

Timur's brothers spent their time fishing and racing canoes in the lagoon. They wrestled each other on the white sand and argued over whose arms were strongest, whose canoe was fastest. Timur, the youngest, kept silent during these arguments. Though he fished every day with his brothers, he was neither big nor strong and could never hope to surpass them. When he tired of their loud voices, he would wander to his mother's hut and listen to her tales instead.

His mother, Likantur, was wise in the ways of the ocean and taught her sons all she knew. Timur loved to listen to her tell of the tides that filled and emptied the lagoon, of the currents that moved like eels beneath the green water, and of the coral reef, whose jagged teeth were as sharp as a shark's.

Most of all, he loved to hear her speak of the wind. "The wind has great power," she would tell Timur. "One minute it will sleep, the next it will roar. If we could catch it, we could go anywhere, perhaps even beyond Ailinglapalap." Timur would look at her in wonder, for how could anyone catch the wind? Then he would stare out over the water and wonder what lay beyond the dancing waves.

At the time of the taro harvest, excitement gripped the village. The king announced a great race all the way across the Ailinglapalap lagoon to Jeh Island. The winner would receive a fine fishing net woven by the king's daughter. At the evening meal, Timur's brothers spoke of nothing else.

"Such a distance!" cried one. "I might have to stop halfway to catch my breath!"

"Not me!" boasted another. "My canoe slips through water so easily, I'll hardly have to lift my paddle!"

"Hah!" snorted a third. "I know the best current. It will grab my canoe and hurl it across the lagoon!"

Timur said nothing. He longed to have the fine net, which would bring him luck at fishing. Although his chances were poor, he began to cherish hopes of winning the race. Long after the others were snoring, he lay gazing at the stars, which seemed to point the way to Jeh Island.

The night before the race, a great storm blew up and battered the village with rain and fierce winds. Timur, worried about his mother, ran through the whipping trees to Likantur's hut. To his surprise, she stood in the rain, holding up a mat of woven pandanus leaves that the storm had ripped from her roof. The wind clutched at the mat, tugging it this way and that. "How strong is the power of the wind!" Timur cried.

Likantur merely nodded and returned silently to her hut. But Timur tossed and turned all night, the wind blowing in and out of his dreams.

The day of the race dawned bright and fair. A brisk wind ruffled the coconut palms and sent tiny clouds scuttling across the sky. All traces of the storm were gone.

Timur went down to the beach to prepare his canoe. As the youngest, he was last in line on the smooth, white sand. How large and powerful the canoes of his brothers looked! But the wind will be with me all the way, he thought. He gripped his paddle and waited for the race to begin.

Suddenly, Likantur's voice rang out across the beach. "My sons, I am here! Who will take me to Jeh Island?" Likantur strode toward them, a large bundle in her arms.

The brothers looked at each other in dismay. What was their mother thinking? Any extra weight in their canoes would slow them down!

The first son said quickly, "I would take you, but my canoe cannot fit two."

Another spoke up, "I would take you, but I fear the ocean spray would ruin your skirt."

"You haven't brought a paddle; otherwise I would take you," a third son declared.

Thwack! came the sound of the king's staff against a coconut, starting the race. Timur's brothers leaped into their canoes and hurriedly pulled away from the beach. Timur looked at his mother. She had raised him and fed him and taught him all she knew. He could not leave her behind.

Shoulders sagging, he said, "Come share my canoe, Mother."

"I have brought the bit of matting from the roof, Timur," Likantur said when they were out on the water. "I thought it might prove useful."

Timur looked into Likantur's eyes, and a seed of excitement began to grow inside him. "Mother, bind your mat to this paddle. Perhaps the wind can help us." With quick fingers and sparkling eyes, Likantur did as he said. Timur raised the paddle toward the sky. As the pocket of matting unfurled, it billowed out in the wind and looked like the round stomach of the king. The canoe shot forward, faster than Timur imagined possible.

"Mother!" Timur cried. "We have caught the wind!"

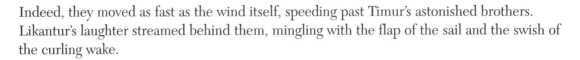

Indeed, they moved as fast as the wind itself, speeding past Timur's astonished brothers. Likantur's laughter streamed behind them, mingling with the flap of the sail and the swish of the curling wake.

Timur's canoe reached the shore of Jeh Island long before anyone else's. He and Likantur were honored by all in a great feast, and Timur proudly claimed the precious net.

Timur made many more sails with Likantur's help, and he showed his brothers how to use them. Over the years, the young men found their way from Ailinglapalap to far-flung islands, where they passed on their skills at navigation and sailmaking.

It is said that when Timur and his brothers died, their bodies rose to the heavens. They became bright stars that help sailors find their way across the vast oceans to this very day.

And when a sail flaps in the breeze, people say, it is really the sound of Likantur laughing, knowing that she has captured the wind.

1. **Read the sentence below.**

> As the pocket of matting unfurled, it billowed out in the wind and looked like the round stomach of the king.

What does the word *unfurled* mean in this sentence?

A   closed up

B   spread out again

C   opened up

D   tore

2. **Read the sentence below.**

> At the time of the taro harvest, excitement gripped the village.

The word *gripped* suggests that the villagers were —

A   greatly excited.

B   a little bit excited.

C   not excited at all.

D   stopped from acting because of the excitement.

3. Read this sentence from the story.

> Timur loved to listen to her tell of the tides that filled and emptied the lagoon, of the currents that moved like eels beneath the green water, and of the coral reef, whose jagged teeth were as sharp as a shark's.

Why does the author use figurative comparisons in this sentence?

A   to suggest that the tides are very beautiful

B   to suggest that the tides are filled with many fish

C   to suggest that the tides are sacred to Timur's people

D   to suggest that the tides could be dangerous

4. **How does the reader know that this is a myth or legend?**

A   It has a happy ending, in which everyone gets what they want.

B   The characters are very colorful.

C   It ends on a note of fantasy, with the brothers turning into stars.

D   It takes place in a fictional location.

5. **What is the overall theme expressed in the tale?**

A   Knowledge and intelligence help people overcome obstacles.

B   Physical strength can help a person achieve any goal.

C   After listening to his mother, Timur harnesses the power of the wind.

D   Older brothers are always outwitted by the youngest ones.

6. **What does this story show about Timur's people at the time in which the story is set?**

A   They are not used to being out in open water.

B   They think that using sails on a canoe in a race is cheating.

C   They have never thought before of using sails on their canoes.

D   They had never believed that wind was strong enough to move a canoe.

7. **How is Timur different from his brothers?**

A   Unlike his brothers, who are brave, Timur is a coward.

B   Timur's brothers all get along well, but none of them like Timur.

C   Timur cannot compete with his brothers in tests of strength.

D   Unlike his brothers, Timur does not enjoy going out in canoes.

8. **What is the dilemma or internal conflict Timur faces?**

A   Timur believes that having his mother on his canoe will slow him down and hurt his chances of winning the race, but he has a sense of duty to her.

B   Timur resents his mother for her thoughtlessness in demanding he take her to Jeh Island, but believes that he will embarrass himself if he does not take her.

C   Timur feels duty-bound to take Likantur, but does not want to embarrass himself in her eyes by losing the race.

D   Timur is angry at his brothers for refusing to take Likantur in any of their canoes and wants even more to win the race, but knows that by taking her, he has less chance of winning.

 9. Why is it important to the plot that Timur decides to take his mother?

A It shows that he loves her very much.

B She brings a bit of matting from the roof.

C This makes his other brothers angry.

D The mother helps Timur row the boat.

 10. In this tale, what does the wind symbolize?

A the love of a mother for a son

B the power to develop self-sufficiency

C the competition among the brothers

D the skill to navigate by the stars

✎ REMINDER

✎ **Write your response to the prompt below.**

✎ **Place a title on your response if you like.**

✎ **Try to sound out words you do not know how to spell. You may not use a dictionary.**

✎ **Write legibly. You may print or use cursive.**

Writing Task:

We value strength, but sometimes it's the weak who succeed against all expectations.

Of the sons, why is Timur the one who can harness the wind, even though he is the weakest? What character traits make him successful? Use details from the tale and your own experience in your response.

Checklist for Your Writing

Use the checklist below to help you do your best work.
Be sure to:

❏ read the description of the writing task carefully;

❏ provide a strong introduction, body, and conclusion;

❏ use specific details to support your response;

❏ demonstrate that you have understood the selection and the author's intent;

❏ write in an interesting style and vary your sentences;

❏ correct any mistakes in grammar, usage, and mechanics.

The following is a rough draft of an essay Armando wrote about Lewis and Clarke. It may contain errors in grammar, punctuation, sentence structure, and organization. Some of the questions may refer to numbered or underlined sentences or phrases. Read the essay and answer the questions that follow it.

Lewis and Clark
by Armando Hernandez

[1] On May 21, 1804, a group of explorers started out from Camp Wood, its winter camp on the Mississippi River north of St. Louis. [2] These sturdy travelers were Meriwether Lewis and William Clark. [3] They had been asked by President Jefferson to explore the Louisiana Purchase. [4] This huge area of land greatly increased the size of the United States. [5] Indians, trappers, plants, and animals were the occupants of the vast land, and Lewis and Clark were going as representatives of the U.S. Government to find out all they could about the region. [6] If they was to return safe, with lots of findings to deliver, Jefferson would be proud.

[7] The band set out northwest, and they followed the Missouri River. [8] As they traveled, Lewis and Clark not only had to find their way, keep their group united, and discover enough food to keep off starvation, but also keeping records of the sights and sounds they noticed. [9] They took notes about plants they found that might have medicinal value. [10] Recorded their first new mammal, the eastern wood rat, in the early weeks of the journey. [11] One of the animals that impressed them most being the pronghorn antelope. [12] On the plains of South Dakota the band saw their first herd of buffalo. [13] Neither Lewis nor Clark had ever seen those creatures before. [14] They estimated the herd to consist of about 20,000 head of the great shaggy beasts. [15] Although they found them to be gentle, they needed food, so a few were killed.

[16] The adventures of Lewis and Clark could fill many books. [17] In fact, the explorers themselves kept long journals which have been published in book form. [18] The grizzly bear, the pronghorn antelope, the mountain goat, and mountain lion and prairie dog are just a few of the well-known creatures that Lewis and Clark saw and described. [19] As they traveled, they found items that might be useful to their nation, including medicinal plants, mineral deposits, new hunting grounds, and areas for farmland. [20] Their expedition helped the United States and is still fun to read about today.

1. Which of the following sentences, if inserted before sentence 1, would make the MOST effective opening sentence?

A Meriwether Lewis and William Clark are two famous American explorers.

B It was the beginning of one of the greatest adventures in our history.

C The territory west of the Mississippi needed to be explored, and Lewis and Clark were the people to do it.

D Can you picture what life was life in 1804 for people living in the West?

 2. Which of the following items is supported by details, or evidence in the essay?

A Lewis and Clark saw many plants and animals that were unknown to the Americans.

B Little is known about the adventures of Lewis and Clark in spite of the many notes they took.

C No one has ever been on as successful a journey as Lewis and Clark.

D Most explorers set off by following a river.

3. Based on the essay, which of the following would be the BEST source of firsthand information on the Lewis and Clark expedition?

A a poster showing the tribes that they encountered

B a museum display of the expedition

C a biography of Meriwether Lewis

D the journals that they kept

4. Which is the MOST effective substitution for sentence 6? If no substitution is necessary, choose "Leave as is."

> If they was to return safe, with lots of findings to deliver, Jefferson would be proud.

A If they returned safely, with abundant findings, Jefferson would be pleased.

B They was to return safe, with lots of findings, to make Jefferson proud.

C Returning safe, and delivering many findings, would make Jefferson be proud.

D Leave as is.

5. Which is the MOST effective substitution for the underlined part of sentence 7? If no substitution is necessary, choose "Leave as is."

> The band set out northwest, <u>and they followed the Missouri River</u>.

A but they followed the Missouri River

B following the Missouri River

C having followed the Missouri River

D Leave as is.

6. Which is the MOST effective substitution for the underlined part of sentence 8? If no substitution is necessary, choose "Leave as is."

> As they traveled, Lewis and Clark not only had to find their way, keep their group united, and discover enough food to keep off starvation, <u>but also keeping records of the sights and sounds they noticed</u>.

A but also keep records of the sights and sounds they noticed.

B but also keeping records of the sights and sounds they were noticing.

C but also kept records of the sights and sounds they noticed.

D Leave as is.

7. What is the BEST way to combine sentences 9 and 10?

> They took notes about plants they found that might have medicinal value. Recorded their first new mammal, the eastern wood rat, in the early weeks of the journey.

A Taking notes about plants they found that might have medicinal value and recording their first new mammal, the eastern wood rat, in the early weeks of the journey.

B They took notes about plants they found that might have medicinal value, having recorded their first new mammal, the eastern wood rat, in the early weeks of the journey.

C To take notes about plants they found that might have medicinal value, they recorded their first new mammal, the eastern wood rat, in the early weeks of the journey.

D They took notes about plants they found that might have medicinal value, recording their first new mammal, the eastern wood rat, in the early weeks of the journey.

8. Which is the MOST effective substitution for sentence 11? If no substitution is necessary, choose "Leave as is."

> One of the animals that impressed them most being the pronghorn antelope.

A One of the animals that impressed them most was the pronghorn antelope.

B One of the animals impressing them most being the pronghorn antelope.

C One of the animals that impressed them most were the pronghorn antelope.

D Leave as is.

9. Which of the following sentences is redundant and so should be removed from the second paragraph?

A Sentence 7

B Sentence 12

C Sentence 13

D Sentence 15

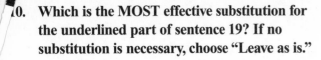

0. **Which is the MOST effective substitution for the underlined part of sentence 19? If no substitution is necessary, choose "Leave as is."**

> <u>As they traveled, they found items that might be useful to their nation, including</u> medicinal plants, mineral deposits, new hunting grounds, and areas for farmland.

A   As they traveled they found items that might be useful to their nation; including

B   As they traveled, finding items that might be useful to their nation, including

C   As they traveled, they found items that might be useful to their nation, and these included

D   Leave as is.

✎ **REMINDER**

✎ **Write your response to the prompt on the next page.**

✎ **Place a title on your response if you like.**

✎ **Try to sound out words you do not know how to spell.
You may not use a dictionary.**

✎ **Write legibly. You may print or use cursive.**

Writing Task:

Scary movies are a staple of the movie industry. What do you think accounts for their popularity?

Write an essay explaining why you think teenagers in particular like to see scary movies. Use specific details to support your response.

Checklist for Your Writing

Use the checklist below to help you do your best work.
Be sure to:
❑ read the description of the writing task carefully;
❑ provide a strong introduction, body, and conclusion;
❑ use specific details to support your response;
❑ demonstrate that you have understood the selection and the author's intent;
❑ write in an interesting style and vary your sentences;
❑ correct any mistakes.

Students' responses will vary. Use the CAHSEE Scoring Rubric: Response to Writing Prompt to evaluate them.

Glossary

A

aesthetic approach a critical approach to a work of literature in which you concentrate on the author's style, or way of writing; a way of evaluating literature that focuses on the author's diction, or choice of language, the tone, mood, or theme of the text; p. 152

allegory a special type of story in which all the characters represent qualities and types; p. 119

alliteration the repetition of initial consonant sounds; p. 125

ambiguity what occurs when the writer leaves details or meanings unclear or uncertain. A text that is *ambiguous* has two or more possible meanings, and which meaning applies best to the text is left up to the reader to decide; p. 131

analogy a comparison that seeks to explain something by comparing it to something else; p. 114

analyze break down the information in a source to examine the individual ideas; p. 65

antagonist the characater in a story or play who opposes the protagonist, or main character; often, the "bad guy"; p. 95

argument a defense of a position or claim, p. 78

aside when a character in a play turns and speaks directly to the audience and is supposedly unheard by other characters; p. 142

B

biographical approach a critical approach to a work of literature in which you look at how the author's life, background, attitudes, and beliefs affect the work; p. 152

biographical narrative a story about a real person; p. 210

business letter a formal correspondence about a business-related matter; business letters are written or printed in special formats; p. 227

C

cause and effect to show reasons and results, such as in discussing the results of a historical event or in explaining scientific facts or theories; p. 167

character foil a character in a play who has traits that are just the opposite of the protagonist's. By illustrating what the protagonist is NOT like, the character foil helps the audience understand what the protagonist IS like; p. 142

characterization the ways that authors reveal a character's traits and put flesh and bones on a character's skeleton. In **direct characterization**, the author tells you directly what a character is like. With **indirect characterization**, the writer presents evidence and the reader must draw inferences about the characters; p. 95

chronological order time order; the sequence in which events happen, such as a story from real life or the steps of a proces pp. 107, 167

clause a group of words that has a verb and a subject; an independent or main clause expresses a complete thought and can stand by itself as a sentence; a dependent or subordinate clause does not express a complete idea and must be linked to an independent clause; p. 194

comedy drama in which characters face certain obstacles that they try to overcome. Sometimes their attempts to overcome these obstacles are humorous. Today, we often use the word *comedy* to refer to stories that make us laugh. However, a comedy does not have to be funny, but it *does* have to end happily; p. 90

compare and contrast to show how things are alike and different; p. 167

conclusion adding up all the evidence available; p. 65

conflict the problem or challenge faced by the main character in a story or play. The conflict may be between the protagonist and the antagonist, the protagonist and a force of nature, or within the mind of the protagonist; p. 95

connotation the feelings and associations a word brings to mind; the emotional impression a word makes; pp. 28, 125

consumer documents publications that help consumers make decisions about what products to buy and how to use them; p. 39

context clues words in a sentence or passage that help you find the meaning of an unknown word or phrase; p. 23

context the words surrounding an unfamiliar word that provide a clue to its meaning; p. 2

contradictions seemingly opposing ideas or inconsistencies; p. 131

critical thinking thinking that involves analyzing, evaluating, and elaborating; p. 65

D

denotation the literal meaning of a word; pp. 28, 125

dialogue what actors say to one another in a play; their words reveal the plot and what the characters are like. In fiction, directly quoted conversation between two or more characters; p. 142

draft the first rough piece of writing done for any given project; p. 184

dramatic literature literature that is meant to be acted out or performed for an audience; drama; pp. 90, 142

dramatic monologue a long speech by one character in which the character reveals a lot about himself or herself; p. 90

E

elaborate to state the individual ideas in a source in detail and add your own ideas; p. 65

electronic media videotapes, audiotapes, CDs, CD-ROMs, audiobooks, etc.; p. 179

evaluate to make a judgment about the ideas in a source; p. 66

evocative words words that stir strong feelings or emotions; p. 152

expository composition a piece of writing that provides information and ideas about a topic; p. 219

F

fact a statement that can be proved true: p. 78

figurative comparison a comparison between two essentially unlike things; p. 114

figurative language expressions whose poetic meaning goes beyond the literal meaning of the words; pp. 114, 152

figurative meaning an imaginative use of a word. When words are used figuratively, they mean something different from their simple dictionary definitions; p. 10

first-person point of view when the narrator in a story is a character in the story who uses first-person pronouns (*I, me, mine*) to describe himself or herself; p. 136

flashback a look at a past event. The author halts the action temporarily in order to look back at an event that happened at an earlier time; p. 107

foreshadowing providing hints at what will happen in the future; p. 107

functional documents documents that provide information that helps you function, or learn how to do things, in the real world; p. 72

G

generalization a general statement drawn from numerous specific observations; p. 78

gerund a verb that acts as a noun; gerunds always end in *-ing*; p. 194

 Measuring Up® to the California Content Standards

H

historical approach a critical approach to a work of literature in which you consider the historical context of the work. You think about the time period and the issues that concerned people and see how they affect the plot, the characters, and the theme; p. 152

I

idioms special expressions that are peculiar to themselves grammatically and cannot be understood if taken literally; p. 10

imagery the use of words to create vivid mental images or pictures in the reader's head; p. 125

incongruities details that do not seem logical or that defy conventional reason; p. 131

inference an educated guess based on evidence in the text and what you already know about the topic; p. 65

infinitive a verb that usually comes after the word *to* and functions as a noun, an adjective, or an adverb; p. 194

irony a kind of discrepancy between what is expected and what is revealed. **Verbal irony** occurs when what someone says is the opposite of what that person means. **Situational irony** occurs when what happens is just the opposite of what you expect to happen. **Dramatic irony** occurs when you, the reader or the viewer, know something crucial that the main character in the story does not know; p. 131

L

literal meaning the dictionary definition of a word; pp. 2, 10

literary response a piece of writing that shows an understanding of a literary work that the writer has read; p. 214

M

main idea the most important idea in a text; pp. 58, 65, 173

mental image an image you associate with a word to help you remember its meaning; p. 2

metaphor a comparison between two basically dissimilar things that does not use the words *as*, *like*, or *resembles*; p. 10

microfilm and microfiche camera-film records of documents; p. 179

mnemonic devices tricks you can use to remember the meaning of words; p. 2

mood the feeling created by a work of literature; p. 125

O

opinion a judgment or personal evaluation; p. 79

order of importance to present ideas and information starting with the most important to the least important point, or from least to most important point, especially when you are presenting a persuasive argument or explaining why something happened; p. 167

P

parallelism the expression of similar ideas in the same grammatical form; pp. 152, 198

paraphrase to restate the information in a text or passage in your own words; p. 58

participle a verb that acts as an adjective; it usually ends in *-ing*, *-ed*, or *-en*; p. 194

periodicals magazines and journals; p.179

persona a personality given to the narrator in first-person narratives that affects what he or she tells; p. 136

personification giving human qualities to animals or things that are not human; p. 10

persuasive composition a piece of writing in which the writer tries to persuade readers to do something or to believe something; p. 223

phrase a group of words without a subject and a verb used as a single part of speech; p. 194

plot the pattern of action of a story; the series of linked events that make up the story; p. 95

prediction a guess about what will happen based on evidence; p. 65

prefix a letter or group of letters added to a base word or root to change its meaning; p. 15

premise a viewpoint, position, or claim; p. 78

protagonist The main character in a story or play, the character who is at the center of the story; often, the "good guy"; p. 95

R

reference books dictionaries, encyclopedias, thesauruses, almanacs, directories, etc.; p. 179

repetition the repeating of a key word or element for effect; pp. 125, 152

research the process of finding out more about a topic; p. 52

rhyme the repetition of sounds at the ends of words; p. 125

rhythm the pattern of stressed and unstressed syllables; p. 125

root the base from which a word is built by adding word parts such as prefixes and suffixes; p. 16

S

simile a comparison between two basically dissimilar things that uses the words *as*, *like*, or *resembles*; p. 10

soliloquy a long speech in which a character in a play speaks to himself. This speech is like an inner conversation that the audience can overhear. Like any inner conversation, it reveals a lot about the speaker; p. 142

soliloquy a long speech by one character which is part of a longer play; pp. 90, 142

sound devices devices such as rhythm, rhyme, and alliteration to create a musical quality; p. 152

spatial order to describe location, such as when you are writing about the arrangement of furniture in a room; p. 167

stage design refers to the way the setting for the play looks on stage. The stage design establishes where and when the events are taking place. Stage design includes everything seen on stage; p. 142

stage directions directions in play scripts telling actors exactly what to do and how to say their lines; p. 142

structural features the features in a book that help you identify at a glance the information you need; p. 39

subtleties fine distinctions between things, such as the distinction between *slighting* someone and *insulting* someone; p. 131

suffix a letter or group of letters added to the end of a base word or root to changes its meaning or part of speech; p. 15

summarize to provide the most important ideas and details in a text in a condensed form, leaving out unimportant details; p. 58

supporting details the facts, examples, statistics, and concepts that back up the main idea; pp. 58, 173

symbol a person, place, or thing that stands for an idea or a concept; a **public symbol** is a symbol that is understood and shared by an entire culture; p. 101, 119

synthesize when you synthesize information, you connect or combine it; p. 58

 Measuring Up® to the California Content Standards

T

text features headings, special type, bullets, or other items and text treatments that highlight information in a text and make it accessible; p. 72

text structure how an author organizes information; five types of text structure are: **cause and effect, comparison and contrast, time order, order of importance**, and **spatial order**; p. 167

theme a general observation about life or human nature expressed through a work of literature; **universal themes** can be found in the literature of many different cultures and from many different times; p. 101

thesaurus a reference book that lists synonyms and antonyms; p. 2

the vertical file a file of pamphlets, circulars, clippings, and miscellaneous printed information on varied topics arranged alphabetically in a file cabinet; p. 179

third-person point of view when the narrator uses the third person, signaled by the pronouns *he, she, him,* and *her.* A **third-person omniscient narrator** knows everything that goes on in the story, possibly including knowing every character's thoughts and feelings. A **third-person limited narrator** looks over the shoulder of one major character, presenting that character's traits in great detail, often including this character's thoughts, but *not* other characters' thoughts and feelings; p. 136

tone the writer's attitude toward the subject he is writing about; p. 167

trade books books written by individuals on specific topics; p. 179

tragedy the opposite of comedy. In a tragedy, the main character, who has great potential, faces a problem that brings about his or her downfall—and often death. Usually, a tragedy deals with serious issues, such as the effects of pride or a terrible crime committed in the past. Unlike a comedy, a tragedy always ends unhappily for the main character; p. 90

V

valid opinion a judgment backed up by facts; p. 78

voice the quality of narration that reveals the persona and the narrator's attitude toward other characters and events; p. 136

W

workplace documents documents designed to provide information about a job and help people get the job done; p. 45

Acknowledgments

p. 3, "Amber" from CRICKET magazine, August 1996, Vol. 23, No. 12, Copyright © 1996 by Marjorie Jackson; p. 6, "One Alaska Night" by Barrett Willoughby, Paul R. Reynolds, Inc., 12 East 41st Street, New York, NY 10017, Copyright © 1936 by Barrett Willoughby; p. 11, excerpt from "Moon Tiger" by Penelope Lively, Copyright © 1987 by Penelope Lively. Used by permission of Grove/Atlantic, Inc.; p. 12, excerpt from "The Baroque Marble" by E. A. Proulx; p. 17, "Old Man Mad About Drawing: Katsushika Hokusai" from LIVES OF THE ARTISTS: MASTERPIECES, MESSES (AND WHAT THE NEIGHBORS THOUGHT), copyright © 1995 by Kathleen Krull, reprinted by permission of Harcourt, Inc; p. 17, The Newark Museum/Art Resource, NY, The Newark Museum, Newark, New Jersey; p. 19, "Around the World on Just One Cent, Rufus Porter: Forgotten Genius of the 19th Century" by Jane Kaplan Naliboff. Reprinted by permission of CRICKET magazine, September 2001, Vol. 29, No. 1, © 2001 by Jane Kaplan Naliboff; p. 20, Flying Ship, W. Greer, reprinted by permission of the Minnesota Historical Society; p. 24, excerpt from "Feared, Revered King Cobras" by Mattias Klum, National Geographic, Copyright © 2001. Reprinted by permission; p. 25, "Keep Your Head" by Dewey Gram, published in Boys' Life, March 2000, published by the Boy Scouts of America, Irving TX. Copyright © 2000 by Dewey Gram. Reprinted by permission of the author; p. 29, excerpt from "The Sphinx" by Edgar Allan Poe; p. 31, excerpt from "At War with Grandma" by Ashley Palmer from *Her Fork in the Road* edited by Lisa Bach. Copyright © 2001 Travelers' Tales, Inc.; p. B25, "The Birth of Big Business" by Peter Barnes from COBBLESTONE's, April 2000 issue: *The Gilded Age*, © 2000, Cobblestone Publishing, 30 Grove Street, Suite C, Peterborough, NH 03458. All Rights Reserved. Reprinted by permission of Carus Publishing Company; p. 40, "Refrigerators: Comparing the Types" Copyright © 200 3 by Consumer Union of U.S., Inc. Yonkers, NY 10703-1057, a nonprofit organization. Reprinted with permission from July 2003 issue of CONSUMER REPORT® for educational purposes only. No commercial or reproduction permitted. To learn more about Consumers Union, log onto www.ConsumerReports.org; p. 42, "eHow to Assemble a Scooter" by Sally Ann Barnes from *How to Do Just About Everything*, eHow.com, Copyright © 2001, 2000, 1999 eHow, Inc.; p. 46, "Tips for Success - The Resume" reprinted from the *WorkSmart* web site by permission of the Employment Development Department, State of California; p. 48, "Copyright Your Work" from *The Big Book of Life's Instructions*, by Sheree Bykofsky and Paul Fargis, © 1995 by Stonesong Press, LLC, pp. 313-315; p. 53, "Is the Monster in the Loch a Myth? Not Nessie-sarily" by Patricia Thomas from FACES' January 2000 issue: *Scotland*, © 2000, Cobblestone Publishing, 30 Grove Street, Suite C, Peterborough, NH 03458. All Rights Reserved. Reprinted by permission of Carus Publishing Company; p. 55, "Sssh! Don't Mention His Name" by Dean Durber, from FACES' January 2000 issue: *Scotland*, © 2000, Cobblestone Publishing Company, 30 Grove Street, Suite C, Peterborough, NH 03458. All Rights Reserved. Reprinted by permission of Carus Publishing Company; p. 59, "A Little Girl from Illinois" by Bonnie Geisert, from COBBLESTONE's March 1999 issue: *Jane Addams: 1860-1935*, © 1999, Cobblestone Publishing Company, 30 Grove Street, Suite C, Peterborough, NH 03458. All Rights Reserved. Reprinted by permission of Carus Publishing Company; p. 61, "The House That Jane Built" by Shawn Hoffelt from COBBLESTONE's March 1999 issue: *Jane Addams: 1860-1935*, © 1999, Cobblestone Publishing Company, 30 Grove Street, Suite C, Peterborough, NH 03458. All Rights Reserved. Reprinted by permission of Carus Publishing Company; p. 61, photograph, Jane Addams Memorial Collections (JAMC neg. 146), The University Library, University of Illinois at Chicago; p. 66, "Daily Life-Making the Most of Everything" by Jane A. Beem, from COBBLESTONE's September 1999 issue: *The Cliff Dwellers*, © 1999, Cobblestone Publishing Company, 30 Grove Street, Suite C, Peterborough, NH 03458. All Rights Reserved. Reprinted by permission of Carus Publishing Company; p. 67, photograph reprinted with permission of the National Park Service; p. 68, excerpt from "Grant and Lee" A Study in Contrasts from *The American Story*, by Bruce Catton, edited by Earl Scheck Miers. Copyright © U.S. Capitol History Society. All rights reserved; p. 73, "How to Get Started with Your Family Tree" by Kimberly Powell from the *What You Need to Know About* website, Copyright © 2003 by About, Inc.; p. 75, "Animals in Disaster" from the Federal Emergency Management Agency website, Copyright © September 2002 by Federal Emergency Management Agency; p. 77, "A Tribute to Eleanor Roosevelt: Address to the First Anniversary Luncheon of the Eleanor Roosevelt Memorial Foundation" by Mrs. Lyndon Baines Johnson. April 9, 1964; p. 81, "Commencement Address" by First Lady Barbara Bush at Wellesley College, June 1, 1990; p. 84, ZIGGY © 2002 Ziggy & Friends, Inc. Reprinted with permission of UNIVERSAL PRESS SYNDICATE. All rights reserved; p. B86, "Iditarod: Trail Dog Sled Race" by Lucid Interactive, Copyright © 1995-2003 by Lucid Interactive; p. 90, "Julie" from *Monologues for Teenagers* by Roger Karshner, published by Dramaline Productions, Copyright © 1995 by Dramaline Productions, reprinted by permission; p. 92, "Jeff" from *Monologues for Teenagers* by Roger Karshner, published by Dramaline Productions, Copyright © 1995 by Dramaline Productions, reprinted by permission; p. 96, excerpt from "Aunt Dan and Lemon" by Wallace Shawn. Copyright © 1985 by Wallace Shawn. Published by Grove Press, Inc.; p. 98, excerpt from "Carrot for a Chestnut" from Field of Thirteen by Dick Francis, copyright © 1998 by Dick Francis; p. 102, "The Atlas Moth" by Ethel Pochocki, Reprinted by permission of CICADA magazine, July/August 2001, Vol. 3, No. 6, © 2001 by Ethel Pochocki; p. 104, "A Tale of Love" from *Mexican Folk Tales*, by Anthony John Campos. © 1977 The Arizona Board of Regents. Reprinted by permission of the University of Arizona Press; p. 108, excerpt from "That's Ghosts for You" by Susan Price, published by CRICKET magazine, October 2001, Vol. 29, No. 2, Copyright © 2001 by Susan Price; p. 115, "Watch Repair" from *Return to a Place Lit by a Glass of Milk* by Charles Simic. Copyright © 1974 by Charles Simic; p. 116, "Cast Up" by Lawrence Ferlinghetti, from A CONEY ISLAND OF THE MIND, copyright © 1958 by Lawrence Ferlinghetti. Reprinted by permission of New Directions Publishing Corp.; p. 117, "The Night Has a Thousand Eyes" by Francis William

Bourdillon; p. 120, "The King and the Shirt" from FABLES AND FAIRY TALES by Leo Tolstoy, translated by Ann Dunnigan, copyright © 1962 by Ann Dunnigan. Used by permission of Dutton Signet, a division of Penguin Putnam Inc.; p. 121, "The Waterfall of White Hair" a tale from *China* retold by Josephine Evetts-Secker. Published by Abbeville Press, Copyright © 1996 by Josephine Evetts-Secker; p. 126, "I Was Sleeping Where the Black Oaks Move" from JACKLIGHT by Louise Erdrich, copyright © 1984 by Louis Erdrich. Reprinted by permission of Henry Holt and Company, LLC; p. 127, "The Writer" from THE MIND READER, copyright © 1971 by Richard Wilbur, reprinted by permission of Harcourt, Inc.; p. 132, "One Perfect Rose", from DOROTHY PARKER: COMPLETE POEMS by Dorothy Parker, copyright © 1999 by The National Association for the Advancement of Colored People. Used by permission of Penguin, a division of Penguin Group (USA) Inc.; p. 133, "The Princess and the Tin Box" from *The Beast In Me And Other Animals* by James Thurber. Copyright © 1948 Rosemary A. Thurber. Reprinted by arrangement with The Barbara Hogenson Agency. All rights reserved; p. 137, "Wallet" by Allen Woodman from *An Anthology of Really Short Stories* published by W.W. Norton & Company, Inc. Reprinted by permission of the author; p. 138, "The Luckiest Time of All" excerpted from the book, *The Lucky Stone* by Lucille Clifton. Copyright © 1979 by Lucille Clifton. Published by Delacorte Press; p. 143, excerpt from "What I Did Last Summer" by A.R. Gurney, from SPRING AWAKENINGS by Frank Wedekind, translated by Tom Osborne. Copyright © 1969, 1978 by John Calder (Publishers) Ltd. And Riverrun Press. This translation, Copyright © 1969, 1977, 1978 by Tom Osborn; p. 147, excerpt from A YOUNG LADY OF PROPERTY by Horton Foote. Copyright © 1955, 1983 by Horton Foote; p. 153, "Destiny", from THE BONESETTER'S DAUGHTER by Amy Tan. copyright © 2001 by Amy Tan. Used by permission of G.P. Putnam's Sons, a division of Penguin Group (USA) Inc.; p. 156, excerpt from "Matchimanito" from *Tracks* by Louise Erdrich. Copyright © 1988. First appeared in The Atlantic Monthly; p. B159, "The Shepherd's Daughter" by William Soroyan, from *75 Short Masterpieces*, Edited by Roger Goodman, published by Bantam Books, Copyright © 1967 by Bantam Books; p. B162, "Talent" from *Is There Really Such a Thing as Talent?* by Annie Dillard in Seventeen Magazine, June 1979. Copyright © 1979 by Annie Dillard. Reprinted by permission of the author and Blanche C. Gregory, Inc.; p. 168, "What Happened to the Anasazi?" By Luz Cepeda; p. 171, "T'ai Chi, the "Supreme Ultimate" by Robert Ling; p. 174, "JFK" by Rena Jankowski; p. 177, "Unintended Inventions" by Urica Simpson; p. 180; "Becoming Mark Twain" by Ronald Yuan; p. 182, "Jupiter, the Mysterious Giant" by Anthony Singleton; p. 185, "How to Make an Omelette" by Guy Collins; p. 190, "Finding the Lost Coast" by Kyoko L. Kishi; p. 195, "Firefighters Fight More Than Fire" by Courtney Kassinger; AFP/Getty Images; p. 196, "Forest Fires" by José Alvarez; p. 199, "The World of Water" by Hi-jing Yu; p. 200, "Gifts from the Sea" by Hi-Jing Yu; p. 203, "My Hero" by Tuyet Tran; p. 204, "Where Did All the Dinos Go?" by Jean-Baptiste Vera; p. 211, "Tio Leon's Wagon" by Nicholas Gutierrez; p. 215, "Behind the Minister's Black Veil" by Francine Choi; p. 216, "Mike and the Grass" by Erma Bombeck from *If Life Is a Bowl of Cherries, What Am I Doing in the Pits?* By Erma Bombeck, published by McGraw-Hill Book Company, Copyright © 1978 by Erma Bombeck; p. 220, "Rome, My Favorite Empire" by Thomas O'Connor; p. 224, "Needed: Speed Bumps on Market Avenue" by Noreen Hughes; p. B231, "The Day Grandfather Tickled a Tiger" A True Story by Ruskin Bond, from CRICKET magazine, September 2003, Vol. 31, No. 1, text copyright © 1973 by Ruskin Bond; p. B237, "Comic Books Made Simple" by Daryl Edelman; p. B241, "Zoo" by Edward D. Hoch, copyright © 1958 by King-Size Publications, Inc., © renewed 1986 by Edward D. Hoch; p. B247, "To Catch the Wind: A Tale from the Marshall Islands" retold by Joyce Sidman. Originally published by CRICKET magazine, January 1997, Vol. 24, No. 5. Copyright © 1997 by Joyce Sidman. Used by permission of the author; p. B253, "Lewis and Clark" by Armando Hernandez

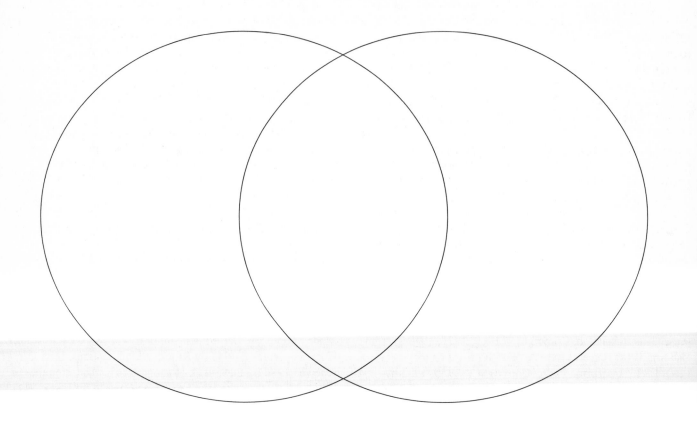

Sequencing List Graphic Organizer

First

Next

Next

Next

Then

Persuasive Graphic Organizer

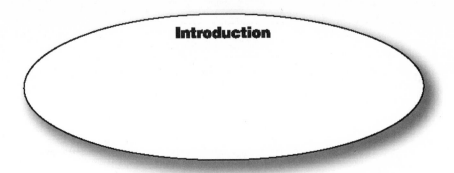

Introduction

Reasons	Supporting Details and Examples

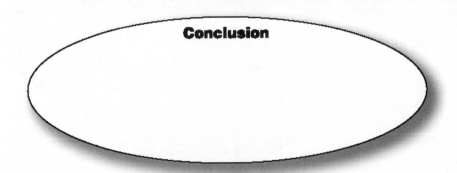

Conclusion

Compare and Contrast Diagram

Introduction

Body

How alike?

How different?

Conclusion

- Summary: How are they alike?

- Summary: How are they different?

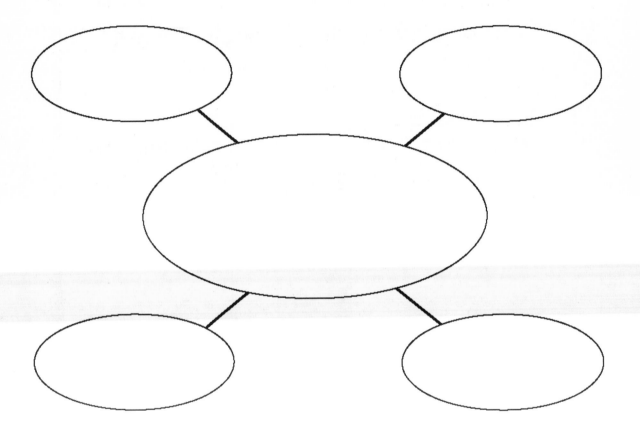

 Measuring Up® to the California Content Standards

K-W-L Graphic Organizer

Topic _____

What I **Know**	What I **Want** to Learn	What I **Learned**

_____

_____

_____

Problem and Solution Chart

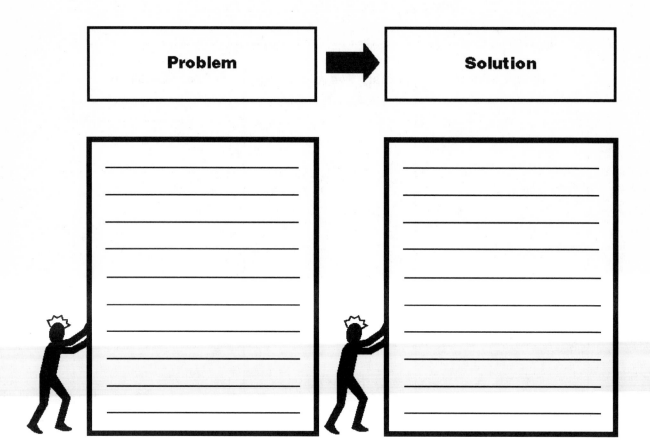

| Problem | → | Solution |

Measuring Up® to the California Content Standards

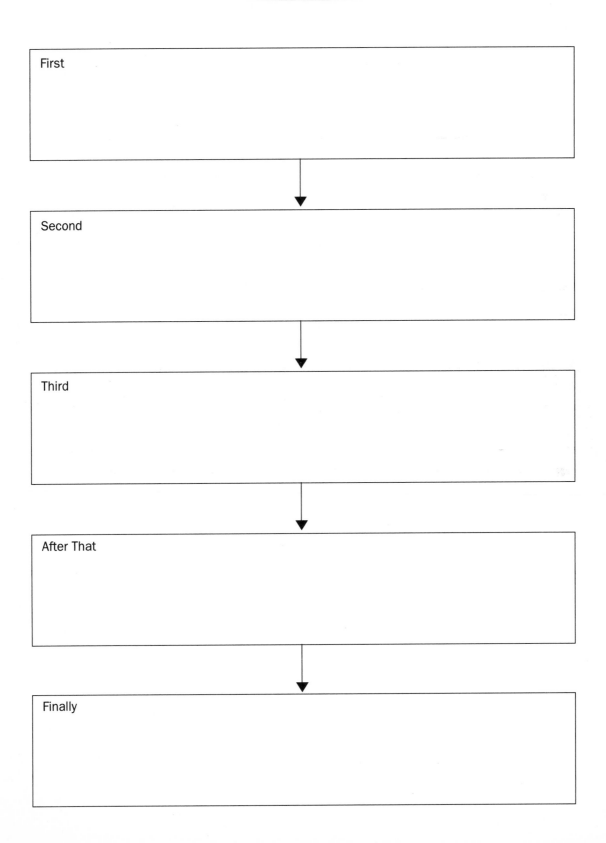

First

Second

Third

After That

Finally

Story Map Graphic Organizer

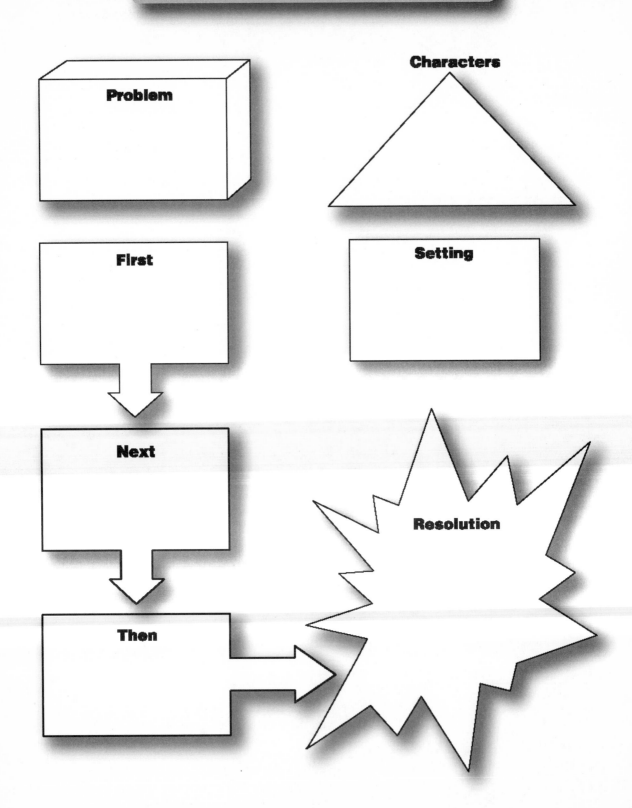

Problem

Characters

First

Setting

Next

Resolution

Then

Measuring Up® to the California Content Standards

Cause and Effect T-Chart

Cause	Effect

What is my topic?	What should be my writing purpose? ___to entertain ___to describe ___to explain ___to persuade
How long should my writing be?	Who is my audience?

What are three ideas or details I will include in my composition?

a. _____

_____

_____

b. _____

_____

_____

c. _____

_____

_____

_____

Writing Prompt Response Rubric

4 The essay —

- provides a *meaningful* thesis that is responsive to the writing task.
- *thoroughly* supports the thesis and main ideas with *specific* details and examples.
- demonstrates a consistent tone and focus, and illustrates a *purposeful* control of organization.
- demonstrates a *clear* sense of audience.
- provides a *variety* of sentence types and uses *precise*, *descriptive* language.
- contains few, if any, errors in the conventions* of the English language. (Errors are generally first-draft in nature.)

A Persuasive Composition:
- states and maintains a position, *authoritatively* defends that position with precise and relevant evidence, and *convincingly* addresses the reader's concerns, biases, and expectations

3 The essay —

- provides a thesis that is responsive to the writing task**.**
- supports the thesis and main ideas with details and examples.
- demonstrates a consistent tone and focus; and illustrates a control of organization.
- demonstrates a *general* sense of audience.
- provides a *variety* of sentence types and uses *some descriptive* language.
- may contain *some errors* in the conventions* of the English language. (Errors do not interfere with the reader's understanding of the essay.)

A Persuasive Composition:
- states and maintains a position, *generally* defends that position with precise and relevant evidence, and addresses the reader's concerns, biases, and expectations.

2 The essay —

- provides a thesis or main idea that is related to the writing task.
- supports the thesis or main idea(s) with *limited* details and/or examples.
- demonstrates an *inconsistent* tone and focus; and illustrates *little, if any* control of organization.
- demonstrates *little* or **no** sense of audience.
- provides *few, if any*, types of sentence types, and *basic, predictable* language.
- may contain *several errors* in the conventions* of the English language. (Errors may interfere withthe reader's understanding of the essay.)

A Persuasive Composition:
- defends a position with *little* evidence and *may* address the reader's concerns, biases, and expectations.

1 The essay —

- *may* provide a *weak* thesis or main idea that is related to the writing task.
- *fails* to support the thesis or main ideas with details and/or examples.
- demonstrates *a lack of* tone and focus; and illustrates **no** control of organization.
- may demonstrate **no** sense of audience.
- may provide **no** sentence variety and uses *limited* vocabulary.
- may contain *serious errors* in the conventions* of the English language. (Errors interfere with the reader's understanding of the essay.)

A Persuasive Composition:
- *fails* to defend a position with any evidence and *fails* to address the reader's concerns, biases, and expectations.

non-scorable: The code "NS" will appear on the student answer document for responses that are written in a language other than English, off-topic, illegible, unintelligible, or otherwise non-responsive to the writing task.

*Conventions of the English language refer to grammar, punctuation, spelling, capitalization, and usage.

This guide describes the attributes of student writing at each score point. Each paper receives the score that best fits the overall evidence provided by the student in response to the prompt. However, papers that do not meet the standard for conventions at a 4 or a 3 score point receive a score that is at most one point lower.